SIVALAYA

The 8000-metre peaks of the Himalaya

SIVALAYA

Explorations of the 8000-metre peaks of the Himalaya

LOUIS C. BAUME

THE MOUNTAINEERS
Seattle

The Mountaineers: Organized 1906 ". . . to explore, study,
preserve and enjoy the natural beauty of the Northwest."

Published by
The Mountaineers
719 Pike Street, Seattle, Washington 98101

Published simultaneously in Canada by
Douglas & McIntyre Ltd.
1875 Welch Street, North Vancouver, British Columbia V7P 1B7

First published in Great Britain in 1978 by
Gastons-West Col Publications

Manufactured in the United States of America

Library of Congress Cataloging in Publication Data

Baume, Louis Charles.
    Sivalaya: explorations of the 8000-metre
peaks of the Himalaya.

    Bibliography: p.
    1. Mountaineering--Himalaya Mountains--
History. 2. Mountaineering--Himalaya Mountains--
Bibliography. I. Title.
GV199.44.H55B38   1979   915.4   79-20964
ISBN 0-916890-97-X
ISBN 0-916890-71-6 pbk.

Cover photo by Galen Rowell: Makalu, Lhotse and Everest
sweep from the front cover to the back.

CONTENTS

MAPS AND DIAGRAMS

Detail from 'A view of the principal mountains   frontis.
throughout the world' by   J. Hulley,   published in
London, 1817 (from a print in the Baume collection)
   One of the earliest artistic impressions of the
   mountain world as known to geographers and explorers at the end of the 18th century. The central
   piece represents Dhawalageri (sic), declared the
   highest mountain then known in the world, and
   ascribed the height of 26,462 ft.

Note: subsequent routes of ascent to main summits or their subsidiary points can be identified on some of the diagrams, but these have not been marked in order to preserve the character of the original drawings by Mario Alfonsi.

ACKNOWLEDGEMENTS

The author wishes to thank Cassell & Collier Macmillan Publishers Ltd. for permission to include a brief résumé from the restricted circulation edition of "Why I Believe in Personal Immortality" by Sir Oliver Lodge.

Robin Collomb for providing the information on currently available maps and West Col Productions for the maps used in this book.

The Alpine Club Library and the Royal Geographical Society Library for permitting him to consult some of their books.

The many persons, too numerous to mention, who have helped in diverse matters of detail.

The mountain drawings are by Mario Alfonsi, and are reproduced from "I Quattordici 8000" by Mario Fantin with the kind permission of Nicola Zanichelli editore, Bologna.

The drawing on page 111 is adapted from an illustration appearing in the Alpine Journal, Vol. 36.

ABBREVIATIONS

AAJ	American Alpine (Club) Journal
AC	Alpine Club (of Great Britain)
AJ	Alpine Journal (published by the AC)
Am	American
AMS	Army Mapping Service (of U.S.A.)
Aus	Austrian
AV	German & Austrian Alpine Clubs
BdW	Berge der Welt (Mountain World, edition in German)
Br	British
c.	(circa) approximately, about
Can	Canadian
DAVJ	Deutscher Alpenverein Jahrbuch (German Alpine Club Yearbook)
DMS	Directorate of (British) Mapping Services
DOAVZ	Deutscher und Österreichischer Alpenverein Zeitung (German and Austrian Alpine Club Journal)
E	East
FNH	Forschungsunternehmen Nepal Himalaya (Research Scheme Nepal Himalaya, Germany)
Fr	French
ft.	foot or feet (lineal measure = 30.479 cm.)
e.g.	(exempli gratia) for example
G, Ger	German
GJ	Geographical Journal (published by the RGS), New Series after 1893
gl.	glacier
GTS	Great Trigonometrical Survey (of India)
HJ	Himalayan Journal
ibid.	(ibidem) in the same book, chapter or passage

i. e.	(id est) that is to say
IGM	Italian Military mapping service
Ind	Indian
ITY	Iwa-to-Yuki maps
Jap	Japanese
JASB	Journal of the Asiatic Society of Bengal
JGP	Harka Gurung (map)
JRGS	Journal of the Royal Geographical Society, Old Series prior to 1893
km.	kilometre (= 3281 ft.)
M	Mountain magazine
m.	metre (= 3.281 ft.)
M & A	La Montagne et l'Alpinisme (French Alpine Club Journal)
MW	Mountain World
N	North
N. C. O.	Non-commission officer (army rank)
Nw	Norwegian
NZ	New Zealand(er)
Pak	Pakistan
PRGS	Proceedings of the Royal Geographical Society
q. v.	(quod vide) which see, (in cross reference)
RCAS	Royal Central Asian Society (now the Royal Society for Asian Affairs)
RGS	Royal Geographical Society
RSOI	Records of the Survey of India
S	South
sic	Latin adverb placed after a word to guarantee it is quoted exactly even though it may appear wrong
SOI	Survey of India
Sp	Spanish
SSAF	Swiss Foundation for Alpine Research
Sw	Swiss
v.	(vide) see, (in cross reference)
W	West
YYJ	Yoshimi Yakushi, Japan (map)

SOURCE REFERENCE EXAMPLES

AJ 12	- Alpine Journal volume 12
GJ 136	- Geographical Journal volume 136
HJ 24	- Himalayan Journal volume 24
Jahrbuch des SAC 37	- Swiss Alpine Club Annual volume 37
M 49	- Mountain magazine number 49
AAJ 1975	- American Alpine Club Journal (year) 1975
LES ALPES 1969/3	- Les Alpes/Die Alpen (year) 1969 number 3 (Swiss Alpine Club)
M & A 1976/2	- La Montagne et Alpinisme (year) 1976 number 2 (French Alpine Club)
MW 1958/59	- Mountain World (years) 1958 and 1959

METRIC CONVERSION

1000m.	equals	3,281 ft.
2000m.		6,562 ft.
3000m.		9,843 ft.
4000m.		13,123 ft.
5000m.		16,404 ft.
6000m.		19,685 ft.
7000m.		22,966 ft.
8000m.		26,247 ft.
1,000 ft.	equals	304.79m.
1 km.	equals	0.62137 miles

Explanatory Preface

This work consists of two principal parts:

1. A Chronicle of journeys, expeditions and ascents relative to the 8000m. peaks.

2. A Bibliography of books pertaining to the above.

These are preceded by an opening chapter on the Himalaya in general, placing the mountains in their geographical and historical settings.

1. CHRONICLE - is divided into 15 sections, one for each main peak and one, preceding the four mountains in the Karakoram, which records the early explorations of the Baltoro glacier, common to all four.

Each section begins with basic details on the mountain followed by a list of currently available maps. Then follow, individually recorded and in chronological order, the significant sightings, early journeys of exploration and reconnaissance, the attempts on and the ascents of the mountain. Omitted are purely scientific expeditions (e.g. topographical, glaciological, botanical). Only the basic data and events are chronicled. After each report appears one or more reference numbers; these are the principal source references from which more complete details can be obtained. These are listed at the end of each section. They are not, of course, the only available sources but generally they are the main ones; many national and club journals carry reports about their own particular national or club expeditions; there are other books, too, published overseas. The principle followed in selecting the listed source references has been as follows:

i) The official book written in or translated into English; failing which

ii) The official book in its foreign language and/or a journal article in English; failing which

iii) A journal article in the original foreign language.

The list of source references is followed by a second list of additional books (and relevant ephemera) mainly in the English language and published in Britain that refer in whole or in part to the mountain. It is not the intention of this present work to record every book published overseas, whether in English or in a foreign language; some however are included as they are considered to be of particular interest.

Foreign language means in general French, German or Italian. Many excellent books have been published, for example, in Japanese; unless they are mainly illustrated books or else incorporate a worthwhile résumé in English, they are not included.

The criterion used in numbering the successful ascents of a mountain is that when two or more parties of the same expedition either reach the summit at the same time but by different routes (v. Mount Everest, American Expedition, 1963) or reach the summit independently on different days (v. Mount Everest, Indian Expedition, 1965) these are counted as separate ascents. When two or more parties of the same expedition reach the summit on the same day and by the same route (v. Broad Peak, Austrian Expedition, 1957) this is counted as one ascent.

The altitudes of summits and all major features are the most recent accepted figures. Those of camps and points reached by climbers are generally as estimated at the time; they are relative rather than absolute.

2. BIBLIOGRAPHY - opens with a list of books dealing with the Himalaya in some aspect relevant to the present work or with the 8000m. peaks in general rather than in particular, bibliographies, books of reference, journals and such.

The main bibliography describes all the relevant books whether mentioned in the chronicle or not and is arranged alphabetically by author. In principle the books are ones in the English language and published in Britain; for reasons already explained, this principle has been applied with flexibility. Excluded are:

Anthologies (other than on a specific 8000m. mountain)
Encyclopaedias covering general subjects
Fictional works (e. g. F. S. Smythe's Secret Mission, 1942)
Film strips or sets of slides, and accompanying handbooks (e. g. "Ascent of Everest" - C. W. F. Noyce)
Guide books (e. g. Baedeker, Murray)
Very young children's books
Journal and newspaper articles (e. g. J. L. Longland's "Everest 1951")
Mountain poetry in general collections
School text books
Theological books (e. g. G. Arundale's Mount Everest, 1933)
Travel books containing only a passing reference to an 8000m. peak.

Inevitably there are a few books that are marginal in their contents and a decision on their merit for inclusion has been somewhat arbitrary; frequently they have been given the benefit of the doubt and included.

Many authors have 'double-barrelled' or compound surnames either inherited or assumed. All surnames correctly hyphenated by origin or usage are listed under the letter of the first of the compound name (e. g. Howard-Bury under H); others are listed under the letter of the second of the compound name (e. g. Kingdon Ward under W).

Many names of foreign origin are preceded by de, du, della, di, d', von, etc. In listing such names these prefixes are ignored (e. g. von Fürer-Haimendorf under F).

Books translated into English are given, where ascertainable, their original place of publication, date, and foreign title. Some books, republished in America, have had their titles changed; where known these are shown.

Illustrations are still sometimes referred to by publishers as plates - the term originally used for engravings and full-page photographs printed separately and inserted in the book at time of binding. Occasionally books are found with two or more illustrations on a page, these being listed as two or more plates; in other books they would be listed as one plate. As far as is possible this present work indicates the number of actual illustrations (or, particularly in some more modern productions, as so many pages of illustrations).

Folding maps imply the large maps that years ago were usual in most books of travel and explorations; some later maps are single fold. Others are listed simply as maps; they may be full page or smaller. Very small maps, in with the text, are described as sketch maps.

Books are octavo (8vo.) size unless otherwise described. However these terms are used in a very simplified way and merely as an indication of size. Strictly, octavo means a sheet of printing paper folded in half three times to give eight sheets or 16 pages; quarto (4to.), folded twice to give four sheets or eight pages. As there are at least a dozen different sizes of the original sheets of printing paper, the exact sizing of books becomes rather complex.

Books of the same edition are sometimes found in different bindings; this is because the publisher had not had the entire printing bound up at one time and for various reasons had varied the cloth used. These variations are not recorded.

Most of the books have been handled by the author but a few

of the less easily found books have not. Reliance for details on the latter has had to be placed on other bibliographies or catalogues. Notification of any errors or omissions will be received with gratitude.

Brooklands   Louis Baume
Bloxham
Oxfordshire

The Himalaya

Formation: The first substantiated and comprehensive proposition regarding the long-held idea of continental-drift was made by the German geologist Alfred Wegener in 1915. His theory was later modified by du Toit; both agreed, however, that the disruption and separation of the land masses, centred on Africa in what is now the Southern Hemisphere, took place relatively late in geological time - probably during the Tertiary period - roughly the last 60 million years. As a result of this drift the two great land masses of Angaraland and Gondwanaland came together in slow collision; the Himalaya range was thrust up by compression from the bed of the Tethys sea, which had separated the drifting continents, and was subsequently overlaid by further nappes squeezed out from below by renewed continental pressures (about 600,000 years ago). The Himalaya range is the youngest in the world, much younger than the European Alps, and is still in a process of formation. It consists of long parallel curvilinear folds in general alignment with and parallel to the edge of the old northward-drifting continent of India, a part of the former Gondwanaland.

Despite the apparent complexity of its formation, the Himalaya comprises three major west-east zones between the plains of the River Ganges in the south and the Tibetan plateau (mean altitude about 4600m.) in the north. These zones are: the Siwalik range or Outer Himalaya, mean elevation 900-1200m., stretching almost continuously from the Punjab in the west to Assam in the east and generally with a broad plain on its

17

northern side; the Lesser or Middle Himalaya, mean elevation 3600-4600m., older, more contorted and eroded by the elements, with high summits; and northernmost, the Great Himalaya, mean elevation 6100m., still aligned generally with the Siwalik range but more fragmented and containing the highest massifs and summits of all.

The Himalaya proper provides the catchment area for the River Ganges and its great tributaries Jumna, Gogra, Gandaki and Kosi. The Himalaya, in a broader sense, is divided for purposes of reference into four zones: (from west to east) - Kumaun Himalaya, about 320 km. wide; Nepal Himalaya, about 800 km. wide; Sikkim Himalaya, a narrow wedge about 100 km. wide; and Bhutan Himalaya, about 300 km. wide. The Sikkim and Bhutan Himalaya provide the catchment area for the Tista river and the other immediate neighbouring tributaries of the Brahmaputra. The Nepal Himalaya are subdivided into three sections: (from west to east) - Karnali, Gandaki and Kosi. These last sections are still further fragmented into their various ranges or 'himal'. As far as this affects the 8000m. mountains, some of the himal are obvious e.g. Dhaulagiri Himal and Annapurna Himal; others are not so self-explanatory e.g. Manaslu is situated in the Gurkha Himal. The Kosi section in which are six 8000m. peaks comprises (from west to east) - Langtang Himal, Jugal Himal, Lapche Kang, Rolwaling Himal, Khumbu Himal, Mahalangur Himal, Khumbakarna Himal (these last two were together known until recently as Mahalangur Himal), Lumbasumba Himal, Umbhak Himal and Nupchu Range. The Singalila Range forms the Nepal-Sikkim frontier.

The term Himalaya is now used to specify a more extensive area than the one just described. In this broadest sense (though neither geographically nor geologically necessarily correct) the Himalaya embraces in the west the complex of ranges continuing into Kashmir and lying within and to the north of the River Indus and its main tributaries Jehlum, Chenab, Ravi and Sutlej; and in the east the area within the great bend formed by the eastward-flowing Tsangpo river round the outlying peak of Namche Bharwa (7755m.) and by its new westerly course, further south, under the name of Brahmaputra. The former area is referred to as the Punjab Himalaya - itself subdivided into Himachal Kashmir and Himachal Pradesh (west and east respectively). The Punjab Himalaya is about 560 km. wide and contains, well to its north, several ranges - Ladakh, Karakoram and Aghil - all still roughly parallel to the general trend-line of the true Himalaya. The latter area, about 400 km. wide, is the Assam Himalaya (or NEFA Himalaya i.e. North Eastern Frontier Agency). North-west of the Punjab Himalaya lie the Hindu Kush and the Pamir, neither strictly within the Himalaya.

This entire range forms a belt (or geosyncline) approximately 240 km. in depth and stretching from west to east for about 2400 km. The snow-line on the southern slopes of the Himalaya varies from about 5800m. in the west to about 4200m. in the east; on the Tibetan side the snow-line is approximately 900m. higher. Within this area are found not only the highest mountains in the whole world - fourteen of them over 8000m. - but also some of the greatest glacier systems outside the Polar regions. The highest summit of all is Mount Everest, 8848m., and the longest glacier is the Siachen in the Karakoram, 72 km. Also in the Karakoram are the Hispar glacier, 61 km.; the Biafo, 59 km.; and the Baltoro and Batura glaciers, both 58 km.

Nomenclature: The origin of the name Himalaya stems from two Sanskrit words, 'Hi-ma', snow, and 'ā-la-ya', abode. In north India the name Himalaya is used to describe the entire mountain range stretching from Chitral (in north Pakistan) to Assam. In Nepal and east of Nepal a contracted form, Himala or Himal, is used together with the appropriate local name to designate individual groups of mountains. Thus Maha Langur Himal (Mahalangur Himal) describes the range stretching south-east from Cho Oyu and including Mount Everest and Lhotse; Mount Everest itself, it is believed, originally had no name. Similarly, the Tibetan appellation of Chomolongma described, it is thought, the Everest group or Himal as a whole.

The correct pronunciation of the name Himalaya may seem academic to many, most people being quite content with the more usual Anglicized version where the stress is on the second 'a', the first and third being short. However, the Tibetans and the Hindi- and Urdu-speaking Indians all pronounce the first 'a' long; any variations lie with the transliteration of the last two syllables. But Himalaya is a Sanskrit word and the correct Sanskrit pronunciation is: first 'a' as in 'car', second and third as in 'Sir'.

The plural form, Himalayas, as commonly used, is wrong. One may refer correctly to the Alps or the Cheviots but the use of hybrid plurals such as Glyders, Berner Alpens, Karakorams and Himalayas is incorrect.

As far as the names of individual mountains are concerned - and this is relevant also to other geographical features - the principle followed by the Survey of India always has been and remains that the name must be of a local or at least indigenous origin. Such names and their spelling in the vernacular are carefully scrutinized before being transliterated phonetically for use by the cartographers. When no likely name exists, as in uninhabited regions, explorers or climbers are permitted to suggest a name but personal names (of reigning monarchs, Presidents or wives, etc.) are not accepted. Preferably these suggested names should have some local basis (e.g. the Matterhorn takes its name from the meadows - or 'matten' - that surround it) or be in some way descriptive (e. g. le Mont Blanc, the White Mountain). Another acceptable consideration is the extent to which a name has been adopted and used by explorers and other travellers, even if that name is a personal one (e. g. Abruzzi Glacier, Conway Saddle, West Cwm).

All the best rules, however, have their exceptions and alone among all the mountains of the Himalaya, the highest two break these rules: Mount Everest and K2. The former was so named in 1865 after (but not by) Sir George Everest, Superintendent of the Great Trigonometrical Survey of India 1823-1843 and Surveyor General of India 1830-1843. The latter is the symbol of identification given to the mountain, seen by Lt. Thomas G. Montgomerie, at the first trigonometrical station from which it was observed. When the final reduction of the Kashmir triangulation was undertaken, this symbol, together with others, was altered so as to conform with the principle of numbering from the right to left. In the Synoptical Volume No. 7 of the G.T.S., 1879, K2 is shown as "Karakoram No. 13".

Survey: The survey of an area as vast as the Himalaya, as complex, as remote, as difficult of access on account of political and dynastic rivalries, an area so hostile climatically, so rugged and forbidding, so overpowering - such a survey would be a daunting project even to-day with all the scientific paraphernalia at modern man's disposal. That this stupendous task was accomplished at all is a near-miracle, a miracle achieved only by the perseverence and devotion of a relatively small number of men - Indian, Pathan, European - over a very long period of years. And yet to-day the maps that result from this historic undertaking are seemingly taken almost for granted, whilst the pioneers who made their production possible are all but forgotten.

The earliest known map that bears any resemblence to the Himalaya is one drawn in 1590 by Father Anthony Montserrate, a Spanish member of the Jesuit mission sent in 1579 to the court of Akbar, sovereign of Hindustan during the time of the Mogul Empire. Nearly a century and a half later, in 1733, Jean Baptiste d'Anville (1697-1782) produced and had published in Paris his 'Atlas of China' in 42 sheets. It was intended as a companion volume to Father du Halde's 'Description de l'Empire de la Chine'. The information and sketch maps from which the Atlas was compiled had been obtained from another Jesuit father, Baptiste Régis of the observatory in Peking. Some of these maps had been produced from surveys carried out by Jesuit missionaries in China but those covering southern Tibet and the Himalaya area were the work of Chinese lamas sent out by the emperor Kang-Li between 1705 and 1717, and were probably not so accurate. The final work, as produced by d'Anville, was an improvement on the earlier map yet still, and inevitably, inexact. Some 15 years later d'Anville produced his 'Carte de l'Inde'.

After the battle of Plassey (in Bengal) in 1757 the New East India Company found itself responsible for the administration of a whole new region about which very little was known. The Company set out to remedy this deficiency by engaging a number of surveyors to carry out surveys of important areas and of routes of communication; one of these surveyors was James Rennell (1742-1830). In 1767 Robert Clive (Clive of India and victor at Plassey) appointed Captain Rennell as the first Surveyor General of Bengal; Rennell later became regarded as the Father of Indian Geography. In 1782, after his retirement, he had published the first edition of his 'Map of Hindoostan' - a great improvement on d'Anville's map except for the Himalaya in Nepal and west of it, for the details of which Rennell was obliged to rely still on d'Anville's Atlas.

During the 17th and early 18th centuries, much information had been gathered by a number of missionaries and travellers - usually Jesuits - on their journeys between India, Tibet, and China. Among these were Stephen Cacella and John Cabral, who crossed the western end of the Assam Himalaya on their journey from Hooghly to Tibet, returning either through Nepal or via Bhutan (1626-1631): Johann Grueber and Albert d'Orville, who crossed from Peking to Lhasa (the first Europeans to visit the city) and thence to Katmandu and Agra (1661-1662); and Ippolito Desideri, who travelled from Delhi to Lhasa over the Pir Panjal Pass and the Zoji La (1714-1716), returning from Tibet via Katmandu to Madras some years later.

This gathering of information and compilation of route-maps continued, though on an increasing and more co-ordinated scale, throughout the latter half of the 18th century and right up to more recent times. Every opportunity, military, political or trade, was used to bring back some description, however slight, of the countries visited and of the routes followed. But the opportunities to penetrate the eastern Himalaya from the south were few during the 18th century. Captain Kinloch was able to sketch a part of the southern border of Nepal when he was despatched to that country in 1767 after an appeal for assistance from its ruler. Twenty-five years later another appeal was sent out by the Gurkhas when involved in their war against Tibet and on that occasion William Kirkpatrick was sent to Katmandu as envoy; Ensign John Gerard, in command of Kirkpatrick's escort, was able to make a sketch-map of the route followed to Nepal's capital. A few years earlier (1774-1775) George Bogle had been despatched on a trade mission to Bhutan and Tibet and he came back with a certain amount of information concerning the route followed. And in 1783 Ensign Samuel Turner was sent to visit the Teshu Lama in Shigatse (Tibet) and he too was able to bring back his contribution to the emerging picture of this part of the Himalaya.

The first proper surveys of Nepal were not made until the turn of the century. These were carried out by Charles Crawford, who commanded the first Resident's escort in Katmandu from 1801-1803. In 1804 Crawford made further surveys in eastern Nepal and it was he who first announced the great height of the snowy peaks observed.

In 1808 Lt. W. S. Webb, under the instructions of Robert Colebrook, Surveyor General of Bengal, and accompanied by Captain F. V. Raper and Hyder Young Hearsey (an Anglo-Indian),

23

explored the upper reaches of the River Ganges, rising in the Kumaun Himalaya - a region then still dominated by Nepal and closed to all outsiders. During his survey, Webb took observations to some of the high peaks and after his return was surprised by the heights obtained (though they confirmed Crawford's earlier findings). He went back in 1809 to measure again the position and height of Dhaulagiri; he calculated its altitude as being 8187m. - a figure ridiculed by geographers outside India, who still regarded Chimborazo (in the Andes) as being the highest mountain in the world.

In 1812, disguised as fakirs and under assumed names, William Moorcroft set off with Hyder Young Hearsey on a journey from Ramnagar to Tibet passing over the Niti Pass (5068m.), the first to cross it. Their report and route-map provided important and conclusive evidence about the sources of the Ganges and its main tributaries, and also of the Sutlej. In the meanwhile Saiyid Mir Ullah, despatched by Moorcroft, had gone off to explore routes through Kashmir to Turkestan and Bukhara. This journey (1812-1813) took Ullah from Leh over the Karakoram Pass to Kashgar in Eastern Turkestan. Later, between 1820 and 1825, Moorcroft carried out further extensive journeys and explored much of Ladakh and Baltistan; he was able to mark on his map the positions of both the Karakoram and Saltoro Passes and to indicate the area in which the Yarkand river rises. His map, however, was not published until 1841, well after his death in 1825 at Andkhui in Afghanistan.

As a result of the Nepalese War of 1814-1816, a new western boundary for Nepal was established on the Kali Ganga. This opened up the whole of the Kumaun Himalaya, previously closed to foreigners, and provided for the first time an opportunity to begin a detailed survey of this hitherto forbidden area. The survey was begun in 1815, the year when John Anthony Hodgson was appointed to the new post of Surveyor of the North-West Mountain Provinces. But Nepal itself continued to remain

closed to outsiders, almost without exception, and this ex-
clusion remained in force right up till 1949.

An interesting side-light on the general knowledge in Britain
at this period of the world's highest mountains is provided by
those Comparative Views so beloved by the Victorians. The
Alpine Journal for 1976 reproduces a short article from "The
Beauties and Wonders of Nature and Science" (London, 1842)
together with an engraved illustration showing the mountains
of the world and their heights before the discovery of Mount
Everest. T.S. Blakeney provides some notes and comments.
Chimboraco is depicted as 21,464 English feet; four higher
summits are shown as Dhawala Gira in Thibet, 26,462 ft.;
Jewahir in Jewahir, 25,749 ft.; Jamatura in Malown, 25,500 ft.;
and Black Peak, also in Malown, 21,155 ft. Dhaulagiri is
reckoned to-day as 26,795 ft. (8167m.). Blakeney suggests
that the next two might correspond with Hooker's estimates
for Jannu at 25,315 and Kabru at 24,000; other possibilities,
he notes, might be Gauri Sankar and Chomolhari, both of which
were known at that time. But their identities, and that of
Black Peak, as well as their locations remain a matter of
conjecture. It is interesting to note that though Kangchenjunga
was known in 1842 no mention of the mountain appears. John
Tallis in his view of the "Waterfalls, Islands, Lakes, Rivers
and Mountains of the Eastern Hemisphere" (London, c. 1850)
shows only Dhawalagir and Jawahir. An earlier view, appearing in William Phillip's "Outlines of Mineralogy and Geology"
(London, 1826), though showing many snowy pinnacles towering
over Chimborazo, 21,451 ft., names only one of them: White
Mountain, 26,452 ft. (White Mountain in Sanskrit is Dhawala
Giri). An even earlier engraving, dated London 1817 and of
unidentified origin, shows a still different set of mountains.
These are Dhawalageri, 26,462 ft.; Jamaturi, 25,500; Dhai-
bun, 24,740; and two mountains in the Valley of Nepal, 24,625
and 23,052 ft.; Chimborazo is shown as 20,900 ft. (see Frontispiece).

At the same time as the survey of the Kumaun Himalaya and of Garhwal and the computation of the heights of their principal peaks were progressing, the exploration of the western Himalaya continued - chiefly in Kashmir, Baltistan, Ladakh and the eastern Karakoram. G. W. Traill was the first, in 1830, to cross the watershed of the Great Himalaya at the head of the Pindari glacier, between Nanda Devi and Nanda Kot, by the pass (5395m.) that still bears his name. Between 1835 and 1838 G. T. Vigne travelled extensively in the area, reaching in 1835 the snout of the Chogo Lungma glacier; in 1838 he penetrated the Saltoro Valley looking for the Saltoro Pass. In the same year, H. Falconer was probably the first to discover the Biafo glacier and to cross the Skoro La.

The Great Trigonometrical Survey of India - the G. T. S. - began with Major William Lambton in 1800; it was he who was its founder. He had obtained permission from the Government of Madras to carry out a mathematical and geographical survey consisting of a triangulation based near Madras and capable of being extended in any direction. This work was begun in 1802 and by 1818 had become recognized as being of such importance that it was taken over by the Government of India and named the Great Trigonometrical Survey of India; Lambton was appointed its Superintendent. George Everest (1790-1866), who had come to India in 1806 as a young Artillery cadet, became Lambton's chief assistant. When Lambton died at Hingan Ghat in 1823, Everest succeeded him as Superintendent; in 1830, Everest was appointed Surveyor General of India and he held these combined posts until his retirement in 1843. During these twenty years, Everest not only developed the Survey by adopting and furthering the basic "grid-iron" system prepared by Valentine Blacker (Surveyor General of India 1823-1826) but he also completed in 1841 the Great Arc astride the 78th meridian, begun by Lambton, as far as the Himalaya - probably his greatest achievement. This Arc forms the foundation upon which are calculated the positions and heights of all Himalayan mountains.

After Everest retired in 1843 he was succeeded as Surveyor General by Andrew Waugh, who linked up the northern ends of other meridional triangulations initiated by Blacker by two primary series: the North-Eastern Himalaya series and the North-Western, both carried out during the years 1846 to 1855. In the course of these operations, geodetic observers working in Bihar made observations in 1849 to a hitherto unnoticed peak to the north - one of many in forbidden Nepal; it was designated "No. XV". Subsequent computation in 1852 revealed it to be the highest summit in the world, topping even Dhaulagiri (XLII) and Kangchenjunga (VIII). It was not until 1865 that No. XV was given the name of Everest.

The G. T. S. was extended to Kashmir, and then to Ladakh, Lahul and Spiti. Here, in the years 1855 to 1865, a very able Engineer officer, Lt. Thomas G. Montgomerie, was operating. It was he who thought up the idea of exploring the little-known areas between India and the expanding Russian Empire further north. In pursuance of this idea he used local men trained in surveying to go, disguised as travellers, lamas or traders, to the Valley of the Oxus, to eastern Turkestan and to Tibet. Montgomerie, during his own explorations, discovered in 1856 the high peak - computed in 1858 as being the second highest in the world - designated in the survey as K2.

The practice of using trained native explorers - pundits as they were called - to penetrate unknown country closed to Europeans continued for many years. They were many but the first, and possibly the greatest of them all, was Nain Singh whose first journey was to Lhasa; his brother and two cousins also became pundits. There were also Abdul Subhan 'the Munshi'; Ata Muhammed 'the Mullah', the first to explore the wild gorges of the Indus; Hari Ram, a Hindu, who made the first circuit of Everest in 1871; Mirza Shuja, later murdered in Bukhara. And there was Kintup, a Lepcha of Tibetan origin from Sikkim, who in the early 1880s, after being sold into slavery in Tibet, escaped and brought back conclusive proof that the Tsangpo and Brahmaputra were indeed one and the same river - something that was not confirmed until nearly 30 years later by Captain F. M. Bailey and Captain H. Morshead.

In 1857 Montgomerie was joined by another officer, Henry Godwin-Austen, an outstanding surveyor and explorer and regarded also as the greatest mountaineer of his day. During most of the following six years Godwin-Austen was surveying in southern and eastern Kashmir and in the Karakoram; he surveyed the Shigar and Saltoro valleys; he explored and mapped the complex of glaciers formed by the Chogo Lungma, Kero Lungma, Biafo, Panmah and Baltoro - areas reached 25 years previously by Falconer, Vigne and other travellers - and he ascended for the first time many of these glaciers. He discovered the Hispar glacier and the Baltoro approaches to K2. Afterwards he carried out surveys in Bhutan and in the North-eastern Frontier among the then still wild tribes of the Khasi and Naga Hills and among the Dafflas. He was often at 6000m. while carrying out his work. It was proposed in 1888 that the great mountain K2 should be given his name but this suggestion, put forward by General J. T. Walker one time Superintendent G. T. S. , was not accepted either in London or in India. Godwin-Austen died in England in 1924 at the age of ninety.

By 1862 the whole of the Himalaya lying west of Nepal was covered by a network of triangles and survey stations and these formed an accurate basis for further detailed topographical surveys. In the course of these operations more than 40 summits over 6000m. had been climbed and observed from. The reconnaissance surveys of Sikkim then began.

It is beyond the scope of this introductory chapter to list all the surveyors, explorers and mountaineers, British, native and European, who contributed to the consolidation of the Survey of India and to its extension to Nepal, Sikkim and the

Assam Himalaya, as well as to the pacification of remote warring areas and the demarcation of boundaries between States - Johnson, Holdich, Cunningham, Strachey, the Schlagintweit brothers, Younghusband, Durand, Collins, Longstaff and so many others. Suffice it to say that the knowledge we possess to-day is due largely to the indefatigable work, the persistence, and the self-sacrifice in face of incredible dangers and difficulties of all these men, about so many of whom too little is known.

Nevertheless it was from their original route-surveys, sketch maps and field notes that the first maps were compiled; these were drawn by hand. But as the demand for maps increased, so new methods of reproduction had to be found. Lithographic printing (a process discovered in Germany in 1796) was adopted for the printing of maps in Calcutta in the 1820s. On these maps there were as yet no contour lines, the hills being represented by hachures or form lines. It soon became apparent that these maps, frequently based on out-of-date information, without contours, and printed in one or at most two colours, no longer served a useful purpose; the urgent need was for modern maps produced by modern methods.

The arrival in India as Commander-in-Chief of Lord Kitchener (Earl Kitchener of Khartoum, 1850-1916), himself an erstwhile surveyor, acted as the spur for a complete reorganization of the Survey of India. In 1906 a complete new survey of India was begun on a scale of one inch to a mile (1:63,360), with maps to be printed in colour and showing contours at intervals of 100 feet (about 30m.), the whole programme to take about 25 years at the end of which time revisions would re-commence. All over India small parties of surveyors went forth armed with plane-table and theodolite; Sir Sidney Burrard, Superintendent of the G.T.S., was appointed Surveyor General in 1910; the triangulation link between India and Russia, proposed at a Potsdam meeting in 1908, was completed by 1913. Interrupted by the First World War in 1914 and curtailed by economic difficulties in the 1920s, the new survey nevertheless slowly progressed, often with the help of vertical air-photography in the more inaccessible areas and of other up-to-date techniques. In 1935 the re-survey of the Kumaun Himalaya was begun under the direction of Major Gordon Osmaston and great assistance was provided over the years by mountaineers of many nationalities. The final maps were published on the scale of half-inch to one mile. Then came the Second World War in 1939 and this put a virtual end to all topographical survey in India for the duration; the surveyors skills were required elsewhere.

Two years after the end of the war in 1945, the Independence and Partition of India and Pakistan took place. Since then all the northern areas of these two countries have been involved in a series of disputes and wars over territories and boundaries not only between India and Pakistan but also between India and China subsequent to the latter's takeover of Tibet in 1959. Russian involvement in Afghanistan and the rivalries between these powers in the highly sensitive and militarily important mountain borderlands exacerbated still further a situation already over-charged with emotion and political ambition. At the same time as Nepal opened its frontiers to foreigners, Tibet slammed shut its frontiers, and Kashmir and the Karakoram became virtually closed to all outsiders.

All these happenings reversed completely the climbing prospects for mountaineers and rendered still more difficult the resumption of a co-ordinated re-survey of the Himalayan ranges. Pakistan, lacking the technical and financial resources required for this work, abandoned any pretence of a systematic survey of its northern territories. But India, backed by vast financial aid provided by the Soviet Government, was able to initiate a very extensive mapping programme; the threat of further Chinese encroachments and infiltration from north of the border was the effective spur to this Soviet-sponsored project. The result has been the publication - though not for

general issue - of a series of maps (1:50,000 and 1:100,000)
of a very high cartographic standard. Officially, these maps
are for the military only.

Further east, isolated for the present from the principal
centre of international geopolitical conflict, lies the independent
kingdom of Nepal, once a vassal state of China but 'cis-alpina'
to the Indians and thus considered by them to lie within their
own sphere of influence, a consideration that also extends to
Nepal's neighbours, Sikkim and Bhutan, both subject to Tibet
in the past.

Nepal, but recently emerged from its mediaeval state, lacked
all knowledge and ability for carrying out a modern survey of
its land. Any mapping that has been done has been accomplished by outside promotion: overall maps produced mainly
from aerial surveys carried out by interested Governments;
local maps of a particular mountain or himal produced from
surveys made by individual or successive mountaineering expeditions e.g. the Dhaulagiri Himal by Y. Yakushi of Japan
and the RGS map of the Everest region compiled mainly from
the pre-war and immediate post-war expeditions; quarter-inch
maps (1/253,440) resulting from an extensive survey carried
out by a team of fourteen Indian topographers (Europeans from
the India Survey Dept. were not permitted into Nepal) between
1924 and 1927 of the territory between the low-lying Terai in
the south, once feared for its miasmic marshes and primaeval
jungle, and the foothills of the Himalaya; one-inch maps
(1/63,360) of the high mountain areas produced some twenty
years ago, also by the S.O.I.; and, foremost, a long-term
systematic survey of the northern frontier regions, begun in
1950 and being conducted by E. Schneider on behalf of the
Research Scheme Nepal Himalaya of Germany under the spon-
sorship of Fritz Thyssen Stiftung. The maps produced so far
(six in number, scale 1/50,000) are printed in Austria and are
of a very high technical standard indeed. They are readily
available to everyone.

SIVALAYA

Heights: The calculation of the heights of Himalayan peaks is a realm of such erudite complexity that not even angels armed with theodolites and plumb-lines would dare to tread therein. The polemics of the problem have lasted for more than a hundred years and still the absolute truth has not been found; perhaps it never will.

Whether the height of Everest be 8848m. or 8848.13m. (as the authorities in Peking inform us) and whether the probable error of its measured mean elevation be in fact in the region of ± 0.24m., are subtleties of little more than academic interest to the layman, particularly as he knows that even a heavy snow-fall could add another 3 or 4m. to the altitude of a high mountain. What is of importance is that Everest is the highest mountain of all. What is also of interest is by how much it surpasses its nearest rival. This figure was 237m. but, since the summer of 1976 when the Survey of Pakistan announced that the altitude of K2 was not 8611m. but 8760m., this difference in heights has been reduced to a mere 88m.

Understandably most interest and most controversy have centred on the highest mountain in the world. The calculations necessary to arrive at the truth regarding its exact height illustrate well the nature of the difficulties to be overcome in assessing the heights of this and of all other mountains. Mount Everest was observed first from six stations in the plains of India and from a distance of about 180 km. in the years 1849-1850. In 1852, as a result of these observations, its height was determined as being 29,002 ft. (1000 ft. = 305m.). During. the years 1905-1907 fresh observations were made from the Darjeeling Hills, 35 km. closer, and Sir Sidney Burrard, by re-computation and by correcting the allowance previously made for refraction, arrived at a figure of 29,141 ft.

Dr. de Graaf Hunter, in 1922, arrived at a value of 29,149 ft. with a probable error of less than 5 ft. and a possible error of less than 15 ft; this value, however, represented the peak's elevation above the spheroid (the earth's theoretical surface outline) - the Everest spheroid having been calculated from the Arc of the Meridian established by Sir George Everest - and by correcting for a then calculable height difference of approximately 70 ft. between the geoid (the earth's true surface of mean sea-level) and the spheroid at the base of Everest, Dr. Hunter amended his figure to 29,079 ft. with a possible error of $\pm$ 25 ft. A few years later the probable height was reduced to 29,050 ft. $\pm$ 15 ft. Nevertheless it was decided to continue retaining officially the original figure of 29,002 ft.

More recent calculations made by Dr. B. L. Gulatee in 1954 revealed an even greater difference between the geoid and the spheroid, resulting in a new height value for Everest of 29,028 ft., $\pm$ 0.8 ft. This last height estimate now replaces officially the original one of 29,002 ft.

So for Everest, so for other mountains. The vertical measurements, as much as the horizontal ones, are in a state of constant revision; and the Himalaya range itself is still in a state of continuing evolution. There are other imponderable factors such as uplift and erosion still to be considered. To the average mountaineer all these may seem but trifles; to the man of science they are vital elements in the quest for truth. To quote from Edward Young:

"Think naught a trifle, though it small appear;
Small sands the mountain, moments make the year."

Orthography: After resolving the difficulties of positioning a mountain correctly on a map, calculating its true height, and resolving the problem of its rightful name, there remains the difficult matter of its spelling. The origin of a name may be lost or merely subject to dispute. It will have different forms in different languages or dialects. Its pronunciation may vary not only between individuals but also from one locality to another. The name may be pronounced differently from what its spelling may indicate, as we find in our own place names: Stiffkey (pronounced Stewky), Cirencester (Cicester), Happis-

33

burgh (Haysborough), etc. The true etymology of names and the correct rendering into our romanized script of these foreign and often more subtle sounds - such as the slightly-sounded Tibetan aspirates - have been and will continue to be debated for a long time.

Kangchenjunga serves as an example, though perhaps as a more extreme one. It is situated on the Sikkim-Nepal border and, like Everest and Dhaulagiri, was visible from the stations of the North-Eastern Himalaya series instituted under Andrew Waugh. It had been designated as "No. VIII". Hari Ram, one of the Hindu pundits, was sent out by Montgomerie to find out what local names existed for various peaks in Nepal; he reported back that No. VIII alone had a name, which according to the Gurkhas of the Tamu Kosi was Kumbhkaran Lungur - though whether in fact that name referred truly to Kangchenjunga or Makalu is a matter of conjecture.

H. Chapman, in his Journal (1836), gives the name as Kanxching-Jinga. H. V. Bayley (1838) refers to Kunching Jinga, as does W. S. Sherwill (1853). B. H. Hodgson (1849) mentions the peak of Kangchan (Kang = snow and chan = abounding in) but he was incorrect for Kangchan is a name applied to a region; Kangchen would have been the correct word. Hooker (1854) spells it Kinchinjunga in the text and Kangchan-junga on his map. Kinchinjunga was adopted by the Imperial Gazetteer, and was used also by the old Survey of India as were Kinchinjinga and Kanchinjunga. Cunningham (1854) chooses the form Kanchinjinga. The mountain appears in J. W. Elder's report as Kinchingunga. In Mahrati it is Kanchanganga; in Bengali, Kanchanjangha or Kanchansrnga; and according to some Sanskrit books, Kanchanadri. The early Alpine Club Journals showed a preference for Kánchanjangá, and Burrard considered either Kanchenjunga or Kanchendzonga to be the correct form. Freshfield, Waddell, and Dr. Kellas all opted for Kangchenjunga, a form also adopted by the Royal Geographical Society.

The mountain name is almost certainly of Tibetan origin -

even though Dr. Shastri, the greatest Sanskrit scholar in Bengal in his time, was of the opinion that the name is Sanskrit (a view subscribed to by Burrard who also believed that Tibetans do not name mountains) and that it derives from Kancan (golden) and Jangha (a thigh). F. W. Bailey, in 1931, contradicted Burrard and others by affirming that Tibetans do name mountains, which are locally named Kang-Chen (big snow) or Kang-Ri (snow mountain).

The evidence in support of its Tibetan origin, however, is now overwhelming. An interesting facet of this problem is illustrated by L. A. Waddell in H. H. Risley's "Gazetteer of Sikhim" (1894), page 263, opposite which is a picture of the god Kang-chhen-dsö-nga - the chief 'country-god of Sikhim', of red colour, carrying a gyaltshén or banner of victory, and mounted on a white lion. His dwelling place is the mountain from which he takes his name and which was formerly an object of worship itself. The mountain was given its name by the adjoining Tsangpa Tibetans. The people of Sikkim are, of course, Tibetans by race and by language.

According to a former Maharaja of Sikkim, who refuted Dr. Shastri's suggestion (as did also Johan van Manen of Calcutta), the name in Sikkimese Tibetan dialect is Kang-chen-mdZod-lNga, pronounced Kang-chen Zod-nga. He accepted the name Kangchenjunga as a reasonable compromise as it has a spelling widely used and understood.

This seems to be an admirable dénouement. Yet the extent of the problem clearly shows the need for very careful scrutiny of the origins and history of names, their meanings and those of their component parts, and their spelling in the vernacular, before they are transliterated phonetically for use by cartographers. This is the responsibility of the respective Surveys.

The name to be given to the mountain "No. XV" has turned out to be an even more controversial issue and the polemics surrounding the subject have continued for over a century and have engaged the pens of men of the greatest erudition. Unlike Kangchenjunga, this mountain apparently had no original native name, even though its locality or massif may have had one. Various suggestions have been put forward during these years but none has withstood a close examination of its pedigree. To add to the complexity of the problem, the mountain lies on the border between Tibet and Nepal and was observed and surveyed under British direction. Finally in 1865, no valid indigenous name having been discovered during the 15 years elapsed since the peak had been first observed, it was given the name 'Everest'. More than fifty different names, or variations of names, have been used as the following list, with brief notes to each, explains:

1. Bya-ma-lung. - Pronounced Cha-ma-lung (the 'u' as in 'put'). Word used in original documents from Lhasa in 1921, 1922 and 1924, according to T. S. Blakeney (AJ 70 p. 305).

2. Cha-Dzi-ma-lung-pa. - A longer version of No. 4, according to Sir Charles Bell, and meaning "the district where birds are kept"; derivation given to him in Lhasa by one of the Dalai Lama's secretaries (HJ 4 p. 193).

3. Chamalung. - Version appearing in passports for the 1933 expedition, according to Ruttledge (Everest 1933 p. 61).

4. Chama Lung. - Version used by the Tibetan Government in correspondence about the early Mount Everest expeditions. 'Cha' means a bird, 'lung' is a valley or district (F. M. Bailey, HJ 4 p. 193).

5. Cha-Ma-Lung. - A version used by Burrard, 1920. Blakeney writes that Cha-ma-lung is customarily used in Lhasa and is thought to indicate a mountain massif rather than a particular peak.

6. Chamo Lung. - Alternative version to No. 4; the spelling of the second syllable is used indiscriminately.

7. <u>Cha-mo-lung.</u> - Version used in one 1922 document, according to Blakeney.

8. <u>Chha-mo-lung-ma.</u> - Version used in passport for the 1921 expedition, according to Howard-Bury (<u>Everest 1921</u> p. 24).

9. <u>Chholungbu.</u> - The name used by the surveyor, Natha Sing, who visited the Dudh Kosi headwaters in 1907 (Blakeney, quoting Burrard, AJ 70 p. 308).

10. <u>Chingopamari.</u> - A Tibetan name put forward by Hermann von Schlagintweit.

11. <u>Choma Kankar.</u> - Meaning "Lord of the Snows", version used by Chandra Das in his narrative of his journey to Lhasa in 1881, quoted by Freshfield (<u>Round Kangchenjunga</u> p. 327).

12. <u>Chomokankar.</u> - Tibetan name put forward by Chandra Das and supported by Waddell, according to Freshfield (<u>Round Kangchenjunga</u> pp. 17 and 357).

13. <u>Chomo Kankar.</u> - Tibetan name put forward by Chandra Das and supported by Waddell, according to Gulatee (HJ 17 p. 133).

14. <u>Chomo-langma.</u> - Thought by Kempson to be the best-known local name (Ruttledge, <u>Everest the Unfinished Adventure</u> p. 288).

15. <u>Chomo Lobzangma.</u> - Meaning "the Liberal-minded Goddess"; the uncorrupted form of No. 18, according to Morshead (HJ 3 p. 128).

16. <u>Chomolomo.</u> - A reported Tibetan name, thought by Lt. Col. Ganesh Bahadur, of Nepal, to apply to the whole northern side of the Maha Langur Himal and not to the mountain itself (Sir E. Tandy, <u>Survey of India, General Report. 1926-1927,</u> quoted by Odell, AJ 47 p. 129).

17. <u>Chomolongma.</u> - A Tibetan name thought by Col. Ganesh

Bahadur Chattari, of Nepal, to apply generally to the whole Everest group and not particularly to the highest peak, according to Sir G. Corbett (HJ 1 p. 84).

18. Chomo Longma. - A corrupt form of No. 15, according to Morshead. The correct transliteration of No. 52, according to Morshead (HJ 3 p. 128).

19. Chomo Longmo. - Form used on $\frac{1}{2}$-inch map Mount Everest and Environs, S. O. I. 1930, according to Odell (AJ 47 p. 127).

20. Chomolung. - Tibetan name referring to the district or range (K. Mason, Abode of Snow p. 73).

21. Chomolungma. - Version used in passport for the 1921 expedition, according to Noel (Through Tibet to Everest p. 101). Meaning "The Mother Goddess of the Country". Name used for both Everest and Makalu (Howard-Bury, Everest 1921 p. 225).

22. Chomo-lungma. - Version attributed to Howard-Bury by Odell.

23. Chomo Lungma. - Name given by the monks of Thyangboche to the whole Everest-Lhotse-Nuptse massif, (Tilman, Nepal Himalaya p. 227). Name appearing on map in Norton's "Everest 1924", south side of Everest.

24. Chomolungmo. - Version used by C. G. Bruce (Everest 1922 p. 123).

25. Chomo-lungmo. - Version (wrongly) attributed to Bruce and to Howard-Bury by Younghusband (Everest 1921 p. 13).

26. Chomo Lungmo. - Name given to Surveyor Nathu Sing when visiting the head-waters of the Dudh Kosi river in 1907 (K. Mason gives the surveyor's name as Natha Singh) and also to C. G. Bruce by some Sherpa Bhottias living in Dhimbuje village (Bruce, Twenty Years in the Himalaya p. 25).

27. Chomo Uri. - Meaning "Goddess of the Turquoise Peak";

a local Tibetan name reported by Howard-Bury (Everest 1921 p. 64).

28. Chu-mu-lang-ma. - Pronounced Jew-moo-lang-ma. A name now (1964) appearing on all Chinese Communist maps, according to Creighton of the Permanent Committee on Geographical Names (AJ 69 p. 144).

29. Devadhunga. - Meaning "Abode of Deity". A local name put forward by Brian Hodgson (1856), Political Officer in Nepal for many years, but never substantiated (Gulatee, HJ 17 p. 132). The name preferred by J. N. Collie in Climbing on the Himalaya (1902).

30. Gans-ri glan-ma. - A name quoted by Kempson from the diary of the Rongbuk Lama, Leaf 287 (Everest the Unfinished Adventure p. 288).

31. Gaurisankar. - Meaning "The bright, or white, bride of Siva". Name given by Hermann Schlagintweit after his visit to Nepal in 1852, resulting from a misidentification of peaks. In his Panoramic Profile of the Snowy Ranges of High Asia, Leipzig 1861, Makalu, Mount Everest and Gaurisankar are wrongly shown as being one and the same mountain - Everest is 17 km. west of Makalu and 38 km. distant from Gaurisankar; the latter was designated Peak No. XX in the original survey. Freshfield, for a time, preferred this name and refused to accept Everest. The name continued to be used, frequently on Continental maps, until quite recent times.

32. Gauri Sankar. - Name used in the Times Survey Atlas of the World, J. G. Bartholomew, 1920.

33. Gaurishankar. - A variation of No. 31.

34. Jolmo Lungma. - Name favoured by China (Mountaineering in China, Peking 1965).

35. Jomo-Gans-Dkar. - Tibetan name given by Sarat Chandra Das in his dictionary.

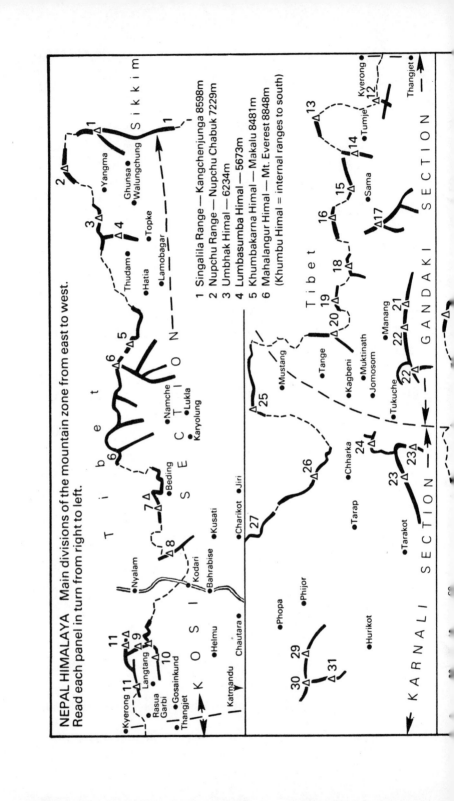

NEPAL HIMALAYA Main divisions of the mountain zone from east to west.
Read each panel in turn from right to left.

1 Singalila Range — Kangchenjunga 8598m
2 Nupchu Range — Nupchu Chabuk 7229m
3 Umbhak Himal — 6234m
4 Lumbasumba Himal — 5673m
5 Khumbakarna Himal — Makalu 8481m
6 Mahalangur Himal — Mt. Everest 8848m
(Khumbu Himal = internal ranges to south)

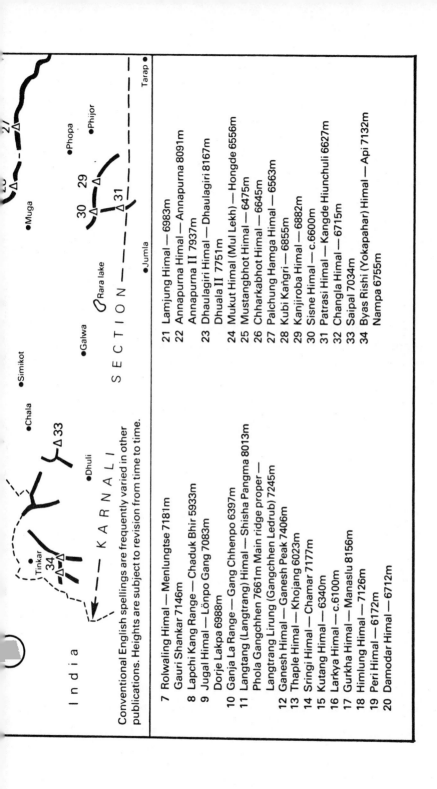

India

Tinkar 34

Chala

Dhuli

Δ 33

Simikot

Galwa

Rara lake

Jumla

Muga

Phopa

Phijor

Phola

30 29

31

Tarap

K A R N A L I

S E C T I O N

Conventional English spellings are frequently varied in other
publications. Heights are subject to revision from time to time.

7 Rolwaling Himal — Menlungtse 7181m
   Gauri Shankar 7146m
8 Lapchi Kang Range — Chaduk Bhir 5933m
9 Jugal Himal — Lönpo Gang 7083m
   Dorje Lakpa 6988m
10 Ganja La Range — Gang Chhenpo 6397m
11 Langtang (Langtrang) Himal — Shisha Pangma 8013m
   Phola Gangchhen 7661m Main ridge proper —
   Langtrang Lirung (Gangchhen Ledrub) 7245m
12 Ganesh Himal — Ganesh Peak 7406m
13 Thaple Himal — Khojang 6023m
14 Sringi Himal — Chamar 7177m
15 Kutang Himal — 6340m
16 Larkya Himal — c.6100m
17 Gurkha Himal — Manaslu 8156m
18 Himlung Himal — 7126m
19 Peri Himal — 6172m
20 Damodar Himal — 6712m

21 Lamjung Himal — 6983m
22 Annapurna Himal — Annapurna 8091m
   Annapurna II 7937m
23 Dhaulagiri Himal — Dhaulagiri 8167m
   Dhuala II 7751m
24 Mukut Himal (Mul Lekh) — Hongde 6556m
25 Mustangbhot Himal — 6475m
26 Chharkabhot Himal — 6645m
27 Palchung Hamga Himal — 6563m
28 Kubi Kaṅgri — 6855m
29 Kanjiroba Himal — 6882m
30 Sisne Himal — c.6600m
31 Patrasi Himal — Kangde Hiunchuli 6627m
32 Changla Himal — 6715m
33 Saipal 7034m
34 Byas Rishi (Yokapahar) Himal — Api 7132m
   Nampa 6755m

36. Jo-mo-glan-ma. - Pronounced Jo-mo-lang-ma ('lang' as 'lung'). Meaning "Lady Cow". Name appearing in booklet presented to some members of the 1936 expedition by the Head Lama of Rongbuk monastery; printed in the Water-Ape Year, i. e. 1932; translated by F. W. Thomas, formerly Boden Professor of Sanskrit at Oxford University. This name appears also in the Rongbuk Lama's diary, Leaf 46 (Everest the Unfinished Adventure p. 288).

37. Jo-mo-glan-mahi gans-ri. - Name appearing in the Rongbuk Lama's diary, Leaf 176 (Everest the Unfinished Adventure p. 288).

38. Jomo-kang-kar. - Name put forward by Pundit Chandra Das in 1885 according to Waddell in Among the Himalayas (Freshfield, AJ 21 p. 35). The Tibetan name for No. 29 according to Collie (Climbing on the Himalaya p. 11).

39. Jomolang-ma-ri. - Meaning "Venerable ? Bull Goddess". According to Creighton, a form appearing in the new Tibetan-Russian dictionary published in Moscow by the Siberian Section of the Soviet Academy of Sciences in 1963 (AJ 69 p. 144).

40. Jomolu. - Meaning "Venerable Goddess ? Redeemer" (ibid.).

41. Jomolungma. - Meaning "Venerable Goddess of the Country" - ? (ibid.).

42. Jo-mo-lung-ma. - Version used by Blakeney when commenting on Creighton's information in AJ 69 (AJ 70 p. 305).

43. Kang-cha-ma-lung. - 'Kang' meaning 'snow'. A local name according to notes left by Sir Charles Bell in 1935 (Blakeney, AJ 70 p. 305).

44. Lho-Cha-dzi-ma-lung-pa. - Meaning "The southern District where the Birds are kept". The full version of No. 45, according to Sir Charles Bell (Odell, AJ 47 p. 128).

45. Lho-Cha-ma-lung. - Meaning "The Bird Country of the

South". A short version of No. 44, according to Sir Charles Bell (ibid.).

46. Mi-thik Dgu-thik Bya-phur Long-nga. - The more correct form of No. 47 (HJ 4 p. 176).

47. Mi-ti Gu-ti Cha-pu Long-nga. - An improbable name reportedly found by the Tsarong Shap-pe, one of the highest officials in Tibet, in some ancient writings (Mason, Abode of Snow p. 73). Name mentioned to Mr. D. Macdonald, the British Trade Agent at Yatung and Gyantse, by an official of Lhasa in 1930 (Odell, AJ 47 p. 128).

48. Mont Everest. - A version first used in a letter signed by Colonel Sir A. Waugh and printed in the Proceedings of the R. G. S. for 1856; very probably due to a slip by a copying clerk. Subsequently used by General J. T. Walker, formerly Surveyor General of India (Freshfield, AJ 21 p. 33-35).

49. Mount Everest. - The official name conferred on the mountain in 1865, after Sir George Everest. Proposed by the Surveyor General, Sir A. Waugh, with the support of Colonel H. Thullier, Deputy Surveyor General, Mr. R. Sikhdar, Chief Computer, and Sir R. Murchison, President of the R. G. S.; finally approved by the Government of India.

50. Qomolangma. - or Qomolangma Feng. Name used by China (Another Ascent of the World's Highest Peak, Peking 1975).

51. Sagarmatha. - Sherpa name, now officially adopted by Nepalese government after researches by Aufschnaiter for the FNH surveying teams, 1955 to date (various FNH survey documents and maps issued by FNH Munich, 1957 to date). A name, meaning 'sky head', derived from Sanskrit and invented and adopted by Nepal during the last decade in response to China's claim over the mountain; China retaliated with Qomolungma Feng (sic.) equally baseless (Odell, AJ 82 p. 258).

52. Tchomolungma. - Sir Charles Bell, in Tibet: Past and Present, states that some French Capuchin Friars, who resided at Lhasa from 1708 to 1733, constructed a rough map of the country and marked on it the mountain "Tchomolungma" in precisely the correct position for the Mt. Everest group. This map by d'Anville is still in existence (HJ 3 p. 128). Odell, who had been shown a copy of the map by Sven Hedin, refers (AJ 37 p. 196).

53. Tchoumou Lancma. - In 1926 Dr. Sven Hedin published "Mount Everest" in German; in it he drew attention to the fact that a range of mountains within sixty miles of Everest had appeared on d'Anville's map of 1733 under this name. He argues that "Mount Everest" should give way to this older name. Sir Sidney Burrard in his paper Mount Everest and its Tibetan Names: A Review of Sir Sven Hedin's Book, Dehra Dun, 1931, refutes this argument. In his critical examination Burrard shows that the name is placed on the lowest ground in the angle between the two rivers Sun Kosi and Arun, some sixty miles south of Everest (HJ 4 pp. 174-175 and 193-195). This would be a district south of Makalu.

54. Tshomo Lungma. - The name found by the 1921 Everest Expedition (so spelt by Sven Hedin) according to Blakeney in his equally critical examination of Burrard's paper Mount Everest and its Tibetan Names (AJ 70 p. 307).

55. Tsungau. - Hooker climbed to the top of Tonglo and described the view: "... in the far north-west ... a white mountain mass of stupendous elevation at 80 miles distance, called by my Nepal people 'Tsungau'". A footnote states: "P.S. - Tsungau is now better known as Mount Everest" (Hooker's Himalayan Journals, Minerva Library edition, 1 volume, 1891, p. 129).

There has been enough controversy and conflict of opinions already without the present author reopening the issue; the purpose of establishing the above list is to collate the evidence in a fair and factual way. The 55 names (and more) used at different times can be pared down to about a dozen basically dissimilar names, the majority of which can be discounted as having no real foundations. The remainder appear to be chiefly variations probably due to local pronunciations, faulty hearing, misinformation, incorrect transliterations, misquotations and perhaps even to mis-prints. The breaking down of names into monosyllables and the use of hyphens may be philologically correct or they may be, as with the use of capital letters, a matter of arbitrary choice. But dare one hope, after a century and a quarter of learned disputation - and irrespective of whether Peak XV did or did not have originally an indigenous name (and the weight of evidence seems to show that the mountain itself did not) - that henceforth surveyors, cartographers, and mountaineers will agree to resolve the matter finally. A resonable solution could be that the mountain be known - in the way that the peak standing on the border between Switzerland and Italy is known as Le Cervin in French, Il Cervino in Italian, and das Matterhorn in German - by any one of three names: Sagarmatha in Nepalese, Chomolungma (or Jomolungma) in Tibetan, and Mount Everest, the first name officially conferred upon it? And that once agreement has been reached, that these spellings be adhered to?

Mountaineering: The first Europeans to cross the Himalaya were Portuguese missionaries, Antonio Andrade and Manuel Marques; in 1624 they went to establish a mission in Western Tibet. They were followed by other missionaries and pilgrims and then by travellers and traders journeying between India, Tibet and China. Then came the first surveyors of the East India Company and those of the Survey of India. At the same time the first explorers began probing and penetrating the remoter areas of the Himalaya, to west and to east but excluding Nepal, which was closed to all foreigners and whose

mountains could be observed only from afar. They were followed towards the end of the 19th century by a number of more
elaborate expeditions organized for mountain climbing as well
as for various scientific undertakings, expeditions such as
those of Martin Conway, the Duke of Abruzzi, de Filippi and
the Workmans; these carried out vast reconnaissances and
photographic and scientific surveys of the ranges and glacier
systems, chiefly in the Karakoram mountains. Concurrently
smaller expeditions were also heading into the Himalaya with
their intentions more specifically climbing and mountain exploration rather than actual surveying; among these many
early mountaineering pioneers were W. W. Graham (notwith-
standing the uncertainty surrounding some of his claims),
Freshfield, Longstaff, Mummery, Bruce, Dr. Kellas, Jacot-
Guillarmod, Mumm, the Neve brothers, together with their
companions.

A number of lesser peaks were ascended in the course of
these mountain explorations and attempts on some of the higher
summits were made. High cols were crossed, routes were
compared and their difficulties assessed. Imperceptibly the
emphasis shifted from climbing mountains in a particular area
to climbing or making a bid for a particular peak. But of the
fourteen 8000m. summits in the Himalaya, K2, Nanga Parbat
and Kangchenjunga alone were attempted; all the others, situated in Nepal or on the Nepal-Tibet border, were beyond the
reach of the mountaineers.

Favourable political relations with the Lhasa authorities,
however, resulted in permission being granted to the British
to climb Mount Everest from the Tibetan side and the subsequent repeated attempts on the world's highest mountain came
to dominate the Himalayan scene during the inter-war years
(1920-1939).

Despite these failures to reach the top - assuming always
that Mallory and Irvine did not do so in 1924 - the 8000m.
'barrier' was broken as early as 1922. That year Norton,

Mallory and Somervell reached an altitude of 8225m. without oxygen; six days later Finch and J. G. Bruce reached an altitude of 8320m. with oxygen. In 1924, Norton attained 8570m. without oxygen; on June 8th of that same year, Mallory and Irvine were seen by Odell "at a point which, if the 'second rock step'" was at a height of 8600m; what may have followed is conjecture.

In 1949 Nepal opened its frontiers to the outside world and within eight years ten of the fourteen 8000m. peaks had been climbed; Annapurna (8091m.) was the first to be climbed, in 1950; this was followed in 1953 by Everest (8848m.) and Nanga Parbat (8125m.). From then on the number of expeditions coming from many different countries of the world multiplied and by 1964 all these Himalayan giants had been climbed, the last one being Shisha Pangma (8046m.) scaled by the Chinese in 1964.

These and most of their subsidiary summits having been successfully reached, the aims of many climbing parties have been diverted to lesser peaks (in height though not necessarily in difficulty) or to alternatives to already known routes. Smaller parties have undertaken these ascents and more recently light-weight, alpine style tactics have been adopted with success.

Hot on the heels of mountaineers have followed trekkers, tourists and trippers. This sudden explosive growth of visitors to a few relatively small but popular areas of the Himalaya, though not without some benefit to the local population, has resulted in many serious problems of congestion, pollution and spoliation of the very environment these visitors have gone to enjoy and risks aggravating the difficulties of adjustment of the inhabitants from a simple, rural culture to a commercially orientated way of life.

The deforestation of the hillsides and the disappearance of the natural vegetation, and hence of much of the wild life too, the building of roads and hotels, insanitary camping sites and the ferrying of tourists and climbers by light aircraft into the

THE EIGHT - THOUSAND METRE PEAKS OF THE HIMALAYA AND KARAKORAM

			1st ascent	
3	Mount Everest	8848m.	29,028ft.	1953 British
14	K2	8611m.	28,253ft.	1954 Italian
		(8760m.)	(28,741ft.)	
1	Kangchenjunga	8598m.	28,028ft.	1955 British
4	Lhotse	8511m.	27,923ft.	1956 Swiss
2	Makalu	8481m.	27,825ft.	1955 French
1a	Yalung Kang	8420m.	27,625ft.	1973 Japanese
4a	Lhotse Shar	8398m.	27,553ft.	1970 Austrian
9	Dhaulagiri I	8167m.	26,795ft.	1960 Swiss
7	Manaslu	8156m.	26,760ft.	1956 Japanese
5	Cho Oyu	8153m.	26,750ft.	1954 Austrian
10	Nanga Parbat	8125m.	26,660ft.	1953 Austro-German
8	Annapurna I	8091m.	26,545ft.	1950 French
11	Gasherbrum I	8068m.	26,470ft.	1958 American
13	Broad Peak	8047m.	26,400ft.	1957 Austrian
12	Gasherbrum II	8035m.	26,360ft.	1956 Austrian
6	Shisha Pangma	8013m.	26,291ft.	1964 Chinese
		(8046m.)	(26,397ft.)	

Chapter mountain sections in order of numerical sequence from East to West shown on map below and listed opposite by the same numbers in order of altitude.

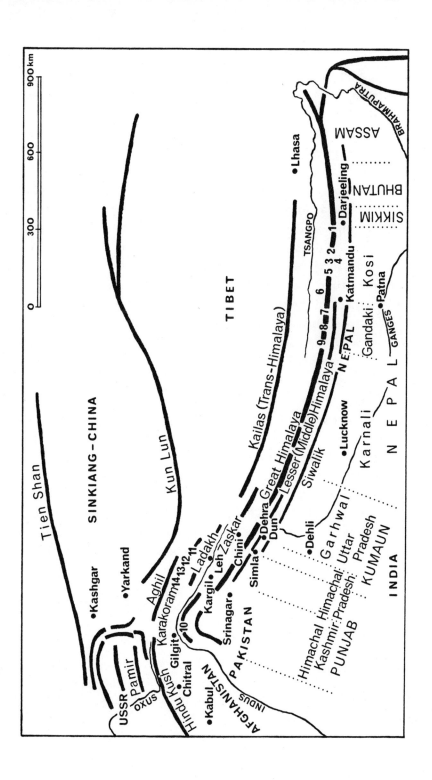

very heart of the mountains - all these, carried to excess, will destroy irrevocably not only the immediate environment but also the social structure of its inhabitants. Already the valleys and the approach routes of the more favoured areas are being vulgarized and the glaciers and mountains fouled by the detritus of countless expeditions who thoughtlessly litter the high cols and camp sites with abandoned tents and discarded bottles, with empty tins and plastic garbage. All credit then to the students of the Evergreen State College from Olympia, U.S.A., who initiated a clean-up project in the Khumbu Valley and by their efforts removed, within a short space of time, between 500 and 700 kg. of trash - and yet but only a token of the total amount of discarded rubbish.

We have seen the results of these self destructive processes in the European Alps and to a lesser extent in our own British Hills; all mountain climbers and walkers are aware that constant vigilance and wise control are necessary to maintain some semblance of natural beauty and peace in those remoter areas. The poor economy of those living in the high Himalayan valleys needs to be improved but the process should be gradual and planned. The excesses of commercial exploitation - usually not to the advantage of the native population - are a threat that must be recognized and countered if the whole Himalaya is not to be blighted and the Throne of the Gods, the Abode of Snow, the Valley of Flowers, are not to become just half-remembered phrases found only within the pages of long-forgotten books.

KANGCHENJUNGA

Yalung Kang 8598 S.summit
8420 8476
Sickle
VI
S.ridge
Great
Shelf
IV
III
II
hump lower icefall
West Buttress
† Pache's grave
BC
Yalung gl.

Alfondi

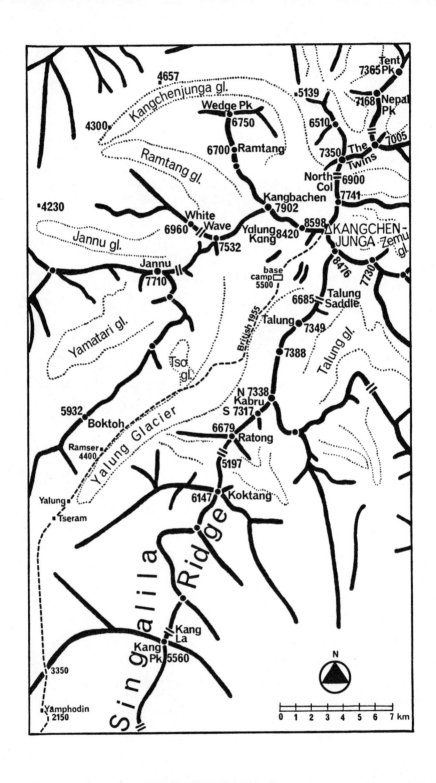

KANGCHENJUNGA   1
and Yalung Kang

Situated: Sikkim Himalaya (on Sikkim-Nepal border) in the Singalila Range (Ridge).

Longitude: 88° 09' 00" E.

Latitude: 27° 42' 09" N.

Altitude: Main summit - 8598m.
Central summit - c. 8496m.
South summit - 8476m.
Yalung Kang (West summit) - 8420m.

(The Alpine Journal Vol. 79, page 256, quotes revised heights as measured by the Japanese 1973 expedition. These would reverse completely the order of the subsidiary summits with Yalung Kang standing at 8505m. These new determinations have been neither confirmed nor accepted yet by the leading authorities).

Early Designation No: Main summit: IX
South summit: VIII

Name: Approximate meaning "The Five Treasuries of the Great Snow".

KANGCHENJUNGA, the most easterly of the 8000m. peaks and the third highest summit in the world, stands, orographically, in some isolation from the main axis of the Great Himalaya. It is unique in as much as it is buttressed north

and south as well as west and east by mountains of equal stature. The main summit stands centrally with ridges extending to all four cardinal points, allowing thereby a variety of approaches. Before 1949, when Nepal was closed, all approaches had to be made through Sikkim;   more recently Sikkim has been closed and all approaches have had to be made through Nepal.
The mountain has been attacked from three different sides but climbed only thrice by two expeditions at 22 years interval. Six men have stood just short of the summit - the first, 50 years after the earliest attempt on the summit.
The total height to be ascended from the Zemu gl. (German Camp 6) is about 3325m.; from the Yalung gl. (British Base Camp near Pache's grave), about 3080m.

MAPS - Good maps of Sikkim and the area of Kangchenjunga are to be found in some of the early books, particularly in Risley's Gazetteer of Sikhim and in Freshfield's Round Kang-chenjunga.
The following modern maps are generally available. Those most recommended are marked with an asterisk (*).

1/506,880 Nepal East Sh. 3rd Ed.-GSGS, 1969, DMS(MoD), London *
1/250,000 Kanchenjunga Sh. NG 45-3, Series U502, 2nd Ed. 1963. AMS, Washington, D.C. (only fair black & white litho reprint available 1977) *
1/150,000 Sikkim Himalaya. 1951. SSAF, Zurich.*

CHRONICLE

1848 J. D. Hooker, one of the greatest of British botanists,
1849 made two remarkable journeys, which together were to take him on an almost complete circuit of the Kangchen-junga range and to within 22 km. of the peak itself. He

described Kangchenjunga in some detail and made a sketch of it from Mon Lepcha. Hooker was accompanied for part of the time by his friend Dr. Campbell, Superintendent of Darjeeling. He travelled also up the Tista valley and reached almost to the Zemu glacier before heading N. E. to Bam Tso and the Dongkya La (5600m.) (1)

1852 Capt. W. S. Sherwill (Br), a Revenue Surveyor, crossed the Singalila ridge from the Kulhait river to investigate the geological structure of the Kangchenjunga range. He also carried out a survey of the area west of Jongri and Kabur and made a map of the headwaters of the Ringbi, Yunga and Yalung rivers. (2)

1855 Hermann von Schlagintweit (Ger), in charge of the Magnetic Survey of India, having failed to obtain permission to travel in Sikkim and on the advice of Dr. Campbell, set off to follow the Singalila ridge northwards. He ascended Tonglo Peak and reached the summit ridge of Phalut. It was from here that Schlagintweit painted his panoramas of Everest and Kangchenjunga. Shortly afterwards his party was turned back by Nepalese soldiers. (3)

1861 Major J. L. Sherwill (Br) and three colleagues travelled from Yoksam and Jongri to the Guicha La (4940m.), overlooking the Talung gl. They also ascended the Kabur ridge to a height of 5030m. (4)

1876 Mrs. Elizabeth Sarah Mazuchelli (who was generally called Nina) made a journey to the southern slopes of Jannu having come via the Kang La and Tseram after crossing the Singalila ridge. (5)

1878 Capt. H. J. Harman (Br) began the regular survey of the
1881 Sikkim Himalaya. He attempted to climb some of the high mountains, including Chomiomo (6836m.), and reached the Dongkya Pass. In 1881 he tried to reach the

foot of Kangchenjunga but his health broke down. He died the same year. The map of his survey (1 inch = 16 miles) was published in 1882. (6)

1879 Two pundit explorers, Lama Ugyen Gyatso, a Tibetan
1881 teacher at Darjeeling, and Babu Sarat Chandra Das, headmaster of a school at Darjeeling, travelled extensively from Darjeeling through the region of Jongri, Kang La, Yalung, Kangbachan to the Chorten Nyima La (north of the massif). A map of the district north of Kangchenjunga (1 inch = 16 miles) was later published. (6)

1882 Major J. W. A. Michell (Br) read a paper before the Alpine Club and in conclusion added that he saw no reason why an expedition to the Himalaya, under the auspices of the A. C., should not succeed, even if an attempt was made to scale Kangchenjunga, "one of its northern spurs at any rate seems to present no insuperable obstacles". (7)

1883 W. Robert (Br) completed Harman's unfinished work, during which time he ascended the rivers flowing down from the eastern face of Kangchenjunga. Earlier (1881) he had produced a map of east Nepal (1 inch = 2 miles). (6)

1883 Rinzin Namgyal (Bhutian), another of the pundits, assis-
1884 ted Robert by exploring the Talung valley. The following year he became the first to explore the Yalung glacier, ascending to 5800m. He then followed Chandra Das' route north to the Jongsong La and to Chorten Nyima La, returning down the Lhonak river valley and, via Lachen, to Darjeeling. He thus completed the first circuit of the Kangchenjunga massif. His map of the country round Kangchenjunga (1 inch = 4 miles) was subsequently published. (6)

1883 The first actual climbing in the neighbourhood of Kangchenjunga was undertaken by W. W. Graham (Br) accompanied at different times by Joseph Imboden (Sw) or by E. Boss (Sw) and Ulrich Kaufman (Sw); both Imboden and Kaufman were professional guides. A number of peaks around 6000m. were claimed to have been climbed including Jubonu (5936m.) and Kabru (7338m.) from the S. E. There is considerable doubt as to whether in fact it was Kabru that they ascended and not Forked Peak (6108m.). Graham also crossed the Guicha La from the south and visited the Talung gl. (Previously he had mistakenly thought that he had climbed Changabang (6864m.) - also with no great difficulty). (8) (9)

1890 J. C. White (Br), Political Officer in Sikkim and resident
1891 in that country for some 20 years, made several journeys of interest. In 1890 he travelled from Jongri (Dzongri) over the Guicha La to the Talung glacier. In 1891, accompanied by T. Hoffmann the Calcutta photographer, he travelled to the Zemu gl. from Talung monastery; they ascended the glacier to a height of 5350m. White then continued on his own northwards up the Lhonak valley to Naku La (5540m.) on the Tibetan border. Hoffmann had taken the first photographs of the northern face of Siniolchu (6887m.). (10) (11)

1896 Major W. A. Waddell (Br) of the Indian Army Medical Corps had made several journeys of exploration in Nepal and Sikkim. In 1896, again accompanied by Kinthup (of the Tsangpo/Brahmaputra episode) as Sirdar, he travelled to Jongri and the Semo La (2 km. W. of the Kang La). From a knife-edged ridge above it he enjoyed a magnificent panorama of the massif though Kangchenjunga itself was blocked from view. As a Government Official, Waddell dared not risk descending into Nepalese territory to set foot on the Yalung gl. and felt obliged to turn back. (12)

1899 A party of six, brought together by D. W. Freshfield (Br) and including Prof. E. J. Garwood (Br), C. Dover (Br), Vittorio Sella and his brother Erminio (It) and the pundit Rinzin Namgyal, made a seven weeks autumn circuit of the mountain in the direction opposite to that followed by Rinzin in 1884 and much of it at a great height. Having travelled up the Tista valley and along the Lachen river, they ascended the Zemu gl. to about 5350m. The party then crossed into Lhonak, headed west over the Jonsong La (6145m.) to the Kangchenjunga gl. from which they trekked to Kangbachen and thence to Tseram, the Kang La and Jongri. From here an excursion was made to the summit of Kabur (4825m.) from where they had an extensive view of the southern face of Kangchenjunga and the upper part of the unexplored Yalung gl. A second excursion was made to the Guicha La before the party headed south again down the Rathong valley back to Darjeeling. (13)

1905 The first attempt to climb this mountain was made by a small Swiss party - Dr. J. Jacot-Guillarmod, C. A. Reymond and A. A. Pache - which placed itself under the leadership of A. Crowley (Br), who invited along an Italian hotel-keeper from Darjeeling, R. de Righi. From the head of the Yalung gl. (never before ascended) they proceeded up the S. W. Face (one of Freshfield's suggested routes) and established Camp 7 at 6200m. (more probably 6000m.); high point reached about 6500m. On Sept. 1 Guillarmod, Pache, de Righi and three natives were descending to a lower camp when they met with an accident. Pache and the three natives were killed, de Righi lay senseless and half buried in the snow. Reymond descended alone on hearing the survivors' cries for help but Crowley remained in his tent drinking tea for "a mountain accident of this sort is one of the things for which I have no sympathy whatever ... To-morrow I hope to go down and find out how things stand. " He considered that "the doctor is old enough to rescue himself, and nobody would want to rescue Righi". But despite Crowley (the self-styled 'Great Beast') all was not in vain: more detailed information of the Yalung gl. basin was obtained and subsequently incorporated into Garwood's map, and much additional information and useful photographs on the climbing prospects of this side of the mountain were brought back. (14) (15)

1907- Dr. A. M. Kellas (Br) visited the Sikkim Himalaya several
1912 times, exploring mainly to the east and north of Kangchenjunga: ascents of Zemu Gap (5880m.) from the north, Simvu Saddle (5390m.), three attempts on Simvu (6815m.), Nepal Gap (6400m.), the Langpo and Kangchenjunga gls. His list of achievements, mostly done only with native companions, is outstanding: in 1910 alone, he made ten ascents over 6000m. In 1912 he was back again and after climbing Kangchenjau (6889m.) he visited the area to the immediate east and north of Kangchenjunga: Green Lake, Tent Peak Pass, Jonsong Peak. (16) (17)

1920 H. Raeburn (Br) paid two visits to the area south of Kangchenjunga. The first with Lt. Col. H. W. Tobin when they crossed the Talung gl. from Guicha La and ascended the Tongshyong gl. in an attempt to reach the Zemu Gap. The second with C. G. Crawford to visit the Yalung gl. and its environs; from about 5800m. on the spur running westward from the Talung Pk. they had a discouraging view of Kangchenjunga's S. W. Face. High point reached, about 6400m. on Kangchenjunga's S. W. slopes. They returned over the Rathong Pass (5197m.). (18)

1920 Kellas made two more visits to the Sikkim Himalaya. He
1921 was in the area south of Kangchenjunga: Kang La, Kabru, Narsing (c. 6100m.) the last of which he climbed. During

these and his earlier tours this tireless and modest
mountaineer had obtained many valuable photographs of
the glaciers to the east of Everest and of the still unknown
high mountains to its north; also many of the Kangchenjunga massif. Immediately after returning to Darjeeling
in 1921 he set off with the first Everest Expedition but
died from heart failure at Kampa Dzong. (19)

1925 A photographic expedition to the southern glaciers of
Kangchenjunga by N. A. Tombazi of Bombay who had
twice been to Sikkim (1919 and 1920), on one occasion
visiting the eastern glaciers (on which he reached a height
of about 6000m.). With his porters, he left Darjeeling
in April and headed north for Jongri and the Guicha La.
They crossed the Talung gl. then ascended the Tongshyong
gl. and climbed to the Zemu Gap (first time reached from
the south). Tombazi concluded that the passage of this
Gap to reach the eastern approaches of the mountain
would not be very advantageous to travellers. After
climbing Kabru and visiting the Rathong gl., Tombazi
returned down the Singalila Ridge. He brought back a
fine collection of photographs of the mountains. (20)

1926 Capt. J. E. H. Boustead (Br) went in May to the Zemu
Gap via the Guicha La. He crossed the Gap and crossed
back again. This would be the first complete crossing
but H. W. Tilman doubted (1936) whether the col Boustead crossed had in fact been the Zemu and not another
one at the very head of the Tongshyong gl. (21) (22)

1929 E. F. Farmer (Am) went to the Yalung gl. from the Kang
La during May with the secret intention of climbing Kangchenjunga alone. Camp 3 was pitched at the foot of the
mountain. May 26 Farmer set off with Lobsang and two
porters to begin the climb; during the morning he continued up on his own (despite warnings), telling his three
porters to wait for him as he wanted to take some

photographs. He did not return that night. The following day he was seen climbing again (apparently towards the Talung Saddle, 6685m.). He was never seen again. (23)

1929 A German expedition of nine members, leader P. Bauer, made the first resolute attack on the mountain. Base Camp (Camp 3) was positioned August 18 not far from the Green Lake (Zemu gl.) which they had reached from Lachen. The plan was to attack the mountain via the N. E. Spur. The crest of the spur was reached September 16; Camps 8, 9, 10 (all were ice caves) followed; Camp 10 was at 7100m. The high point reached was about 7400m. A difficult retreat under bad weather conditions terminated the attempt. (24)

1930 An International expedition of five Germans, three British, two Swiss and one Austrian; leader Prof. G. O. Dyhrenfurth who had received permission to pass through Nepal. They left Darjeeling early April and, via the Kang La and Kangbachen, reached the Kangchenjunga gl; Base Camp was placed close to Pangperma. The plan was to climb up to the N. Ridge from below the N. Col (i. e. by the N. W. Face). When setting off to establish Camp 3 on the first snow terrace above the ice-cliff, E. Schneider and Sherpa Chettan were caught by a great ice fall and Chettan was killed (May 9). The attempt then shifted to the N. W. Ridge with the hope of climbing up from below Kangbachen; U. Wieland and Schneider reached 6400m. before giving up. The expedition then turned its attention to other peaks to the north of Kangchenjunga. (25) (26)

1931 Second German expedition, 10 members, leader P. Bauer. They followed the 1929 route; Advanced Base (Camp 6) was established at the foot of the N. E. Spur July 13. Incessant bad weather delayed the placing of Camp 11 (an ice cave at 7360m.) until September 15. A few days later the highest point of the N. E. Spur was reached (7700m.) but between it and its juncture with the main N. Ridge there lay a depression then a steep snow slope up to the Ridge; it was in too dangerous a condition to attempt so once again the climbers were obliged to retreat. Earlier H. Schaller and porter Pasang had been killed in a fall while climbing up to Camp 8; Sirdar Lobsang and porter Babulall had also died from illness. (24)

1933 Houston-Mount Everest Expedition (Br). The second flight was organized for April 4; two planes were to fly over and photograph Kangchenjunga: Air Commodore P. F. M. Fellowes, pilot, and A. L. Fisher, cinematographer, in one and Flying Officer R. C. W. Ellison, pilot, and S. R. Bonnett, cinematographer, in the other. They approached the mountain at 10,400m. but a huge cloud cap 500m. thick obliterated the summit, over which they were not able to fly. From a photographic point of view the flight was only partially successful. (27)

1937 A small British party planned and organized by C. R. Cooke included H. C. J. Hunt, Mrs Hunt. One of the principal objects was to examine the N. Col (6900m.) and to assess its feasibility as an alternative approach to Bauer's 1929 route. Between November 14 and 19 Cooke and two Sherpas set off from the Twins gl. and tackled the 760m. high wall of rock and ice. It proved too much for such a small group and Cooke was obliged to turn back when only 200m. from the top. The route was not thought to be a practicable one on account of its difficulties and dangers. (28)

1940 A New Zealand expedition of eight members, leader S. Conway, obtained permission to climb Kangchenjunga; preparations were nearing completion and sailing dates were fixed for an attempt in May 1940. The outbreak of war caused its cancellation. (29)

1947 K. Neame, a pilot in the R. A. F. , made two scheduled
flights over Kangchenjunga and its environs towards the
end of March; the object was to take photographs for an
American, Dr. Church, in connection with plans for a
new irrigation scheme. Cloud prevented good photographs
from being taken. (30)

1953 G. C. G. Lewis (Br), who had accompanied G. Frey (Sw)
and Sirdar Tenzing for part of the time on Frey's reconnaissance of the Yalung gl. and its tributaries in October
1951, and J. W. R. Kempe (Br) together returned to the
Yalung gl. during May. From Darjeeling they went up
the Singalila Ridge and crossed by the Chumbab La
(4496m.). During their reconnaissance they were able
to examine more closely the S. W. Face of Kangchenjunga
and came to the conclusion that, despite F. S. Smythe's
adverse view (1930), a possible route up the face might
indeed exist. (31)

1954 British Reconnaissance Expedition, six members, leader
J. W. R. Kempe. The object was to discover a practicable
way up to the great ice-shelf running across the S. W.
Face. Three possible routes were investigated during
May: the 1905 route (to the left of the main ice-fall,
facing the mountain), another from below the Talung
Saddle, and a third more centrally in the vicinity of the
main ice-fall. A safe route was worked out nearly to the
top of the lower part of the ice-fall via the Rock Rib, at
the top of which Camp 7 was placed (5790m.). (32) (33)

1955 FIRST and SECOND ASCENTS: A British expedition of
nine members, leader Dr. R. C. Evans, left Darjeeling
early in March and approached the Yalung gl. through
Nepal, Sikkim being still closed. An attempt was made
to force a route up from Kempe's 1954 Camp 7 site by
N. D. Hardie (NZ) and G. C. Band but this was found to
be too difficult and was abandoned. The route finally

63

decided on started from a new Base Camp (5519m.), just below Pache's grave, and ascended the snow and ice slopes to the left (west) of the Western Buttress, crossing the Hump to the upper ice-fall and the great shelf from where it continued up by the Gang-Way, to the right (east) of Freshfield's Horseshoe, now referred to as the Sickle, and thence to the summit. Camp 6 was placed at the top of the Gang-Way (8200m.) and from there, May 25, Band and J. Brown climbed to just short of the top in accordance with a promise given to the Maharajah of Sikkim that the top of the mountain would remain inviolate. The following day, May 26, Hardie and H. R. A. Streather repeated the climb. Oxygen was used both times. Sherpa Pemi Doje, exhausted after his carry to Camp 5, died at Base Camp a few days later. (34)

1967 A Japanese reconnaissance party of two, H. Higuchi and T. Matsuda, travelled in April to the Yalung gl. and examined the possibility of climbing Yalung Kang (Kangchenjunga West) via the Western Buttress and the Hump. (35)

1973 Yalung Kang, FIRST ASCENT: A Japanese expedition of 15 members, Organization Head Dr. E. Nishibori, leader H. Higuchi, approached the Yalung gl. through Nepal. They succeeded in climbing the summit by its S. W. Ridge, after following approximately the 1955 route at the very start. Y. Ageta and T. Matsuda reached the top very late on May 14 from Camp 5 at 8000m. The two climbers bivouaced on the way down at about 8300m. Next morning they were seen to have difficulty in finding their way down; a support party rescued Ageta but Matsuda had disappeared - only his broken ice-axe was found. (35)

1974 Japanese expedition, 12 members, leader S. Toriumi, attempted YALUNG KANG by its S. E. Ridge. Camp 5 was placed at 7850m. R. Hiro and Sherpa Pasang failed to reach the summit by a mere 20m. on account of bad weather, May 14 (36)

1975 Yalung Kang, 2nd, 3rd, 4th ASCENTS: An Austro-German expedition of 11 members, leader S. Aeberli made a new route up the South Face of this summit after following approximately the 1955 route as far as the great shelf. Three separate parties reached the top: M. Dacher, E. Lackner, R. Walter on May 9; G. Baur, P. Vogler, H. Wagner on May 12; S. Mayerl, G. Sturm, R. Zintl on May 13. (37) (38)

1977 THIRD ASCENT: Indian Army expedition, leader Col. N. Kumar, approaching from Sikkim and the Zemu gl., ascended the N.E. Spur (1931 route) and reached the N. Ridge May 24. Their highest camp was placed on the ridge at 7990m. From there Major Prem Chand and Naik N.D. Sherpa established a high bivouac May 30 and the following day they continued to the top, stopping just short of the actual summit. Oxygen was used. Earlier in the month Havildar S. Singh was killed in a fall while descending fixed ropes below Camp 2. (39)

KANGCHENJUNGA

Principal Source References:

(1) Hooker Himalayan Journals

(2) Sherwill Notes Upon a Tour in the Sikkim Himalayah Mountains

(3) Schlagintweit Reisen in Indien u. Hochasien Vol. 2

(4) Sherwill "Journal of a Trip undertaken to Explore the Glaciers of the Kangchenjunga Group" JASB 31 p. 457

(5) A Lady Pioneer (Mazuchelli) The Indian Alps and how we Crossed them

(6) RSOI Vol. 8 1915

(7) Michell "Twenty Years Climbing and Hunting in the Himalayas" AJ 11 pp. 203-215

(8) Graham "Up the Himalaya" in "Good Words" 1885, 21 pp.

(9) Graham "Travel and Ascents in the Himalaya" AJ 12 pp. 25-52

(10) Hoffman "Exploration in Sikkim: to the North-East of Kangchinjinga" PRGS 14 pp. 613-618

(11) White Sikhim and Bhutan

(12) Waddell Among the Himalayas

(13) Freshfield Round Kangchenjunga

(14) Jacot-Guillarmod "Vers le Kangchinjunga" Jahrbuch des SAC 41 pp. 190-205

(15) (G. Yeld, Ed.) "The Disaster on Kangchenjunga" AJ 23 pp. 51-54

(16) Kellas "The Mountains of Northern Sikkim & Garhwal" AJ 26 pp. 113-142

(17) Kellas "A Fourth Visit to the Sikkim Himalaya, with Ascent of the Kangchenjau" AJ 27 pp. 125-153

(18) Raeburn "The Southerly Walls of Kangchenjunga & the Rathong Pass" AJ 34 pp. 33-50

(19) Tobin "Exploration & Climbing in the Sikkim Himalaya" HJ 2 p. 11

(20) Tombazi Account of a Photographic Expedition in Sikkim

(21) Boustead "An Adventure to Kangchenjunga" GJ 69 pp. 344-350

(22) Tilman When Men and Mountains Meet

(23) W. S. Ladd "The Fatality on Kangchenjunga" AAJ 1929 pp. 195-199

(24) Bauer Himalayan Campaign

(25) Dyhrenfurth Himalaya, Unsere Expedition 1930

(26) Dyhrenfurth "The International Himalayan Expedition 1930" HJ 3 pp. 77-91

(27) Fellowes, etc. First Over Everest

(28) Hunt & Cooke "A Winter Visit to the Zemu Glacier" HJ 10 pp. 49-70

(29) Temple The World at Their Feet

(30) Neame "Alone Over Everest" MW 1955 pp. 133-141

(31) Kempe "The Yalung Valley, 1953" AJ 59 pp. 316-322

(32) Kempe "Kangchenjunga Reconnaissance, 1954" AJ 59 pp. 428-431

(33) Tucker Kanchenjunga

(34) Evans Kangchenjunga the Untrodden Peak

(35) Higuchi "The First Ascent of Yalung Kang" AJ 80 pp. 17-28

(36) AAJ 1975 p. 193

(37) Sturm Erfolg am Kantsch 8438m.

(38) AAJ 1976 p. 512

(39) M 57 p. 13

Additional books and ephemera relevant to Kangchenjunga, not already listed. (The dates in brackets refer to the expeditions written about).

BAUER   Kangchenjunga Challenge (1929, 1931)

BOUSTEAD   The Wind of Morning (1926)

BRAHAM   Himalayan Odyssey (1954)

BROWN   The Hard Years (one chapter, 1955)

CLARK   The Splendid Hills (in part)

DOUGLAS & CLYDESDALE and M'INTYRE   The Pilots Book of Everest (1933)

DYHRENFURTH   Das Buch vom Kantsch (up to 1955)

GRAHAM   "Climbing the Himalayas" in From the Equator to the Pole

HUXLEY   Life and Letters of Sir Joseph Dalton Hooker

IRVING   Ten Great Mountains (one chapter)

JACKSON   More than Mountains

KYOTO A. A. C.   The First Ascent of Yalung Kang (1973)

MACINTYRE   Attack on Everest (one chapter, 1929, 1930, 1931)

MATTHEWS   Medicine my Passport (1954)

MILLER   On Top of the World (includes Mazuchelli)

SMITH   Pioneers of Mountaineering (one chapter)

SMYTHE   The Kangchenjunga Adventure (1930)

SMYTHE   Spirit of the Hills (in part, 1930)

SMYTHE   The Mountain Scene (part)

SMYTHE   Adventures of a Mountaineer (one chapter, 1930)

SNAITH   At Grips with Everest (briefly)

STYLES   First on the Summits (one chapter)

SYMONDS   The Great Beast (Crowley, reference to 1905)

ULLMAN   Man of Everest (Tenzing, briefly 1951)

YOUNGHUSBAND   Everest the Challenge (1929, 1931)

MAKALU

8481

8208

NE ridge

SE ridge

NW ridge

KANGCHUNGTSE

MAKALU LA

Twins

Barun gl.

BC

Alfonsi

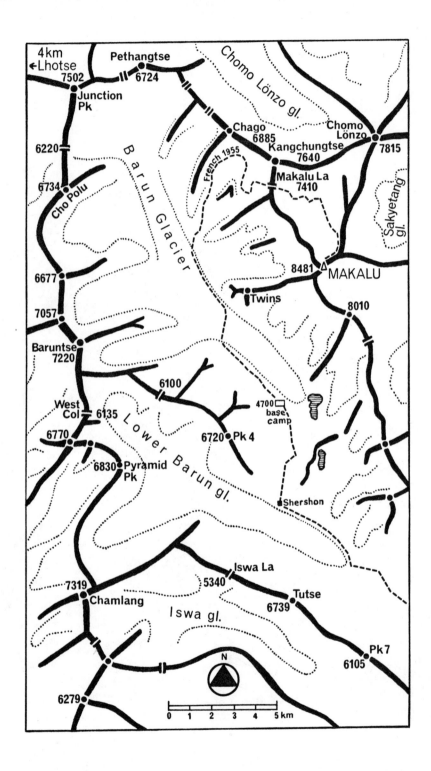

MAKALU

Situated: Nepal Himalaya (Kosi Section) in the Khumbakarna Himal (Nepal-Tibet border).

Longitude: 87° 05' 29" E.

Latitude: 27° 53' 23" N.

Altitude: Main summit - 8481m.

S.E. Peak - 8010m.

Early designation No: XIII

Name: In 1884, the Survey of India explorer Rinzin Namgyal gave the name Khamba Lung to the mountain on his panorama. The name is derived from the adjoining Khamba district of Tibet. Kama-lung is the valley to the north of the massif down which flows the Kama-chu. It has been suggested that the name Makalu derived from a transposition in the Tibetan words Kama-lung. Another opinion is that the name is a local corruption of Maha-kala. In Sanskrit this means 'Great Weather', attributive to the fierce qualities of the Hindu god Siva who controls the weather. In Tibetan, and this would seem to be the most probable origin, Maha-kala means 'The Great Black One' - aptly descriptive of the mountain's dark granite formation.

MAKALU, a close neighbour to Mount Everest and fifth in altitude among the 8000m. summits, leapt into prominence some 25 years ago just after the two Shipton reconnaissance expeditions had visited the area. Since then its summit has been reached no less than ten times by five different routes. The total height to be ascended from Base Camp area is about 3775m.

There can be some confusion concerning the exact position of the summit. The R.G.S. and the F.N.H. maps show the summit at the highest point of the N.W. Ridge. The map in Franco's book Makalu, p. 105, shows his climb as terminating at the summit situated a little to the east; neither the route drawing on page 206 nor the text quite bears this out. Terray in Conquistadors of the Useless, p. 328, shows the summit also as being to the east. Fantin in I Quattordici "8000", p. 164, does the same before quoting extensively from Franco and Terray. On the other hand Paragot and Seigneur in Makalu: Pilier Ouest, p. 81, show the summit as being to the west and Franco's summit as being a shoulder of 8208m. height. Doubtless the artist who drew the sketch map for Franco's book made an error, and this error was probably copied by Terray and repeated by Fantin, surprisingly without anyone noticing (Bordet's work was not published until about six years later). A significant passage occurs in Makalu: Pilier Ouest, p. 204; Seigneur, on the summit, records: "Bernard speaks and shows me the east ridge up which the 1955 expedition climbed." - this can refer only to the short ridge linking point 8208 with the true summit.

MAPS - The following modern maps are generally available. Those most recommended are marked with an asterisk (*)

1/506,880 Nepal East Sh. 3rd Ed.-GSGS, 1969. DMS(MoD), London*

1/250,000 Kanchenjunga Sh. NG 45-3, Series U502. 2nd Ed. 1963. AMS, Washington, D.C. (only fair black & white litho reprint available 1977)

1/100,000 Mount Everest Region. 2nd Ed. 1975. RGS, London *

1/50,000 Khumbu Himal. 1965. FNH, Munich *
1/50,000 Trekking Map: Khumbu Himal. 1975. Mandara maps,
Katmandu (fair dyeline copy of artwork)

CHRONICLE

1921 Valuable sightings and photographs of Makalu and of other
peaks and glaciers surrounding it were obtained, mainly
from the north and the north-west, during the reconnaissance of the eastern approaches to Everest by the British
Expedition, post monsoon period. G. H. Bullock, Lt.
Col. C. K. Howard-Bury and G. H. L. Mallory explored
the Kama valley and the Kangshung gl. and in the area
around Pethang Ringmo. Howard-Bury climbed to a high
point (c. 5950m.) on a ridge to the east of Pethangtse
(6724m.) for a view of the west side of Makalu. (1)

1933 During the first flight, April 3, of the British Houston
expedition (q. v.) the two machines passed very close to
Makalu and some excellent pictures, mainly of the south
and west sides, were obtained. (2)

1934 The French received permission from the Tibetan Government to climb Makalu, but this was cancelled.

1951 E. P. Hillary (NZ) and E. E. Shipton (Br) of the Everest
Reconnaissance expedition, during one of their exploratory
journeys to the south of Mount Everest, travelled from
the Imja Khola to a 6000m. pass leading over to the Barun
gl.; from there they were able to take some photographs
of the West Face of Makalu. (3)

1952 The main purpose of the British expedition to the Cho Oyu
having been completed, R. C. Evans, Hillary, G. Lowe
and Shipton headed south from Namche by the same route
as the previous year. From Hongu Lake they crossed
over to the Barun gl. and ascended it as far as the foot of

Pethangtse. They were able to observe the west side of Makalu very closely and to assess the climbing possibilities. This was the very first time that this area had been visited. (4)

1954 An American expedition of 10 members, leader W. Siri, and with Ang Tharkay as Sirdar, set off for the first attempt on the mountain. From Jogbani (on the frontier) the party headed due north, via Khandbari, to the Barun valley; Base Camp was established April 5 at 4725m. Two possible routes were examined: the S. E. Ridge and the N. W. Ridge; the former was selected. Three attempts were made on the summit via the southern col; the highest point reached was about 7150m. before continuous storms and deep snow drove the climbers back. (5) (6)

1954 While the Californian team was engaged in its attempt, a New Zealand party of 10 members (including Dr. R. C. Evans and Dr. M. Ball, both British), leader Sir E. P. Hillary, arrived at the head of the Barun Khola, also from Jogbani, April 21. Six members of the party (Hillary and C. J. McFarlane had been injured early on in a crevasse accident) ascended the 'Makalu' gl. (Chago gl.) and then divided. N. D. Hardie, W. G. Lowe and C. M. Todd climbed to a saddle (6550m.) N. W. of Makalu II (Kangchungtse, 7660m.) and from there were able to observe the northward flowing Chomo Lönzo gl. coming down from Kangchungtse and Chomo Lönzo (7815m.); they were able also to examine the Makalu N. W. Ridge. W. B. Beaven, Evans and G. Harrow were in the meanwhile progressing up to the Makalu La (7410m.) but before they could reach it Hillary, who despite his earlier injuries had come up to join them, was taken suddenly and seriously ill and his evacuation from the mountain (May 18) took overriding priority to any continued climbing. (7)

1954 That autumn a French Reconnaissance expedition of eight
members, leader J. Franco, planned by L. Devies,
arrived at the snout of the Barun gl. and there, September 15, established Base Camp. By October 15 J. Bouvier
and P. Leroux reached the Makalu La, their route having
again followed up the 'Cirque N. W.' (Chago gl.); several
attempts were made to climb higher from Camp 5 near
the col but these generally were frustrated by bad weather;
a high point of 7800m. appears to have been reached.
Franco, L. Terray, Sirdar Gyaltsen Norbu and Pa Norbu
climbed Kangchungtse October 22 (FIRST ASCENT);
J. Couzy and Terray also climbed Chomo Lönzo October
30 (?) (FIRST ASCENT). D. B. Verma, the young Nepalese liaison officer, died of pneumonia at Base Camp
September 23. (8)

1955 FIRST, 2nd, 3rd ASCENTS: A follow-up French expedition, 11 members, leader J. Franco, also planned by
L. Devies, returned to the Barun Khola and established
Base Camp at 4700m., April 4. They succeeded in
gaining the summit from the Makalu La, reached May 9,
by moving out onto the N. Face and up to the N. E. Ridge.
Camp 6, the last, was placed on a small terrace on the
N. Face at 7800m. Three teams reached the top: May
15 - Couzy and Terray; May 16 - Franco, G. Magnone
and Sirdar Gyaltsen Norbu; May 17 - Bouvier, S. Coupé,
Leroux and A. Vialatte. All three achieved in good conditions. Dr. A. Lapras performed a difficult appendi-
sectomy on porter Sona at Base Camp. Sona survived.
(8)

1961 A mixed expedition of 10 members (Am., Australian,
Br., NZ), leader Sir E. P. Hillary, drawn from the
1960-61 Himalayan Scientific & Mountaineering Expedition, left their hut south of Ama Dablam and after crossing
three high passes arrived at the Barun gl. They sought

to climb Makalu following generally the 1955 French route but without oxygen. The attempt however was marred by ill luck. Hillary suffered a transient stroke while at Camp 3 (6400m.) May 6 and had to be evacuated. P. D. Mulgrew when going for the summit from Camp 7 (8230m.) with the second assault team consisting of himself, J. Harrison, T. O. Nevison and Sherpa Annulu, May 18, suffered a pulmonary embolism when only some 120m. below the summit. That same day Dr. M.P. Ward, who had assumed the leadership from Hillary, was also taken seriously ill when descending from Camp 6 (6860m.) to which he had climbed to attend to Ang Temba's ankle damaged in a 200m. fall with five other Sherpas on May 17; Ward was delirious for two days - then began a gruelling descent. In the meantime Mulgrew, more dead than alive, was being rescued under desperate conditions. A tremendous effort was made by everyone, including the low level Sherpas, and all concerned survived. (9) (10)

1969 A Japanese reconnaissance expedition of five members, leader Dr. M. Matsuura, having waited since 1965 for Nepal to remove its ban on mountaineering, set out to take a close look at the S. E. Ridge. They climbed up to the S. Col to a height of 6500m. during May. (11)

1970 FOURTH ASCENT: Japanese scientific and mountaineering expedition, Commander-General K. Kumazawa, including 16 climbing members under the leadership of M. Hara, arrived at their Barun Pokhari Base Camp (4700m.) March 22 after an approach march from Dharan Bazar of 30 days. Camp 3 (Advance Base Camp) was established at 6500m. just below the S. Col; Camp 6 was pitched at 7850m. Though the first pair, Y. Ozaki and A. Tanaka, who had sited Camp 6, had originally stuck to the S. E. Ridge and had ascended over the difficult Black Gendarme, the route was afterwards modified so as to outflank this major obstacle: this alternate route dropped down from a little above Camp 4 onto the northern glacier and then climbed back to the S.E. Ridge to a point above the saddle, where Camp 6 was placed. May 21, T. Goto and Y. Kawaguchi reached about 8400m. in poor weather and were obliged to bivouac in a snow cave at 8300m. on their way back. May 22, Ozaki and Tanaka attained the summit in good weather. (11)

1971 FIFTH ASCENT: French expedition, 11 members, leader R. Paragot. From Base Camp they ascended the Barun gl. to Camp 1 (5300m.) from where they climbed up by the West Ridge, over the Twins and up over the formidable 'West Pillar' (entailing great technical difficulties). May 23, B. Mellet, J-P. Paris and Y. Seigneur left Camp 6 (7770m.); Paris dropped out at 8300m. and the other two continued to the summit. (12) (13)

1972 Yugoslavian expedition, including 10 climbers, leader A. Kunaver, attempted to reach the summit by a new route up the South Face from the Barun gl. with the line of ascent leading up towards the upper part of the West Ridge, above the 'West Pillar'. J. Azman and M. Malezic from their Camp 5 reached to about 7900m., October 26, but were turned back by adverse weather. (14) (15)

1973 Czechoslovakian expedition, 14 members, leader I. Galfy, made an attempt by a new route up the S.W. Ridge that leads up to Point 8010. The high point reached above Camp 5 was about 8000m.; at this point J. Kounicky's oxygen failed, he removed his mask, fell about 100m. and was seriously injured. After spending five days back in Camp 5 he died; the expedition was abandoned. (16) (17)

1974 Austrian expedition, 10 members, leader W. Nairz, attempted the South Face route but were forced back by bad weather after reaching 7500m. May 9. (18)

1974 International expedition, eight members, leader F. Stammberger (Am) made an attempt by the South Face. A. Larcher (Aus) and M. Malezic (Jugoslav.) reached a high point above Camp 4 of about 7800m., October 18, before being forced to turn back. (19)

1975 6th, 7th, 8th, 9th ASCENTS: Jugoslavian expedition, 21 members, leader A. Kunaver. They succeeded in climbing the South Face by their 1972 line of ascent and despite Camps 3 and 4 being struck by avalanches September 25. Seven men were placed on the summit. October 6: S. Belak and M. Manfreda; October 8: J. Azman and N. Zaplotnik (of four men); October 10: V. Groselj and I. Kotnik (of three men); October 11: Z. Beslin and J. Dovzan made the 4th bid but Beslin failed just 10m. below the top, which Dovzan reached alone. The last Camp 5 had been pitched at 8050m. (20)

1976 10th ASCENT: Spanish expedition, 12 members, leader J. M. Fabregas, achieved the second ascent of the S. E. Ridge. J. Camprubi reached the top from Camp 6 (7850m.) May 24 with two Czechoslovakian climbers.

While the Spaniards were climbing their ridge, a Czechoslovakian expedition of 18 members, leader I. Galfy, was attempting again the S. W. Ridge. Arrived at the top of the juncture with the S. E. Ridge (Point 8010, sometimes referred to as the S. E. Peak) they were frustrated from proceeding very much further by oxygen failure and deep snow. The two expeditions then decided to join forces (with the added advantage that the Czechoslovakians could use the Spanish Camps on the S. E. Ridge for the descent rather than have to come down the more difficult S. W. Ridge). Together they placed Camp 6 at about the final saddle and on May 24 M. Krissak, M. Orolin and K. Schubert - together with Camprubi of Spain - set off using oxygen for the summit. Orolin failed to reach the top and returned to Camp 6. The three successful climbers returned individually; Schubert however was obliged to bivouac in the vicinity of the juncture of the W. Ridge with the S.E. Ridge and next day he failed to return to Camp 6. The remaining three climbers were unable to reach or search for Schubert, who perished. (21) (22)

1977 American expedition, 13 members (including one British and one Yugoslavian?), leader J. Long, left Katmandu about March 19. They are reported to have attempted the W. Face without Sherpas and not using oxygen. The attempt was abandoned after one of the camps had been overwhelmed by an avalanche.

MAKALU

Principal Source References:

(1) Howard-Bury Mount Everest: the Reconnaissance 1921

(2) Fellowes, etc. First Over Everest

(3) Shipton The Mount Everest Reconnaissance Expedition: 1951

(4) Evans "The Cho Oyu Expedition, 1952" AJ 59 pp. 9-18

(5) Dunmire & Unsoeld "Makalu 1954" AAJ 1955 pp. 7-24

(6) Meyer & Lippmann "First Attempt on Makalu, 1954" HJ 19 pp. 57-67

(7) Hillary & Lowe East of Everest

(8) Franco Makalu

(9) Hillary & Doig High in the Thin Cold Air

(10) Mulgrew No Place for Men

(11) Hara & Asami Makalu 1970: the First Ascent by the South-East Ridge (Reprinted in HJ 30 pp. 129-140)

(12) Paragot & Seigneur Makalu: Pilier Ouest

(13) "The French Expedition to Makalu West Ridge 1971" (Translated and summarized by J. Russell from original accounts in La Montagne) AJ 78 pp. 44-52

(14) M 28 p. 12

(15) AAJ 1973 p. 481

(16) Wolf Reka Jmenem Cervankya

(17) AAJ 1974 p. 203

(18) AAJ 1975 p. 194

(19) Stammberger "International Makalu Expedition" AAJ 1975 pp. 194-195

(20) Kunaver "Makalu South Face Climbed" M 48 pp. 32-35

(21) Fabregas Makalu, Expedicion Española Himalaya 1976

(22) AAJ 1977 p. 238

Additional books and ephemera relevant to Makalu, not already listed. (The dates in brackets refer to the expeditions written about).

BORDET   Recherches géologiques dans l'Himalaya du Népal, région du Makalu

DOUGLAS & CLYDESDALE and M'INTYRE   The Pilots Book of Everest (1933)

GILL   Mountain Midsummer (1961, 1 chapter)

HAGEN   Mount Everest

HILLARY   Nothing Venture, Nothing Win

LOWE   Because it is There (1952, 1954)

SHIPTON   That Untravelled World

TEMPLE   The World at their Feet (1954, 1961)

TERRAY   Conquistadors of the Useless (part, 1954, 1955)

WARD   In this Short Span (part, 1961)

MT. EVEREST

8848

8393 steps

S. summit

LHOTSE

South Col

N col

W. ridge

éperon

VIII

VII

VI

V

West Cwm

IV

Lho La

III

icefall

BC=I

Khumbu Gl.

Alfonsi m.

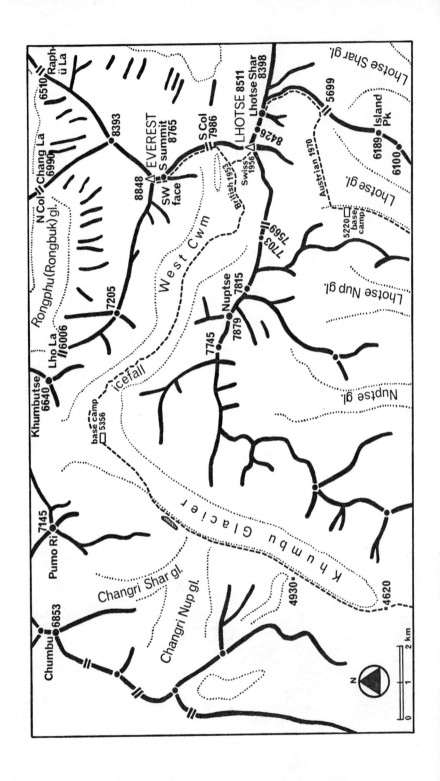

MOUNT EVEREST 3

Situated: Nepal Himalaya (Kosi Section) in the Mahalangur Himal forming the Nepal-Tibet border along the N. boundary of the Khumbu Himal.

Longitude: 86° 55' 40" E.
Latitude: 27° 59' 16" N.

Altitude: Main summit - 8848m.
South summit - 8765m.
NE Shoulder - 8393m.

Early Designation No: XV

Nepalese name: Sagarmatha
Tibetan name: Chomolungma (or Jomolungma); approximate meaning "The Mother Goddess of the District"

EVEREST, the highest mountain in the world, has attracted more attention from geographers, mountaineers and writers than probably any other mountain - with the possible exception of Mont Blanc (4807m.), the highest mountain in Europe.
Everest was first observed in 1849 and the first attempt to climb it was made 72 years later; it was another 32 years before the summit was reached.
Before 1949 all approaches had to be made from Tibet as Nepal was closed; since then all attempts have been made from Nepal as Tibet is closed, except to the Chinese.

The successful British expedition of 1953 was the 9th attempt on the mountain - excluding three solo bids and a rumoured Russian attempt - and up to June 1977 there have been in all 31 expeditions (again excluding three solo, one unauthorized, the rumoured Russian, and a doubtful Chinese attempt). The summit has been attained by 22 independent teams. A total of 54 people including two women have stood on the summit; there is a faint possibility that two others - Irvine and Mallory - may have done so and a strong probability that one other - Burke - may have done so too. One man has been to the summit twice: Sherpa Nawang Gombu.

The mountain has been climbed by four different routes and has been traversed once.

The total height to be ascended from the West Cwm via the S.W. Face, once close to the mountain, is about 2225m.; from the Rongbuk gls., or from the West Cwm via the S. Col, about 2450m.; from the Lho La via the W. Ridge, about 2850m.; and from below the ice-fall via the S. Col, about 3500m.

A little-known facet of the 1924 tragedy, which may not be without interest, is revealed by the late Sir Oliver Lodge, a well-known and respected believer in life after death, in his book Why I believe in Personal Immortality, pp. 73-80. He tells of a communication received from a spirit (Frederic Myers) on September 14, 1924. The message was that Irvine and Mallory had reached the top of Everest, had planted a flag, and that their bodies were lying frozen on a ledge a hundred feet down on their return journey, to the left of their ascending path. Another communication on November 15, addressed to his friend Arnold Lunn by Irvine himself, revealed that his body would be found crouching under a shelf of rock and that in the left-hand inside pocket of his coat were his papers in which he had entered his last record: "Summit reached, flag planted, food giving out, we begin to descend". No information seems to have been given about a lost ice-axe.

MAPS - Well produced maps are to be found in the earlier books on Everest; for instance in the first three books on Everest - 1921, 1922, 1924 - and also in Ruttledge's Everest 1933. Thereafter, with the exception of books of general reference such as Hagen's Mount Everest or Kurz's Chroniques Himalayennes, the maps tend to become smaller and more local.

The following modern maps are generally available. Those most recommended are marked with an asterisk (*).

1/506,880 Nepal East Sh. 3rd Ed. -GSGS, 1969. DMS(MoD), London*

1/250,000 Mount Everest Sh. NG 45-2, Series U502, 1955, AMS, Washington, D. C. (Only poor black & white litho reprint available 1977). Ecological version 1974 by CNRS, Paris.

1/126,720 Trekking Map: Lamosangu to Mt. Everest. 1975. Mandara maps, Katmandu (fair dyeline copy of artwork).

1/100,000 Mount Everest Region. 2nd Ed. 1975. RGS, London *

1/50,000 Khumbu Himal. The so-called "Schneider map". 1965. FNH, Munich *

1/50,000 Trekking Map: Khumbu Himal. 1975. Mandara maps, Katmandu (fair dyeline copy of artwork).

1/25,000 Chomolongma - Mount Everest - Mahalangur. 1957. AV (DAV + OAV), Munich & Innsbruck *

CHRONICLE

According to a family legend, Julius Behrens (1827-1888) (Br), at one time contemplated making an attempt on Everest. This was probably no more than a vague ambition as he had climbed Mont Blanc, the highest mountain in Europe, in September 1851. (1)

1876 Miss "Meta" Brevoort (Am) considered climbing Everest with her nephew, Wm. A. B. Coolidge, while staying at Bel Alp, Switzerland. She thought the R.G.S. might help them if they went out. (2)

1892 Clinton Dent (Br) published an article entitled "Can Mount Everest be Climbed?" in the Nineteenth Century of Oct. 1892. He firmly believed it could be. (3)

1893 Lt. C. G. Bruce first suggested to Capt. F. E. Younghusband, while they were on a mission to Chitral, the idea of climbing Mount Everest. According to Bruce, it was Younghusband who made to him a proposition for the first exploration of Everest. (4) (5)

1899 Lord Curzon, when Viceroy of India, wrote to D. W. Freshfield, July 9, saying he hoped soon to visit Nepal and would try to get permission for an attempt on Everest. (6)

1904 Capt. C. G. Rawling, who had joined the Younghusband mission to Lhasa in 1904, afterwards led a party, which included Capt. C. Ryder, on a journey from Lhasa to Gartok and on to Simla, during which time they obtained views of Everest from the north. (6)

1905 The A. C. Committee minutes of June 6 record that Freshfield had received from Lord Curzon a proposal to encourage a systematic attempt to reach the summit of Kangchenjunga or of Mount Everest. The A. C. believed that any success attained would largely depend on the presence in the party of Major Bruce or an officer like him together with a band of trained Gurkhas. (7)

1907 The A. C. Committee minutes record regretfully that the Secretary of State for India had vetoed the idea of climbing Everest. February 19. (7)

1907 A letter appeared in The Times of March 18 from Sir

George Goldie (President of the R. G. S.) quoting his letter of January 23 to the Rt. Hon. J. Morley, Secretary of State for India, explaining the proposed expedition conceived by Lord Curzon and planned to be led by Major the Hon. C. G. Bruce and including Dr. T. G. Longstaff, A. L. Mumm, three Alpine guides and half a dozen Gurkhas from the 5th Rifles; the attempt to be made from the Tibetan side. And quoting Morley's reply refusing the request for reasons of public policy. (8)

1908 Bruce made a second plan to approach Everest through Nepal, up the valley of the Dudh Kosi. The plan fell through in 1909. (3)

1911 Curzon wrote in October to the Maharaja of Nepal expressing the hope that the latter would sanction an Everest expedition. (6)

1913 Capt. J. B. L. Noel, disguised as a Mohammaden from India and with a few native companions, made a journey from Darjeeling through N. W. Sikkim and round the north of Kangchenjunga in an attempt to reach Everest. They enjoyed a good view of the mountain from the Langbu Pass but when within 65km. of the mountain they were stopped and turned back by a posse of Tibetan soldiers. (9)

1914 The A. C. Committee minutes of May 19 record a serious attempt to arrange an expedition to Everest that year and an invitation to the President (Lord Justice Pickford) from Major C. G. Rawling asking him to accept a seat on the advisory committee of a 2-year expedition being organized. But war broke out in 1914 and Rawling was killed in France in 1917. (6)

1918 Sir Thomas Holdich, President of the R. G. S. reopens negotiations in December by writing to the Secretary of State for India on behalf of the R. G. S. and the A. C. (10)

1920 Lt. Col. C. K. Howard-Bury visited India to confer with Sir Charles Bell, Political Officer in Sikkim, and with the Viceroy; the former was opposed to an expedition. (10)

1920 In December the India Office received a telegram from the Viceroy of India, Lord Chelmsford, informing them that the Tibetan Government had given their consent to the exploration of Mount Everest and to the need to travel through Tibetan territory. (10)

1921 First (Br) Reconnaissance Expedition. Nine members, leader Lt. Col. C. K. Howard-Bury. Possible approaches from the east and the north were explored. G. H. L. Mallory and G. H. Bullock explored the Rongbuk and West Rongbuk gls. from where they attempted to reach the West Cwm that they had viewed from a col N. E. of Pumori. They thought the glacier looked terribly steep and broken, and the chances for reaching the col between Everest and the South Peak (Lhotse) from the west not good. Bullock, Mallory and Major E. O. Wheeler reached the Chang La (North Col), 6990m., from the Kharta and E. Rongbuk gls. Sept. 24. Dr. A. M. Kellas died during the approach march (near Kampa Dzong). (11)

1922 Second (Br) expedition. 13 members and 5 Gurkhas, leader Brig. Gen. C. G. Bruce. The North Col was reached from the E. Rongbuk gl. Mallory, Major E. R. Norton and Dr. T. H. Somervell reached a height of 8225m. - above their Camp 5 - without oxygen, May 21. Capt. J. G. Bruce (nephew of the leader) and Capt. G. I. Finch reached a height of 8320m. - above their Camp 6 - with oxygen, May 27; Lance-naik Tejbir Bura reached a height of just over 7900m. A third attempt, June 7, by C. G. Crawford, Mallory and Somervell plus 14 porters ended in disaster when the whole caravan was carried down by an avalanche just below the North Col; 7 porters lost their lives. (12)

1924 Third (Br) expedition. 10 members and 4 Gurkhas and again the indefatigable interpreter Karma Paul; leader C. G. Bruce, who went down with malaria during the approach march and was obliged to hand over command to Norton. From Camp 4 on the N. Col, Norton and Somervell - with porters Narbu Yishé, Llakpa Chédé and Semchumbi - pitched Camp 6 at 8160m. From there, June 4, Norton and Somervell continued up to about 8540m., without oxygen; then Norton pressed on alone to about 8570m. A second attempt was made by A. C. Irvine and Mallory who, with four porters, reached Camp 6 on June 7. N. E. Odell went up to Camp 6 on June 8 while Irvine and Mallory made a bid for the summit. From a point at about 7950m. Odell observed - during a momentary clearing of the weather - "a tiny object moving and approaching the rock step. A second object followed, and the first climbed to the top of the step". If they were at the second step, which is not certain, Irvine and Mallory had reached a height of 8600m. They were never seen again. Did they reach the top? Would the outcome have been different if Mallory had taken Odell instead of Irvine? These questions will long be debated. (13)

1933 Another (Br) expedition. 14 members with two Signals officers and five Gurkha N. C. Os; also Karma Paul; leader, H. Ruttledge. The N. Col was reached from the E. Rongbuk gl. P. Wyn Harris, J. L. Longland and L. R. Wager and 8 porters pitched Camp 6 at 8350m. The first assault was made by Wyn Harris and Wager, May 30. About 20m. below the crest and about 230m. east of the 'first step' they found an ice-axe that can have belonged only to Irvine or to Mallory. They reached a height of about 8570m. The second assault was made by E. E. Shipton and F. S. Smythe but the former had to return to Camp 6 as he was unwell; Smythe continued and reached about the same spot as the first party. Hopes for a third attempt did not materialize. Police-ie, their Tibetan mastiff dog, attempted to climb to Camp 4 on the N. Col but got no further than the foot of the rope-ladder (6700m.); later it disappeared, probably down a crevasse. (14)

1933 Houston-Mount Everest Expedition (Br). The first flight over Everest. A highly complex and technical feat of organization that resulted in two flights over the summit, each by two Westland biplanes. The first, April 3, by Sqdn. Ldr. the Marquess of Douglas and Clydesdale with Col. L. V. S. Blacker, chief observer (and a descendent of Col. Valentine Blacker, the first Surveyor General of India 1823-1826); and by Flt. Lt. D. M'Intyre with S. R. Bonnett, cinematographer. The second, April 19, by Clydesdale and Blacker and by M'Intyre and A. L. Fisher, cinematographer. Expedition leader, Air Commodore P. F. M. Fellowes; administrator, Col. P. T. Etherton. These flights resulted in a valuable series of vertical survey strips and many oblique photos of the mountain massifs revealing areas hitherto never seen. (15)

1934 Solo attempt by M. Wilson, ex-Captain of the British Army, by the N. Col route; Wilson crossed Tibet disguised as a deaf-and-dumb Tibetan priest. His body was found by the 1935 party close to Camp 3 on the E. Rongbuk gl. He had died at the end of May in his tent from exhaustion after making more than one rash attempt to reach the N. Col. (16)

1935 A small, light reconnaissance party (Br). Eight members and Karma Paul; among the porters was Tenzing who carried to the N. Col; leader, E. E. Shipton. New equipment was tried out, the Nyönne Ri Range and the N. E. Face of Everest were surveyed under the direction of M. Spender, and the N. Col was occupied (early July)

in less than a week after leaving Rongbuk via the E. Rongbuk gl. Valuable sightings were obtained by Shipton and
L. V. Bryant (NZ) into the West Cwm and the route up it
was judged not impossible. H. W. Tilman and E. H. L.
Wigram viewed the W. Ridge from the Lho La (6006m.)
and considered its lower section to be utterly impracticable. 7100m. was reached in an attempt on Changtse;
several other peaks were climbed before the expedition
withdrew via the Kharta valley. It was during the march
up the E. Rongbuk gl. that the body of Wilson was found.
(17)

1936 British Expedition of 12 members with three Gurkhas and
the dependable Karma Paul; leader H. Ruttledge. They
left Darjeeling as usual and, passing through Tibet and
up the E. Rongbuk gl., established Camp 4 on the N. Col
(Shipton and Smythe) May 15. But the monsoons reached
the Everest area early (May 23) and the expedition was
unable to make any further progress. In June they moved
round to the Rongbuk gl. to reconnoitre the W. side of
the N. Col. Wyn Harris and Smythe failed to reach the
Col owing to heavy snow and avalanches but judged the
slope to be practicable though not easier than the E. side.
Shipton's party (including G. N. Humphreys, aged 52)
reached about 7150m. on North Peak before being turned
back by adverse conditions. (18)

1938 Small expedition (Br) of seven members, and Karma Paul
whose 6th expedition this was; leader H. W. Tilman.
Frustrated by not getting much beyond Camp 4 (to 7450m.,
May 30) from the E. Rongbuk gl. owing to a very early
monsoon (May 5), they went round to the western side.
From there they succeeded in climbing again the N. Col;
then Shipton and Smythe placed Camp 6 at 8290m. on June
7 but the following day got only a little further. P. Lloyd
and Tilman made a second attempt on June 11 but without

93

greater success. One of the porters who carried to Camp 5 (7850m.) was Tenzing. (19)

1942 Col. R. L. Scott, an American airman, made an unauthorised flight over the Himalaya, twice over Everest. (20)

1945 Sqdn. Ldr. C. G. Andrews (NZ) and C. Fenwick (Br) made an unauthorised flight over Everest. (21)

1945 The Committee of the A. C., October 22, considered a letter from Shipton suggesting that preparatory steps should be taken to mount an expedition in the near future. The Committee asked Shipton to act as leader and make all arrangements. The President (Rt. Hon. L. S. Amery) wrote informally to the Viceroy of India (Lord Wavell); a reply made it clear that the Tibetans would not permit even a small party in either 1946 or 1947. (22)

1947 K. Neame, a pilot in the R. A. F., made an unscheduled flight around the Everest massif towards the end of March, taking many oblique photographs from about 9000m. (23)

1947 Another solo attempt by E. Denman (Can) with Tenzing and Ang Dawa. They travelled surreptitiously through Tibet to Rongbuk and tackled the N. Col from the E. Rongbuk gl. Ill-prepared and ill-equipped, they were forced to turn back by poor conditions at about 7150m., just above the Col, May 9. (24)

1950 A small party of five, organized by O. Houston (Am), travelled across Nepal to the Sola Khumbu. From Namche Bazar (reached Nov. 14) they travelled to Thyangboche; C. Houston and Tilman then went up the Khumbu gl. and from a vantage point about 5500m. high they had a good view of the entrance to the West Cwm, barred by its great ice-fall. Tilman noted that the old climbing route was free from snow and formed the opinion that October might be a favourable month for a future attempt. (25)

1951 A third solo attempt (unauthorized and unrecorded), this
time by R. B. Larsen, a Dane. He left Darjeeling at the
end of March and headed for the Dudh Kosi valley and
for Namche Bazar. He then made his way towards the
Khumbu gl. but failed to get anywhere near the West Cwm.
So from Namche Bazar he is supposed to have headed N. W.
up the valley of the Bhote Kosi, crossed the Nangpa La
(5716m.), west of Cho Oyu, into Tibet, and from Kyetrak
to have gone to Rongbuk (six days travel from Namche
Bazar). He attacked the N. Col on May 7; his Sherpas
refused to camp on the Col and went down at once. The
return journey was by the same route. (26)

1951 A reconnaissance expedition, initiated by M. P. Ward,
of six members, leader E. E. Shipton. The party from
England left at short notice in August; E. P. Hillary and
H. E. Riddiford (both NZ) met them at Dingla in Nepal.
By the end of September they were examining the lower
part of the ice-fall and having a good look right up the
Cwm to its very head from a high point on one of Pumori's
buttresses; a possible route to the S. Col was observed.
The party succeeded in climbing up to the lip of the Cwm
and in observing its gently sloping glacier. (27)

1952 Spring expedition (Sw) of eight climbers and various
scientific personnel; leader Dr. E. Wyss-Dunant. Base
Camp was established at 5050m., April 22; they proceeded up the West Cwm, climbed to the S. Col (7986m.),
established Camp 7 at 8400m. on Everest's S. E. ridge,
and reached a high point of 8600m. on May 28 before
turning back (R. Lambert and Tenzing). (28)

1952 Second Swiss expedition of seven members, leader G.
Chevalley, returned during the post-monsoon period.
Abandoning the earlier Éperon route for the Lhotse face,

Lambert, E. Reiss, Tenzing and seven Sherpas set up Camp 8 on the S. Col Nov. 19. Next day they reached 8100m. but were then forced back. Earlier Mingma Dorje had died from injuries resulting from a fall of ice debris from the upper part of Lhotse, just above Camp 5. (28)

1952 Many rumours and press reports of a large Russian expedition, 35 climbers and 6 scientists, attempting Mount Everest from the north during the last quarter of the year. Camp 8 was established at 8200m. then all communications ceased; the summit party of six, including the leader, were supposedly lost. A search proved unavailing and the expedition was abandoned December 27. A further search is reported to have been carried out in the spring of 1953. These stories have been neither confirmed nor denied by the Russians.

1953 FIRST ASCENT: British expedition of 14 members including a physiologist, a cameraman, Sirdar Tenzing, and the leader Col. H. C. J. Hunt. The route was via the glacier of Lhotse and the Lhotse Face; Camp 8 was erected on the South Col May 21. The first assault party, R. C. Evans and T. D. Bourdillon, reached the South Summit (8765m.) May 26. The second assault party, Hillary and Tenzing, from Camp 9 (8500m.) reached the summit May 29. This was Tenzing's 7th expedition to the mountain. (29)

1953 An Indian Air Force plane, captained by Flt. Lt. A. E. Paul and with a supporting crew of four and four photographers, flew over Everest June 6. Valuable photographs in colour and in black and white were taken from a height of 9800m. (30)

1956 SECOND and THIRD ASCENTS: Third Swiss expedition of 11 members, leader A. Eggler. They approached the mountain by the West Cwm. Camp 6A was pitched on the

Lhotse Face May 9, a little below the South Col at nearly 8000m. From there F. Luchsinger and Reiss achieved the first ascent of Lhotse (8511m.) on May 18. Camp 7 was placed on the S. E. Ridge (about 8400m.). The first assault party, J. Marmet and E. Schmied, reached the summit May 23. The second assault party, H. von Gunten and A. Reist, reached the summit May 24. Sherpa Da Norbu carried twice to the highest camp. (31)

1960 Claim by China to have climbed Everest from the N. Col. The expedition consisted of 214 men and women, Chinese and Tibetan. The highest camp was placed at 8500m. It apparently took 19 hours to climb the last 350m. to the top - three members reached the summit in the dark (May 25) and, it appears, in good weather. The claim has lacked so far any credible evidence. (32)

1960 Indian expedition, including 13 members of the climbing group, leader Brig. Gyan Singh. May 25, Nawang Gombu (Sherpa instructor at the Mountaineering Institute), S. Gyatso and Capt. N. Kumar left Camp 7 (about 8400m.) to attempt the summit but they were turned back by harsh winds and driven snow at about 8625m., just short of the South Summit. (33)

1962 Another unauthorized attempt - some consider it to have been a rash adventure; three Americans and a Swiss, leader W. W. Sayre. Having deceived the Nepalese authorities by asking permission to climb Gyachung Kang (to the east of Cho Oyu), the party instead crossed from the Ngozumpa gl. (April) by the Nup La to the W. Rongbuk gl. (without Tibetan permission). They then made their way to the North Col via the E. Rongbuk gl. and attained a height of about 7600m. on the N. Ridge. (34)

1962 Second Indian expedition. Nine members, two doctors and one cameraman; leader Major J. D. Dias. Camp 6 was erected on the South Col May 21 and Camp 7 at 8450m. May 28. H. Dang, Gyatso and M. Kohli attempted the summit May 30 but were forced back by adverse conditions when at about 8720m. Sirdar Angtharkay, though aged 55, carried up to Camp 7; and Da Norbu made his 4th trip to the same camp. Earlier a Sherpa, Nawang Tsering, had died from injuries received during an ice and rock fall from the Lhotse Face, just above Camp 4. (35)

1963 4th, 5th, 6th ASCENTS: American expedition, 20 members, leader N. G. Dyhrenfurth. Base Camp established March 21; a few days later J. Breitenbach was killed in the ice-fall. At Advanced Base Camp in the West Cwm the expedition divided for a two-pronged attack. The South Col team placed Camp 5 on the Col April 16 and J. Whittaker and Nawang Gombu reached the summit May 1. The West Ridge team in meantime reached the site of Camp 4W (7650m.) April 12. Two tents, with their six occupants, were blown 30m. down the mountainside in a storm on May 16; the following morning the 3rd tent was all but blown away. Nevertheless Camp 4W was re-established May 20. Camp 5W (8300m.) was placed on the N. Face May 21. May 22 L. G. Jerstad and B. C. Bishop climbed Everest again from the South Col; a few hours later W. F. Unsoeld and T. F. Hornbein reached the summit from the West Ridge and descended by the South Col, meeting up with the first two as pre-planned on the S. E. Ridge (FIRST ASCENT by the West Ridge and FIRST TRAVERSE of Everest). (36)

1965 7th, 8th, 9th, 10th ASCENTS: Third Indian expedition, 17 members, leader Lt. Cdr. M. S. Kohli. Base Camp was established March 22. The South Col was reached April 16. No less than nine men were placed on the summit: Capt. A. S. Cheema and Nawang Gombu (the latter's second visit) May 20; Sonam Gyatsu and Sonam Wangyal May 22; C. P. Vohra and Ang Kami May 24; Capt. H. P. S. Ahluwalia, H. C. S. Rawat and Pha Dorji May 29. (37)

1965 A ban on all mountaineering imposed by the Nepalese Government.

1966-There were various rumours of further Chinese attempts
1968 on Everest during these years, but none has been substantiated. They probably arose as a result of the Scientific expedition operating in the Everest area; it is thought that a station was established on the North Col as part of the Chinese research programme.

1969 Japanese Reconnaissance Party, April-June. Four members, leader Y. Fujita. They reached 6500m. in the West Cwm and observed the S. W. Face. (38)

1969 Second Japanese Reconnaissance Party, August-November. 12 members, leader H. Mihashita. H. Nakajima and Y. Satoh reached about 8050m. on the S. W. Face, November 1. During the expedition the Japanese found the body of J. Breitenbach (killed in the ice-fall 1963). Sirdar Phu Dorje of the Ski Expedition section of the reconnaissance was killed in the ice-fall, October 18. (38)

1970 11th and 12th ASCENTS: Japanese expedition (postponed from 1966) with 30 members (including reporters, etc.), leader S. Matsukata. Divided into two parties: Eight S. W. Face members, leader M. Konishi, and sixteen S. E. Ridge members, leader T. Matsuura. The former party failed to improve on the 1969 performance. The latter party, from the South Col, placed two teams on the summit: T. Matsuura and N. Uemura May 11; K. Hirabayashi and Sirdar Chotare May 12. K. Narita died of heart-attack at Camp 1; Sherpa Kyak Tsering was killed by a fall of seracs in the ice-fall. Miss S. Watanabe reached an altitude of 8020m. (38) (39)

1970 Japanese Everest Skiing Expedition. 34 members, including two skiers and 10 film cameramen; also 800 porters employed to help carry the 27 tons of equipment. Y. Miura made a ski descent from the South Col of some 2000m. to the West Cwm in a little over two minutes; it is reported that a speed of 150 km. per hour was reached, even though he had a parachute to restrain him. Six Sherpas were killed, April 5, at 5700m. by a glacier avalanche. (38) (40)

1971 International expedition, 30 members from 13 countries, leader N. G. Dyhrenfurth and Col. J. O. M. Roberts. It was divided into two sections: a S. W. Face party and a W. Ridge party, the latter to climb the ridge along its full length. Dogged by terrible weather, the early death (April 18) of Major H. V. Bahuguna (Ind) in a blizzard while descending from W. Ridge Camp 3 (6900m.), illness and epidemics, an excess of publicity, and by personal ambitions and conflicts, the expedition all but broke up. However, the scaling of the S. W. Face reasserted itself and in the end the assault team of D. Haston and D. D. Whillans (the British pair), having been strongly supported by the Sherpas and by R. Ito and N. Uemura (the Japanese pair) and Camp 6 having been placed at 8250m., pushed to a height of 8380m. but, with supplies petering out, was then forced to turn back (May 21). (41) (42)

1971 Argentinian expedition, 18 members, leader Col. H. C. Tolosa. An attempt made during the post-monsoon season by the South Col route. They were turned back when at about 8230m. by adverse weather and lack of supplies. (43)

1972 European expedition, 22 members, leader Dr. K. M. Herrligkoffer. Their objective, the S. W. Face. Camp 5 was pitched at 7800m. May 11. From Camp 6, 8200m., May 20, F. Kuen (Aus) and A. Huber (Aus) reached about 8350m. while reconnoitering a route for the summit bid next day; but no attempt was made owing to intense cold and high winds. The expedition was plagued with personality problems and mutual suspicions; the three British members - H. MacInnes, D. K. Scott, Whillans - decided to quit the expedition May 20. (44) (45)

1972 British expedition, 11 members, leader C. J. S. Bonington. Another attempt on the S. W. Face. A height of 8300m. was reached before the climb was abandoned (November 14) due to cold and high winds by Haston and Scott. T. Tighe (Australian), a visitor helping out at Base Camp, was killed in the ice-fall as the expedition was pulling out. (46)

1973 13th and 14th ASCENTS: A large Italian expedition (mountaineering and scientific), 64 members, leader G. Monzino; also 100 Sherpas and 2000 local porters. Three helicopters were used (one of which had crashed in the West Cwm). Two teams reached the summit from the South Col: May 5 - R. Carrel, M. Minuzzo, Sambhu Tamang (Nepal), Sirdar Lhakpa Tenzing. May 7 - C. Benedetti, V. Epis, F. Innamorati. (47)

1973 15th ASCENT: Japanese expedition, 48 members, leader M. Yuasa. Divided into two sections, one for the S. W. Face and the other for the South Col route. The former climb was abandoned at about 8400m. October 26; Sherpa Jangbu lost his life in an avalanche between Camps 2 and 3, Oct. 12. Success was achieved from the South Col when H. Ishiguro and Y. Kato, without any intermediary camp, reached the summit October 26, the first post-monsoon ascent. (48)

1974 Spanish expedition, 16 members, leader J. I. Lorente Zugaza. Camp 6 was established above the South Col at 8530m. May 12, but the attempt on the summit was frustrated by strong winds. (49)

1974 French expedition of 10 Chamonix guides, leader G. Devouassoux. An attempt by the West Ridge from the proximity of the Lho La (about 6000m.) was planned. However in the evening of September 9 Camps 1 and 2 were completely destroyed by an avalanche; Devouassoux and 5 Sherpas were killed. That same morning Camp 3 had been established on the crest of the shoulder at 6950m. The expedition was abandoned. (50) (51)

1975 16th ASCENT: Japanese Ladies expedition, 15 members, leader E. Hisano. The summit was reached via the South Col May 16, Mrs. J. Tabei and Sherpa Ang Tsering. Mrs. Tabei is the first woman to have climbed Mount Everest. (52)

1975 17th ASCENT: A very large Chinese expedition, leader Shih Chan-chu, approached the mountain from the north. Military type trucks were used to transport supplies to Base Camp at 5000m.; yaks helped transport supplies as far as Camp 3, 6500m., on the E. Rongbuk gl. Camp 4 was placed on the North Col and two other camps and two bivouacs were placed along the N. Ridge, the final assault camp being at 8680m. Three assaults were launched, the first two unsuccessful; Wu Tsung-yueh, deputy commissar of the expedition, died at 8500m. May 27, nine members (8 Tibetan and one Chinese) set off from the high camp and reached the summit (of what the Chinese now call Qomolangma Feng): Phanthog, a Tibetan woman - Sodnam Norbu - Lotse - Hou Sheng-fu - Samdrub - Darphuntso - Kunga Pasang - Tsering Tobgyal - Ngapo Khyen. (53)

1975 18th and 19th ASCENTS: Second British S. W. Face expedition. 19 members, leader C. J. S. Bonington. Camp 6 was placed at 8320m. September 24, Haston and Scott set out for and reached the summit - the first ascent by the S. W. Face. Two days later P. D. Boardman, M. Boysen, M. Burke and Sirdar Pertemba left for the summit; Boysen was obliged early on to return to Camp 6 owing to oxygen failure and a lost crampon. Boardman and Pertemba pulled ahead and reached the summit. On the way down again and only a couple of hundred metres or so from the top, they were surprised to meet Burke who told them he was going to the summit and would then catch them up on the descent. The weather suddenly deteriorated and Burke was never seen again. (54)

1976 20th ASCENT: Joint British-Nepalese expedition, 29 members, leader Lt. Col. H. R. A. Streather, Sirdar Sonam Girme. Two climbers reached the summit May 16 by the South Col route, Cpl. M. P. Lane (Br) and Sgt. J. H. Stokes (Br). During their return they had to bivouac just below the South Summit and suffered serious frostbite. Earlier, Capt. T. Thompson fell into a crevasse near Camp 2 and was killed. (55)

1976 21st ASCENT: American expedition, 12 members including H. Bruyntjes (Dutch) plus a film crew of four, leader P. R. Trimble. The French having surrendered their own permit, the Americans decided to attempt the mountain by the South Col route. They left Katmandu August 3 and established Base Camp August 25; Sherpa Pasang Kame was Base Camp Manager. Camp 2 (erected September 8 at 6580m.) served as Advanced Base Camp. Camp 5 was sited on the South Col October 1. C. Chandler, R. Cormack and Ang Phurba left from the Col and erected a higher Camp 6 October 7. The following day the party of three set off for the summit; Ang Phurba had to turn back very soon owing to oxygen failure but the other two reached the top. A second summit team was turned back by bad weather before reaching the South Col. (56)

1977 New Zealand expedition, 8 members, leader K. Woodford, The plan was to climb the mountain via the South Col without using Sherpas. Base Camp was established March 14 and the highest camp was placed at 7570m. on the Lhotse Face during April. M. Brown and M. Mahoney reached the South Col towards the end of the month. The undertaking, however, proved to be beyond the powers of the expedition and no further progress was made.

1977 22nd ASCENT: South Korean expedition. They did a very rapid ascent also by the South Col route. Base Camp was established early August and on Sept. 15 Ko Sang Do and Sherpa Pemba Norbu reached the summit.

MOUNT EVEREST

Principal Source References:

(1) Blakeney "Early Ascents of Mont Blanc" AJ 66 p. 322

(2) Clark Eccentric in the Alps p. 100

(3) Longstaff This My Voyage p. 152

(4) Seaver Francis Younghusband p. 155

(5) Bruce Himalayan Wanderer p. 124

(6) Blakeney. AJ 69 pp. 143-144

(7) Blakeney. AJ 68 p. 155

(8) AJ 23 pp. 466-468

(9) Noel Through Tibet to Everest

(10) Blakeney "A. R. Hinks and the First Everest Expedition, 1921" G. J. 136 pp. 333-343

(11) Howard-Bury Mount Everest: the Reconnaissance 1921

(12) Bruce The Assault on Mount Everest 1922

(13) Norton The Fight for Everest 1924

(14) Ruttledge Everest 1933

(15) Fellowes, etc. First Over Everest

(16) Roberts I'll Climb Mount Everest Alone

(17) Shipton "The Mount Everest Reconnaissance, 1935" AJ 48 pp. 1-14

(18) Ruttledge Everest: the Unfinished Adventure

(19) Tilman Mount Everest 1938

(20) Scott God is my Co-Pilot

(21) "Tararua" 1947, pp. 6-10

(22) AJ 55 pp. 314-315

(23) Neame "Alone Over Everest" MW 1955 pp. 131-141

(24) Denman Alone to Everest

(25) Tilman Nepal Himalaya

(26) MW 1953 pp. 33-34

(27) Shipton The Mount Everest Reconnaissance Expedition:1951

(28) Dittert, etc. Forerunners to Everest

(29) Hunt The Ascent of Everest

(30) Jayal "Indian Air Force Flights over Everest" HJ 18 pp. 65-66

(31) Eggler The Everest-Lhotse Adventure

(32) People's Physical Culture Publishing House Mountaineering in China

(33) Singh Lure of Everest

(34) Sayre Four against Everest

(35) Dias Everest Adventure

(36) Ullman Americans on Everest

(37) Kohli Nine Atop Everest

(38) Ohtsuka "Japanese Mount Everest Expedition, 1969-1970" HJ 31 pp. 100-112

(39) JAC Official Report of the Japanese Mount Everest Expedition 1969-1970

(40) Kotani & Yasuhisa Japan Everest Skiing Expedition 1970

(41) Steele Doctor on Everest

(42) Wilson & Pearson "Everest, Post Mortem of an International Expedition" M 17 pp. 10-29

(43) Brignone "Ill Expedición Argentine en los Himalayas. Everest 1971" Montaña 15 (1971) pp. 32-36

(44) Herrligkoffer Mount Everest: Thron der Gotter

(45) Herrligkoffer "Mt. Everest, 1972" HJ 33 pp. 14-17

(46) Bonington Everest, South West Face

(47) Monzino La Spedizione Italiana all'Everest 1973

(48) M 30 p. 10

(49) Lorente Zugaza "Expeditions Tximist to Everest" HJ 34 pp. 146-147

(50) Mollier Everest 74, Le Rendez-vous du Ciel

(51) AAJ 1975 p. 198

(52) M 44 p. 9

(53) Foreign Languages Press Another Ascent of the World's Highest Peak - Qomolangma

(54) Bonington Everest the Hard Way

(55) Fleming & Faux Soldiers on Everest

(56) Trimble "The American Bicentennial Everest Expedition" AAJ 1977 pp. 30-34

Additional books and ephemera relevant to Everest, not already listed. (The dates in brackets refer to the expeditions written about).

AHLUWALIA   Higher than Everest

ALPINE CLUB   Catalogue of the Exhibition of Photographs from the Mount Everest Expedition 1921

ALPINE CLUB   Catalogue of the Exhibition of Photographs and Paintings from the Mount Everest Expedition 1922

ALPINE CLUB   Catalogue of Paintings and Photographs from the Mount Everest Expedition 1924

BARNES   After Everest (Tenzing)

BENSON   Mountaineering Ventures (one chapter)

BOUSTEAD   The Wind of Morning (1933)

BRIDGES & TILTMAN   More Heroes of Modern Adventure (one chapter)

BROUGHTON   Climbing Everest (Anthology)

BRUCE   Himalayan Wanderer

BRYANT   New Zealanders and Everest (1935 and later)

BUCHAN   The Last Secrets (one chapter)

BURRARD   Mount Everest and its Tibetan Names

CHARTWELL PRESS   Everest, a Guide to the Climb (folding chart, 1953)

CHINA PUBLICATION   A Photographic Record of the Mount Jolmo Lungma Scientific Expedition 1966-68

CLARK   Six Great Mountaineers (including Hunt, Mallory)

CLEARE   Mountains (2 chapters)

COLLINS   Mountain Climbing (one chapter)

CREMER   Mount Everest and other Poems

DOLBIER   Nowhere near Everest (1953)

DONOUGHUE   The Ascent of Mount Everest

DOUGLAS & CLYDESDALE and M'INTYRE The Pilots Book of Everest (1933)

ENGEL They came to the Hills (including Mallory, Smythe)

EVANS Eye on Everest (1953)

FINCH The Making of a Mountaineer (1922)

FINCH Climbing Mount Everest

FRESHFIELD The Conquest of Mount Everest

GEOGRAPHICAL MAGAZINE Special Number, October 1953

GOSWAMI Everest, is it Conquered? (1953)

GREENE Moments of Being (1933)

GREGORY The Picture of Everest (1953)

GULATEE Mount Everest, its Name and Height

GULATEE The Height of Mount Everest, a new Determination (1952)

HAGEN and others Mount Everest: Formation, Population and Exploration of the Everest Region

HASTON In High Places (1971)

HEDIN Mount Everest

HILLARY High Adventure (1951, 1953)

HILLARY Nothing Venture, Nothing Win (1951, 1953)

HORNBEIN Everest, the West Ridge (1963)

HUNT Our Everest Adventure (1953)

INDIAN MOUNTAINEERING FEDERATION Indian Mount Everest Expedition 1965

IRVING Ten Great Mountains (one chapter)

IZZARD An Innocent on Everest (1953)

LODGE Why I believe in Immortality (1924) Restricted edn. only

LONGLAND and others Tight Corners (one chapter, "Caught in an Everest Blizzard" 1933)

LONGSTAFF This My Voyage (one chapter, 1922)

LOWE Because it is There (1953)

McCALLUM Everest Diary (1963)

MACINTYRE Attack on Everest (to 1936)

MALARTIC Tenzing of Everest

MARSHALL Men against Everest (to 1953)

MAZEAUD Naked Before the Mountain (one chapter, 1971)

MEADE   Approach to the Hills (one chapter)

MORIN   Everest: from the First Attempt to Final Victory

MORRIS, James   Coronation Everest (1953)

MORRIS, John   Hired to Kill (1922)

MULLICK   The Sky was his Limit (1965)

MURRAY   The Story of Everest (to 1953)

NATIONAL GEOGRAPHIC Magazine   Volume 124 No. 4 October 1963 (1963)

NORTON   Memoires d'un Sherpa (Ang Tharkay)

NOYCE   South Col (1953)

NOYCE & TAYLOR   Everest is Climbed (1953)

PARES   Himalayan Honeymoon (references to 1938)

PROGRAMME   Ascent of Everest 1953

PYE   George Leigh Mallory: a Memoir

REBUFFAT   Mont Blac to Everest (briefly)

ROBERTSON   George Mallory

ROCH   Everest 1952

SEAVER   Francis Younghusband

SEREILLIER   Everest Climbed (1953)

SHIPTON   Upon that Mountain (1933,1935,1936,1938)

SHIPTON   The True Book about Everest (to 1953)

SHIPTON   Mountain Conquest (to 1965)

SHIPTON   That Untravelled World (1933, 1935, 1936, 1938, 1951 and briefly 1953)

SMITH   True Stories of Modern Explorers (one chapter)

SMYTHE   Camp Six (1933)

SMYTHE   Adventures of a Mountaineer (one chapter, 1933)

SMYTHE   British Mountaineers (in part)

SMYTHE   The Mountain Vision (one chapter, 1933)

SNAITH   At Grips with Everest (to 1934)

SOMERVELL   After Everest (1922,1924)

STOBART   Adventurer's Eye (1953)

STYLES   Mallory of Everest

SUNDAY TIMES MAGAZINE   Interview of Capt. J. B. L. Noel by P. Gillman (1924)

SUNDAY TIMES MAGAZINE   "Man at the Top"   photographic coverage (1975 S. W. Face)

SWINSON   Beyond the Frontiers (one chapter)

SWISS FOUNDATION FOR ALPINE RESEARCH   Everest, the Swiss Expeditions (1952)

TIMES, The   Mount Everest Reconnaissance Expedition 1951 Special Supplement

TIMES, The   Challenge to Mount Everest. Special Supplement

TIMES, The   The First Ascent of Everest. Special Supplement

TIMES, The   Everest 1953. Special colour Supplement

ULLMAN   Kingdom of Adventure; Everest (to 1942)

ULLMAN   Man of Everest (Tenzing: 1935, 1936, 1938, 1947, 1952, 1953)

UNSWORTH   Because it is there (including Bruce, Mallory, Smythe)

VERGHESE (Ed)   Himalayan Endeavour (1953, 1953, 1960)

WARD   In this Short Span (1951, 1953)

WIBBERLEY   The Epics of Everest (to1953)

WILLIAMS   Women on the Rope (briefly, 1971)

WOLLASTON   Letters and Diaries of A. F. R. Wollaston (1921)

YOUNGHUSBAND   The Epic of Mount Everest (1921, 1922, 1924)

YOUNGHUSBAND   Everest, the Challenge (1st edn. to 1933; 2nd imp. to 1936)

Addenda:

ETHERTON   The Last Strongholds (1933 Houston Expedition)

FINCH   Der Kampf um den Everest (1921, 1922, 1924)

STYLES   First on the Summits (1953)

MOUNT EVEREST NORTH SIDE ATTEMPTS 1922-1924

A. Camp VI, 8160m. (1924).
B. Point reached by Mallory, Norton and Somervell in 1922.

C. 'The First Step'.
D. Point reached by Finch and Geoffrey Bruce in 1922.

E. 'The Second Step' where Mallory and Irvine were last seen.

F. Point reached by Somervell in 1924.

G. Point reached by Norton in 1924.

H. Summit, 8848m.

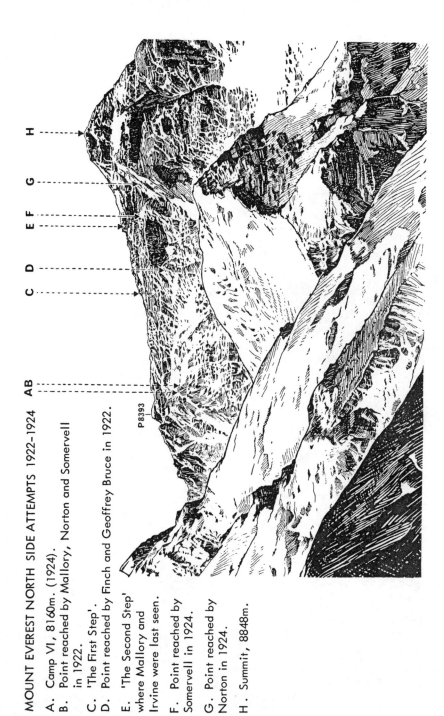

LHOTSE   4
and Lhotse Shar

Situated: Nepal Himalaya (Kosi Section) in the Mahalangur Himal forming the Nepal-Tibet border along the N. boundary of the Khumbu Himal.

Longitude: 86° 56' 10" E.
Latitude: 27° 57' 43" N.

Altitude: Lhotse - 8511m.
            Central summit - 8426m.
            Lhotse Shar - 8398m.

Early Designation No: E1

Name: means "South Peak"

LHOTSE is the principal summit in a long range running from west of Nuptse to Pethangtse. It is separated from Everest by the South Col. The central section of this range forms a ridge that never falls below 8000m. for a distance of about 4 km. This section presents to the south a formidable wall nearly 3000m. high.

It was not until relatively recently that the mountain, less of a status symbol than its famous neighbour to the immediate north, has been regarded as an objective in its own right for an expedition. Lhotse has been climbed four times by two expeditions and Lhotse Shar has been climbed once.

The total height to be ascended from the upper West Cwm is about 2000m., from the Lhotse gl., about 3100m.

The mountain was named Lhotse because it is the peak south of Everest. The peak north of Everest is called Changtse and the intervening col, Chang La (North Col); the South Col has no Tibetan name. West of Lhotse is Nuptse (West Peak) and west of Everest is the Lho La (South Col).

This appeared illogical to many Swiss and, without reference to anyone else, they changed the name of the South Col in their reports and books to 'Lho La' and changed the name of Lho La to 'Khumbu La'. There is indeed some force in their point of view: it is more symmetrical and much tidier. But it ignores the origins of names and the important historical associations that lie behind them. Professor N. E. Odell took this matter up very strongly in a letter to the Editor of the Alpine Journal (AJ 60 pp. 132-134) and pointed out that the name Lho La was in fact perfectly logical to anyone approaching up the Rongbuk gl. from Tibet as had done the earlier pioneers; he added that the Swiss arbitrary decision was unacceptable. The Swiss point of view is supported by H. W. Tilman and N. D. Hardie.

The Swiss argument and decision, forcefully declared by M. Kurz and G. O. Dyhrenfurth inter alia, would have been more consistent had it been decided to rename the Lho La not 'Khumbu La' but 'Nup La' (West Col) and to give some other name to the Nup La though it, too, has perfectly logical and historical origins.

Fosco Maraini makes an impassioned plea on this score (Karakoram p. 158) "In this whole matter, nothing is worse than systematization. System is the catalogue, the tags and labels; it is a museum, death; and place-names are too important, too charged with spiritual magnetism, to be left in the hands of bureaucrats and commissions. They need the touch of life! "

MAPS: These are as for Mount Everest, q. v.

CHRONICLE

1921 Lt. Col. C. K. Howard-Bury, leader of the 1921 Everest Reconnaissance expedition, recounts how from Pethang Rimgmo he enjoyed a view up the Kangshung gl. to Everest, 5 or 6 km. distant, from which "swept a huge amphitheatre of mighty peaks culminating in a new and unsurveyed peak, 28,100 ft. in height, to which we gave the name of Lhotse, which in Tibetan means the South Peak". The mountain was also partly seen from the west by G. H. Bullock and G. H. L. Mallory. (1)

1950 H. W. Tilman (Br) also had a view of Lhotse from the south and the west during his journey with O. Houston (Am) to the Khumbu gl. (2)

1951 A very close view of Lhotse from the top of the ice-fall leading into the West Cwm was obtained during E. E. Shipton's reconnaissance. The South Face was seen from the upper basin of the Imja Khola. (3)

1952 During the ascents from the West Cwm to the South Col,
1953 the Lhotse Face, to the north west of the peak, was used as the line of ascent in preference to the earlier Geneva Spur.

1955 An International expedition, leader N. G. Dyhrenfurth (Am), was in the Khumbu Himal for six months chiefly for mapping purposes but also to make an attempt on Lhotse - then the highest unclimbed peak. Included in the party was E. Schneider (Ger), the cartographer, who began work on the 1/50,000 map Khumbu Himal. Base Camp was placed at the foot of the ice-fall at 5250m. Early in October E. Senn (Aus), A. Spöhel (Sw) and two Sherpas camped out just below the Lhotse Terrace at 7800m. October 15 Senn, on his own, made a bid for the summit. He reached 8100m. before turning back. He was cut off, all alone, in his Camp 5 for several days by raging snow storms. (4) (5)

1956 LHOTSE - FIRST ASCENT: During the 3rd Swiss Everest Expedition (q.v.) Camp 6A was established on the Lhotse Face, a little below the South Col at nearly 8000m. From here, May 18, F. Luchsinger and E. Reiss set off and after climbing up the Lhotse Couloir reached the top during the afternoon. (6)

1965 Japanese expedition, 11 members, leader H. Yoshikawa, made an attempt on Lhotse Shar S. E. Ridge from the Col north of Island Peak (6189m.) but failed to get much higher than about 8000m. During the climb T. Narukawa slipped but was held by his companion; however he was seriously injured and they both had to spend the night in the open while awaiting help. Narukawa was badly frost-bitten as a result. (7)

1970 LHOTSE SHAR - FIRST ASCENT: Austrian expedition, 11 members, leader S. Aeberli, established Base Camp at 5220m. by the Lhotse gl. They climbed to the col (5699m.) on the S. E. Ridge then ascended the ridge. S. Mayerl and R. Walter reached the summit May 12. A traverse of the Lhotse Ridge to the main summit - a distance of about 1200m. - was considered but not carried out owing to the smallness of the party. (8)

1971 South Korean expedition, 10 members, leader Park Shulam, attempted to climb Lhotse Shar by a route slightly to the east of the Austrian one. High point reached about 8000m., May 13, by Choi Soon Nanam and Sherpa Sange. (9)

1972 German team of two members, G. Lenser (leader) and M. Holz, supposedly went for Lhotse but were reported to have attempted peaks east of Lhotse and Pethangtse (6724m.). (10)

1973 Japanese expedition, nine members, leader R. Uchida. Base Camp was established at 5300m. next to the Lhotse gl. The plan to attempt a new route up the 3000m. South Wall had to be abandoned on account of constant avalanches. Instead, the expedition turned its attention to the West Ridge via the long ridge projecting southward between the Lhotse and the Lhotse Nup gls. Three camps were placed before the climbers were forced to give up the climb at 7300m., May 8. (11)

1974 Austro-German expedition of four members, leader G. Lenser - thwarted in their wish to try a new route on Lhotse from the West Cwm - set off from the Barun gl. to attempt the mountain from the east: a route involving the ascents of Shartse (Junction Peak, 7502m.), Peak 38 (7589m.), and Lhotse Shar. They set up Base Camp in the upper Barun gl. at 5500m. Between Base and the top of Shartse's South Ridge 6 camps were placed, the highest at 7100m. May 23 K. Diemberger and Dr. H. Peter-Warth reached the summit (first ascent). This apparently completed their 'exploration' and they came down again. (12)

1974 Polish expedition of 16 members (including film crew and driver), leader A. Zawada, Pemba Norbu as Sirdar, made an attempt on the N. W. Face from the West Cwm. This was the first time a major Nepalese peak had been tried in winter. The expedition flew from Katmandu to Lukla and established Base Camp on the Khumbu gl. October 21. Four camps in all were established, the highest well up the Lhotse Face at 7800m. Intense cold and winds of hurricane force rendered the climb hazardous. December 25 A. Heinrich and A. Zawada made a bid for the summit and reached 8250m. before being forced back by blizzard conditions. Earlier, December 17, S. Latello (one of the film crew) died of exposure and exhaustion while coming down the fixed ropes below Camp 3 (13)

1975 Italian expedition, 15 members including R. Messner (Aus), leader R. Cassin, originally intended to climb the direct route up the South Face but, as with the 1973 Japanese expedition, this proved to be too hazardous. So they switched their attention to the long south ridge followed by the Japanese. Base Camp had been established April 3 at 5300m.; Camps 1 and 2 were erected by April 12. Then on April 20 an avalanche came down on Base Camp, hurting four Sherpas; the camp was re-sited and because of continued bad weather on the face all climbers were recalled to Base. On May 3, Camp 3 was set up (7200m.) and from there a high point of 7500m. was reached; but four days later the camp was nearly swept away by another avalanche. It continued to snow heavily and the decision was taken May 13 to abandon the attempt. (14) (15)

1976 Second Japanese expedition, leader K. Kamei, failed in its bid to climb Lhotse by the 1973 route. Camp 3 was placed at 7250m. with a light 'advance camp' 50m. higher. Camp 4 was planned for 7780m. but bad weather with heavy snow prevented any advance beyond 7600m. (16)

1977 2nd, 3rd, 4th ASCENTS: German expedition, 13 members, leader Dr. G. Schmatz. Their line of ascent was up the N. W. Face from the West Cwm. Base Camp was established about mid-March. Three teams reached the summit: May 8, J. von Kanel, H. Warth and Sherpa Urgen; May 9, G. Sturm, P. Worgetter and F. Zintl; May 11, M. Dacher, M. Lutz, P. Vogler and one other. During the night of May 12/13 Lutz left his tent at Camp 4, fell down the mountain and was killed. (17)

LHOTSE

Principal Source References:

(1) Howard-Bury Mount Everest: the Reconnaissance 1921

(2) Tilman Nepal Himalaya

(3) Shipton The Mount Everest Reconnaissance Expedition 1951

(4) Dyhrenfurth "Lhotse, 1955" AAJ 1956 pp. 7-20

(5) Senn's account in Herrligkoffer's Mount Everest: Thron der Götter pp. 86-90

(6) Eggler The Everest-Lhotse Adventure

(7) Dyhrenfurth "Chronique Himalayenne" Les Alpes 1966/4 pp. 273-274

(8) Dyhrenfurth "Chronique Himalayenne" Les Alpes 1971/4 pp. 218-220

(9) Dyhrenfurth "Chronique Himalayenne" Les Alpes 1972/4 p. 235

(10) Brief note HJ 32 p. 201

(11) Uchida "Lhotse, 1973" HJ 33 pp. 18-23

(12) Diemberger "Austro-German Lhotse Expedition, 1974, and the Ascent of Shartse" HJ 33 pp. 207-209

(13) Zawada "Winter at 8250 Metres" AJ 1977 pp. 28-35

(14) Cassin and Nangeroni Lhotse '75

(15) Messner The Challenge

(16) AAJ 1977 p. 239

(17) M 56 p. 11

CHO OYU

8153

IV

III

II

6446

Gyabrag Gl.

BC

Alfonfin

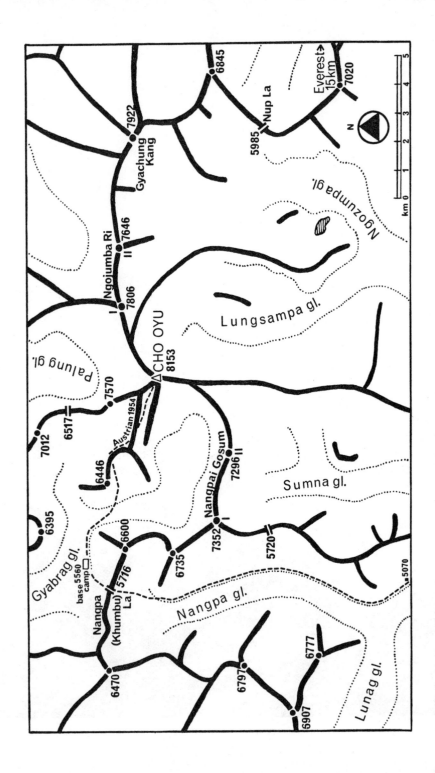

CHO OYU   5

Situated: Nepal Himalaya, Kosi Section in the Mahalangur
Himal (on Nepal/Tibet border).

Longitude: 86° 39' 51" E
Latitude: 28° 05' 32" N

Altitude: 8153m.

Early Designation No: (none)

Name: Tibetan. Meaning probably "Goddess of the Turquoise"

Though the Nangpa La has been used for long ages as an important trade route between Nepal and Tibet, Cho Oyu itself
began to attract the attention of 'outsiders' only in the last
few decades. 30 km. west of Everest, it is separated from it
by a long ridge with five summits over 7000m. high: Ngojumba
Ri I (7806m.), Ngojumba Ri II (7646m.), Gyachung Kang
(7922m.), Lingtren (7020m.) and Pumo Ri (7145m.). Albeit
regarded as the easiest of the 8000m. peaks to ascend, its
entire southern perimeter presents continuous and precipitous
faces to the would-be climber. The easier northern and western
approaches all involve passing through forbidden Tibetan
territory.
The mountain has been climbed three times, twice for certain,
and all from much the same direction. Pasang Dawa Lama
has been to the summit twice. The last of five expeditions
was made more than 15 years ago.

The total height to be ascended from Base Camp (Nangpa La approach) is about 2600m.

MAPS - The following modern maps are generally available. Those most recommended are marked with an asterisk (*).

1/506,880 Nepal East Sh. 3rd Ed.-GSGS, 1969. DMS(MoD), London *
1/126,720 Trekking Map: Lamosangu to Mt. Everest. 1975. Mandara maps, Katmandu (fair dyeline copy of artwork).
1/100,000 Mount Everest Region. 2nd Ed. 1975. RGS, London *
1/50,000 Khumbu Himal. 1965. FNH, Munich *
1/50,000 Trekking Map: Khumbu Himal. 1975. Mandara maps, Katmandu (fair dyeline copy of artwork).

CHRONICLE

1921 During the British Mount Everest Reconnaissance, Lt. Col. C. K. Howard-Bury left Kyetrak, south of Tingri, for the Khumbu Pass (Nangpa La, 5716m.). During this part of the journey they were able to observe Cho Oyu from the west and the north-west. Cho Oyu was seen also from the east, from the Rongbuk gl. north of Everest. Good photographs were obtained. (1)

1951 In the course of E. E. Shipton's Mount Everest Reconnaissance, W. H. Murray, H. E. Riddiford (NZ), T. D. Bourdillon and M. P. Ward made an October journey westward from the Khumbu gl. over to the Ngozumpa gl. from where they tried without success to reach the Nup La (5985m.) previously reached from the West Rongbuk gl. by J. de V. Hazard in 1924. They were within the cirque formed by Cho Oyu and Gyachung Kang (7922m.) for two or three days but could find "not one chink in its icy armour" on the east side. Then, early November, the expedition travelled westward towards the Gauri Sankar; en route Murray and Bourdillon made a quick trip north up to the Nangpa La. From near the pass they saw two possible ways of climbing Cho Oyu: by the North Ridge (i.e. N.N.W. Ridge) or, apparently better still, by the N.W. Face; they judged that autumn would be better than the spring on account of wind direction. (2)

1952 A British expedition was organized to select and train men for a later attempt on Everest and to try out equipment and oxygen gear. The party consisted of seven British and three New Zealanders, leader again E. E. Shipton. From Namche Bazaar they headed north to the Nangpa La. In an attempt on Cho Oyu in early May, E. P. Hillary and W. G. Lowe (both NZ) reached a height of 6850m. on the N. W. Face but were turned back by ice cliffs that could not be circumvented with the limited resources at their disposal. (3)

1954 FIRST ASCENT: An Austrian expedition of three members and seven Sherpas, leader H. Tichy, though severely repulsed during its first assault, succeeded in climbing the mountain from the Nangpa La. Base Camp was established September 27 on the Tibetan side of the Pass at 5560m. From there they climbed to the West Ridge (i.e. W.N.W. Ridge) and managed to negotiate the ice cliffs. From Camp 4 (7000m.) three members crossed the N.W. Face and reached the summit October 19: S. Jöchler, H. Tichy, Pasang Dawa Lama. It was the third highest summit to have been climbed to date and the first to have been achieved in the autumn. (4)

1954 While the Austrian expedition was on Cho Oyu, for which it had received specific permission from the Nepalese Government, there suddenly arrived on the scene a Swiss party of five (plus two botanists) fresh from the Ganesh

Himal, with R. Lambert as leader. Certain difficulties arose as a result but it was finally agreed that Tichy's party should be given priority for an attempt on the summit. The Swiss, too, attacked the N. W. Face but the start of their route onto the main W. Ridge was a little further north than that of the Austrians. A Camp 4 was placed at 7150m. Madame Claude Kogan (Fr) and Lambert attempted the summit October 28 but had to renounce owing to intense cold and high winds. High point reached, about 7700m. (5)

1958 SECOND ASCENT: Indian expedition, leader K. F. Bunshah. S. Gyaltsen and Pasang Dawa Lama reached the summit May 15. Major N. D. Jayal, aged 32, the first Director of the Mountaineering Institute at Darjeeling, died of pneumonia or heart failure when ascending rapidly from Base Camp to Camp 1. (6)

1959 An International Women's expedition (four French, three British, three Nepalese, one Belgian and one Swiss), leader Mme. C. Kogan (Fr). Base Camp was again established at 5600m. Kogan, C. van der Stratten and Sherpa Ang Norbu occupied Camp 4 (7100m.) on the N.W. Face prior to a bid for the summit. October 2 Sirdar Wangdi and Sherpa Chhowang left Camp 2, despite persistent bad weather, to render help to the summit team now isolated; they were swept away by an avalanche and Chhowang was killed. At much the same time an avalanche obliterated the Camp 4 and its occupants. (7) (8)

1964 THIRD ASCENT (?): German Ski expedition, five members, leader R. Rott; including also Sirdar Dawa Tensing. From the Nangpa La the same approach was made and Camp 4 was placed on the N. W.Face at about 7200m. F. Stammberger claims to have reached the summit April 25 alone; Sherpa Phu Dorje II claims they were together. The photographs supposedly taken on the summit were in all probability not taken there nor at the hour claimed. That same day G. Huber and A. Thurmayr, the second team, decided to bivouac at about 7500m. without tent or anything but finally came down to Camp 4 with Stammberger and Phu Dorje. They waited there for two wasted days; their butane gas gave out; both Huber and Thurmayr were unwell. April 27 Phu Dorje was sent down to fetch provisions and gas. April 28 Stammberger went down to fetch help; at Base Camp he collapsed. The result of this ill-judged operation was that 61 year old Sirdar Dawa Tensing was the only person left capable of rendering any assistance. Alone he climbed up to Camp 4, May 2, but alone he could not bring down the two dying climbers. Then Khagda Bahadur, the Nepalese Officer, went for help to the village of Thami. It was only on May 5 or 6 (the testimonies vary) that the rescue column of Stammberger, Phu Dorje, Dawa Tensing and one other Sherpa reached Camp 4 again. Huber was already dead; Thurmayr died while being carried down. (9)

CHO OYU

Principal Source References:

(1) Howard-Bury Mount Everest: the Reconnaissance 1921
(2) Murray "The Reconnaissance of Mount Everest, 1951" AJ 58 pp. 433-453
(3) Evans "The Cho Oyu Expedition, 1952" AJ 59 pp. 9-18
(4) Tichy Cho Oyu
(5) Lambert & Kogan White Fury
(6) G. O. Dyhrenfurth "Chroniques Himalayennes" Les Alpes 1959/4 p. 246
(7) La Montagne February 1960 pp. 193-195
(8) Harper Lady Killer Peak
(9) G. O. Dyhrenfurth "Chroniques Himalayennes" Les Alpes 1965/3 pp. 190-191

Additional books relevant to Cho Oyu, not already listed. (The dates in brackets refer to the expeditions written about).

HILLARY High Adventure (2 chapters, 1952)
HILLARY Nothing Venture, Nothing Win (in part)
MULLICK The Sky was his Limit (1958)
SHIPTON The Mount Everest Reconnaissance Expedition 1951
WILLIAMS Women on the Rope (in part)

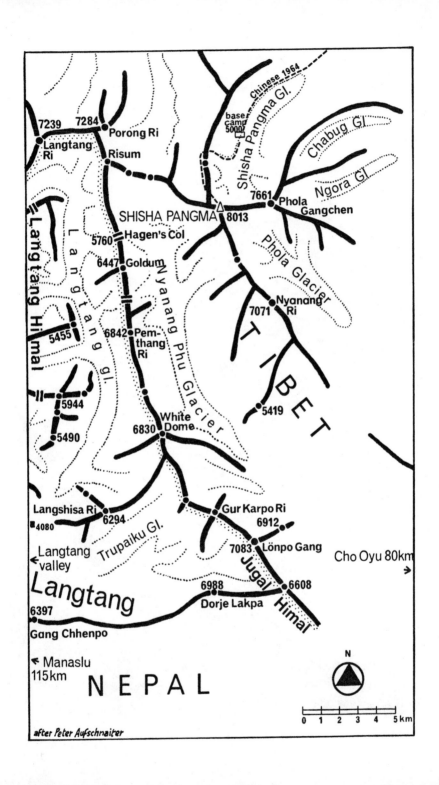

SHISHA PANGMA   6
(Gosainthan)

Situated: Nepal Himalaya, Kosi Section adjoining the Langtang Himal (the mountain, in fact, is situated on a secondary crest zone just north-east of the Langtang Himal and entirely within Tibet).

Longitude: 85° 46' 55" E
Latitude: 28° 21' 07" N

Altitude: 8013m.

Early Designation No: XXIII

Name: Tibetan: Shisha Pangma meaning "The Crest above the Grassy Plain". Sanskrit: Gosainthan meaning "The Place of the Saint" or "Abode of God". Since the Chinese occupied Tibet the name Kao-seng-tsan Feng has appeared in mountaineering literature.

Until the last few years the mountain has been known generally by its Sanskrit name and the fact that a mountain entirely within Tibet should have such a name has caused some perplexity. 40 km. north of Katmandu and about 18 km. distant from Gosainthan lies Gosainkund, the largest of numerous lakes in the area. The latter is associated closely with Siva, paramount god of Nepal, Mahadeo, one of the Hindu Triad, whose celestial home is Mount Kailas (also in Tibet). To millions of Asiatics Mt. Kailas is a place of veneration and pilgrimage, the holiest of holy mountains, the most sublime of all. To unbelievers it is little more than an interesting geological specimen consisting of horizontally stratified conglomerate masses with erratic admixture, 6713m. high, known also as Kang Rimpoche.

Gosainkund is one of the most important religious centres outside the Valley of Katmandu and a place of pilgrimage and worship too. A connection between Gosainkund and Gosainthan seems highly probable, more so since according to Perceval Landon (Nepal Vol. II p. 36 note 2) "the frontier line, as traced on the Nepalese maps, includes access to the summit of the mountain" - itself an important place of Hindu sanctity.

The Chronicle of Gosainthan, or Shisha Pangma, is one of endeavours to glimpse the mountain rather than one of attempts to climb it. This most elusive of mountains - geographically, politically and literally - has been climbed but once, from the north, though whether the actual summit or only the fore-summit was attained is still in some slight doubt. Doubt also exists as to the exact position of the summit along the main E.-W. ridge of the mountain, and the highest point could be situated further W. than indicated in the accompanying map.

The total height to be ascended from Base Camp (Shisha Pangma gl.) to summit is about 3000m.

In 1976 it was announced by the Survey of India that Shisha Pangma had been remeasured as 8046m. If this figure becomes acceptable it displaces Gasherbrum II which would go to the bottom of the fourteen 8000m. peaks table.

Peter Aufschnaiter, a recognized authority on this part of the Himalaya, considers that 'Langtrang' is more correct than 'Langtang'; the latter, nevertheless, is used here as this form is the one generally found in the literature quoted.

MAPS - A good map of the Langtang-Shisha Pangma area, after P. Aufschnaiter, is produced as the Frontispiece of Kurz's Chronique Himalayenne Vol. II. The following map is generally available.

1/506,880   Nepal East Sh. 3rd Ed.-GSGS, 1969. DMS(MoD), London

CHRONICLE

1921 Major H. T. Morshead and Dr. A. F. R. Wollaston with interpreter Gyaldzan Kazi and surveyor Gujjar Singh, all of the British Mount Everest Reconnaissance expedition, travelled from Tingri during July to visit the village of Nyenyam, to the south-west. While descending from the Tang La (5480m.) they caught sight of the twin summits of Gosainthan, 45 km. to the west. They did not see the mountain again but at Nyenyam Wollaston did find a new deep-blue primula (P. Wollastonii). (1)

1945 P. Aufschnaiter and H. Harrer, interned at the outbreak of war in 1939 on their return from the Austrian Nanga Parbat reconnaissance (q. v.), escaped from their Dehra Dun camp in April 1944 and headed north for Tibet. They spent 10 months in Kyerong and there planned their escape route to Lhasa. In November 1945 (ironically, long after the war had ended) they left Kyerong and passed Lake Pelgu; from here they had a view south to the Pungrong range with Gosainthan and Lapchi Kang in the background. They sketched this panorama. (2)

1949 A British expedition of four members, including botanist O. Polunin and Sherpa Tenzing Norkay, leader H. W. Tilman, obtained permission to travel and climb in the Langtang Himal to whose immediate north, in Tibet, was an area of country marked on the 1/4 inch maps as "Unsurveyed". In this area was Gosainthan, or Shisha Pangma. From Katmandu the party travelled up the Trisuli valley in early June to Langtang village and thence to the Langtang gl. From a high ridge at the head of the

Lirung gl. Tilman had the only view of Gosainthan: its West Face, some 20 km. away. Thereafter it eluded them. (3)

1950 While carrying out his geological explorations in the Nepal Himalaya, Dr. T. Hagen (Sw) flew over the Langtang area and obtained the first photograph of Shisha Pangma - from a south-westerly direction. (4) (5)

1951 In October P. Aufschnaiter (Aus) travelled to within about 10 km. of Shisha Pangma's eastern side and was able to photograph it from a point above Kong Tso Lake. (6)

1952 While still engaged on his geological survey Hagen left Katmandu in the autumn and journeyed up to the Langtang Valley. Setting out from Langshisa village, he ascended the Tunga Phu gl. and reached a col (5760m.) that now bears his name; it is on the frontier ridge. But he found himself too close to the mountain for a photograph so went to a prominent point on the opposite side of the Langtang gl. from where an excellent picture was obtained. (7)

1962 A mixed party (Br) led by Lord Glentworth visited the Langtang Himal. During their tour four members climbed up to near the head of the Langtang gl. and thence to a col on the frontier ridge, about 5860m., north of the one reached by Hagen. From there they were able to see the S. W. Face of Shisha Pangma. (8)

1963 A Chinese party reconnoitered the northern side of the mountain to study the environment, weather and topography of the area. They reached a height of 7160m. on the northern slope. (9)

1964 FIRST ASCENT: Chinese expedition of 195 members, leader Hsu Ching (the deputy leader of the 1960 Chomo Lungma expedition), and including many scientists, claims to have reached the summit. Base Camp was established at 5000m. March 18. The final Camp 6 was placed at 7700m. May 2, ten members (including the leader) set off to climb the final 312m. (the Chinese give the summit a height of 8012m.); this took nearly $4\frac{1}{2}$ hours to achieve. Unfortunately details about the route followed are scant and the photographs accompanying the accounts are inconclusive. (9) (10)

1973 K. Yamada (Jap.) made a flight in a Pilatus Turbo Porter, pilot A. Moreaux, on October 31 from the Rolwaling to the Langtang Himal. During the flight he obtained a good aerial photograph from the south-west. (11)

SHISHA PANGMA

Principal Source References:

(1) Howard-Bury Mount Everest: the Reconnaissance 1921
(2) Harrer Seven Years in Tibet
(3) Tilman Nepal Himalaya
(4) Hagen "Das Gebirge Nepals: Die Shisha Pangma-Gruppe" Les Alpes 1956 pp. 165-166
(5) Hagen & others Mount Everest (pp. 22-31)
(6) Dyhrenfurth To the Third Pole (page 157)
(7) Hagen "Dans la plus haute Fromagerie du Monde: Langtrang, Himalaya Nepalais" Les Alpes 1959 pp. 194-199. (This includes his photograph, No. 86, and also Aufschnaiter's map completed during 1954.)
(8) AJ 68 p. 291 (Expedition note)
(9) Chou Cheng "The Ascent of Shisha Pangma" AJ 69 pp. 211-215
(10) Peoples Physical Culture Publishing House Mountaineering in China
(11) Yamada & Yakushi The Himalaya from the Air

Additional book, not already listed:

KRUPARZ Shisha Pangma (slight reference only)

MANASLU

8156
7895
S.E.RIDGE
E.RIDGE
PLATEAU
VI
PINNACLE
North Pk.
V
IV
N. COL
III
II
NAIKE COL
Dep.
MANASLU GL.
BC

Alfonsi
m

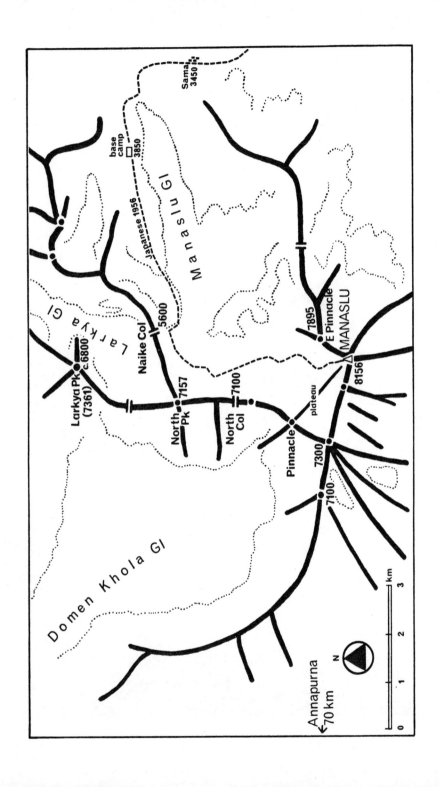

MANASLU   7

Situated: Nepal Himalaya, Gandaki Section, Gurkha Himal (also sometimes referred to incorrectly as the Larkya Himal).

Longitude: 84° 33' 43" E
Latitude: 28° 33' 00" N

Altitude: 8156m.

Early Designation No: XXX

Name: Derived from the Sanskrit word 'Manasa' meaning intellect or soul. Name is approximately "Mountain of the Intellect" or "Mountain of the Spirit". Earlier referred to as Kutan I, 'tang' in Tibetan meaning a flat place - descriptive of Manaslu's general summit. Called Kambung in Sama after a local god.

The summit of Manaslu has been reached from the north, the west and the south; it has been attempted from the east too by the east ridge. There have been 15 expeditions on the mountain, eight of them successful, and nine teams have reached the summit.
The total height to be ascended by the original Manaslu glacier route is about 4300m., by the N.W. Wall about 4600m., by the southern route about 3800m., and by the East Ridge about 3700m.

MAPS - The following modern maps are generally available. Those most recommended are marked with an asterisk (*)

1/506,880 Nepal East Sh. 3rd Ed.-GSGS, 1969. DMS(MoD), London *

1/506,880 Nepal West Sh. 2nd Ed.-GSGS, 1967. DMS(MoD), London *

1/250,000 Jonga Dzong Sh. NH 45-13, Series U502. 1963. AMS, Washington, D.C. (only fair black & white litho reprint available 1977).

CHRONICLE

1950 Following up the old salt route from Thonje to Bimtakhoti in the Dudh Khola valley, H. W. Tilman and three members of his party passed close by Manaslu; they were able to admire its long north ridge in some detail. Three months later, after an unsuccessful attempt on Annapurna IV, Tilman's party retraced its steps but from Bimtakhoti it headed north in the direction of the Larkya Bhanjyang Pass. Major J. O. M. Roberts crossed over to Larkya and reported having seen what he thought might be a direct route to the summit plateau. Some of the first photographs of Manaslu were obtained during the tour. (1)

1950 In the course of his geological survey of Nepal Dr. T. Hagen
1951 (Sw) flew over the area and photographed Manaslu from the south-east. (2)

1952 Japanese reconnaissance party of six, leader Dr. K. Imanishi. They first examined during October all the western side of the mountain from the Dudh Khola but, like Tilman, they found these sides quite terrifying. Then in November they crossed the Larkya Bhanjyang Pass (5213m.) and found a possible route from the head of Manaslu gl. and via the North Col (7100m.). They also reached a height of 5275m. on the East Ridge. (3)

1953 Japanese expedition, 13 climbers and two scientists, leader Y. Mita, went from Katmandu up the Buri Gandaki to Sama. Base Camp was established April 12 beyond Sama village on the left bank of Manaslu gl. at 3850m. The plan was to ascend the glacier then to advance southward up the northern ramparts of Manaslu. Camp 4 was placed on the Naike Col (5600m.) May 3; Camp 8 was placed above the ice-fall on the North Col (7100m.) May 15. Two days later the first attempt on the summit was made but the team could go no higher than 7400m. on account of unsettled weather and withdrew back to Camp 4. A second attempt was made May 31 from a new Camp 9 (7500m.) but when at about 7750m. J. Ishizaka, K. Kato and J. Yamada realized they were still a long way from the summit and turned back because of shortage of time. (3)

1954 Second Japanese expedition of 13 members, leader Y. Hotta. They went up the Buri Gandaki and reached Ngyak April 1. At Sama they met trouble: the villagers claimed that the heathen Japanese had profaned their holy mountain and that the gods in their anger had sent down avalanches and pestilence on the valley and on a local gompa (lamasery). The intermediaries and indeed the whole expedition were threatened with physical violence if they persisted in their advance. The better part of valour being discretion, the expedition withdrew to the Ganesh Himal. (4)

1955 Two members of the Himalayan Committee of the Japanese Alpine Club, Dr. Nishibori and I. Naruse, went to Katmandu in April to negotiate for permission to be on Manaslu in the post-monsoon period and also during the spring of 1956. That autumn an advance party of three passed without let or hindrance through Sama to the old Base Camp site from where they reconnoitred as far as the Plateau above the N. Col (to about 7500m.). (5)

1956 FIRST & SECOND ASCENTS: Third Japanese expedition, 12 members, leader Y. Maki, returned by the usual route to Sama, reached March 26. Despite some local opposition the expedition was able to establish Base Camp (no number) beside the Manaslu gl. as previously. In carrying out a plan to reduce the number of camps and to speed up operations, Camp 2 was placed on the Naike Col and Camp 3 (an Advanced Base Camp) was placed above the ice-fall at 6200m. April 25. From Camp 4 at 6550m. the climbers took a line that avoided the N. Col and by keeping more to the east they reached the Plateau via the 'Snow Apron'. There at 7800m. Camp 6 was pitched. May 9 the first team, T. Imanishi and Sirdar Gyalzen, reached the summit. May 11 the second team, M. Higeta and K. Kato, reached the summit. (6)

1970 A two-man Japanese reconnaissance party went in the autumn to find a Base Camp site and a route to an Advanced Base Camp for the 1971 expedition from the north-west; also to sound the feelings of the people of Sama. (7)

1971 South Korean expedition, leader Ho Sup Kim, attempted the mountain during the spring from the north (Manaslu gl.) but failed to reach the top. During the climb Ki Sup Kim,brother of the leader, fell down into a crevasse close to Camp 5 (7600m.) and was killed. The expedition was abandoned. (8)

1971 THIRD ASCENT: A Japanese expedition, 11 members, leader A. Takahashi, set out to climb the mountain by the N.W. Wall and the W. Ridge. From Pokhara the expedition went to Tonje then followed up the Dudh Khola and the Domen Khola. Base Camp was established March 15 at 3500m. on the moraine of the glacier tumbling down from the north-west side of Manaslu (clearly seen in Plate 22 of G. O. Dyhrenfurth's To the Third Pole). Camp 2 - Advanced Base Camp - was placed at 5500m. on the broad basin-like snow-field above the ice-fall, within the N. W. Cwm or 'West-side Sanctuary'. The line of ascent then ran approximately southward up to the W. Ridge where Camp 3 was pitched (6500m.). Camp 4 was placed at about 7100m. above a pyramidal pinnacle (called Kasa-iwa or Umbrella rock) perched astride the main ridge; this last obstacle proved to be particularly difficult to overcome, with pitches up to Grade 6. Camp 3 had been established April 8, Camp 4 not until May 6; loads had to be hoisted up the overhanging face of Kasa-iwa by cable. The next section of the route up to the Plateau on which Camp 5 was to be placed proved to be almost equally daunting; another 10 days were required before the camp could be established (7360m.). Finally, May 17, K. Kohara and M. Tanaka were able to stand on the summit. (7)

1972 Second South Korean expedition, about 12 members including one Japanese, leader Ho Sup Kim. The plan was again to climb the mountain from the Manaslu gl. and up the northern face. But during the night of April 10 Camp 3 (6500m.) was overwhelmed by an avalanche; four Koreans (amongst them the leader), the Japanese and 10 Sherpas perished. Only Yae Sup Kim, brother of the leader, and two Sherpas survived after being swept 760m. down the mountain; while lying there they were caught by a second avalanche and carried a further 300m. down; this also they survived. They and the seven other participants abandoned the climb. Highest point reached was about 6950m. (9)

1972 FOURTH ASCENT: Austrian expedition of nine Tyrolean guides, leader W. Nairz, approached the mountain via the Marsyandi valley and the Dona Khola. Base Camp was established March 29 on the Thulagi gl. to the south at 4300m. One intermediary and four other camps were established by April 24, the last Camp being at 7400m. on the edge of the summit plateau. The following day F. Jäger and R. Messner made a bid for the summit while H. Fankhauser and A. Schlick came up to Camp 4 in support. When on the final and easy snow plateau Jäger turned back for Camp 4 and Messner continued alone and without oxygen to the summit. After spending only a few minutes on the summit because of a change in the weather, Messner headed down but was caught on the way by a terrible snowstorm; it was a desperate struggle to find Camp 4 in the failing light. Jäger was not there. Fankhauser and Schlick immediately went out to search for him but fate struck again; Schlick too failed to return to the tents. Further searches proved useless, an abundance of snow fell, and the expedition was abandoned. (10) (11) (12)

1973 FIFTH ASCENT: German expedition of eight members, leader Dr. G. Schmatz. Base Camp was established March 20 at 3900m. on the Manaslu gl. beyond Sama. Camp 2 was placed on Naike Col and Camp 3 above the ice-fall at about 6350m. From there they reached the N. Col and placed Camp 5 at 7550m. April 14. Leaving this camp, S. Hupfauer, Schmatz and Sherpa Urkien climbed to the summit April 22. (This is reported as being a new East Face route yet it appears to have followed generally the Japanese 1953 route. It is surely confusing to refer to this and similar routes as "East Face" just because the start of the climb from Base Camp is in a westerly direction; the main attack is on the northern quadrant. The true East Face is the one falling away from the ridge linking the main summit and East Pinnacle down towards the Pongern gl.) (13)

1973 Spanish expedition, 12 members, leader J. G. Orts, made an attempt by the Japanese 1956 route during the post-monsoon period. The climb was abandoned after Camp 1 (5150m.) and Camp 2 (5600m.) had been swept twice by avalanches between October 10 and 13. Fortunately the camps were unoccupied. High point reached was 6100m. (14)

1973 A Japanese reconnaissance party investigated the possibilities of a route by the East Ridge and fixed some pegs and ropes up a gully leading from the Manaslu gl. to the ridge. (15)

1974 SIXTH ASCENT: Japanese Ladies expedition, 13 members, general leader K. Sato, left Katmandu with the intention of climbing by the E. Ridge. Base Camp was established west of Sama at 4400m., March 3. Camp 2 was placed on the ridge, just east of the col on March 26. But the ridge proved to be very unstable and difficult so they withdrew to Base Camp. Having decided to tackle the 1956 route instead, they moved Base Camp April 1 to the opposite side of the glacier. Camp 5 was placed on the Plateau at 7650m., May 1. Two ropes reached the summit May 4: M. Uchida with Sherpa Jambu and M. Mori with N. Nakaseko; only one person used oxygen that day. May 5 a third summit party, T. Ito with T. Suzuki, left Camp 4 for Camp 5, preceded by some Sherpas. The latter, when returning down from Camp 5, met Suzuki followed by Ito at 7550m. But neither climber reached Camp 5. That night Ito was found standing absentmindedly outside Camp 4: in a blizzard she had lost both Camp 5 and her companion. Next day, despite continuing blizzard conditions, a search was mounted and close to Camp 4 the Sherpas found Suzuki's ice-axe, cylinder and rucksack; a short distance away were her red jacket and safety-belt. Nothing else. This was the first 8000m. mountain to be climbed by women. (15)

1975 SEVENTH ASCENT: A Spanish expedition, 12 members, leader J. G. Orts, succeeded in climbing the mountain by the northern route. The expedition began in March and Camp 5 was established at 7500m. on April 24. Three days later G. B. Garcia and J. L. Martinez with Sherpa Soman reached the summit. A frozen body thought to be that of one of the missing Austrians, F. Jäger or A. Schlick lost in 1972, was found on the summital plateau. (16)

1976 A third South Korean expedition, 19 members, leader Jung Sup Kim - whose brothers were on the 1971 and 1972 expeditions - attempted to climb the original route (referred to in M 51 as the East Face, original route, and in AAJ 1977 as the East Ridge). Camp 1 was set up at 5195m., April 5, and Camp 4 at 7300m., April 27. Camp 5 was being erected at 7800m., May 5, when an avalanche struck it; Sirdar Dawang Chuk and two Sherpas had lucky escapes but the leader and the climbing leader, Kyoung Bae Kim, had to be evacuated back to Katmandu by air. The expedition was abandoned May 12. (17)

1976 EIGHTH ASCENT: An Iranian-Japanese post-monsoon expedition, joint leaders Brig. Gen. M. Khakbiz (Iran) and N. Tamura (Jap). They approached the summit again from the north and pitched Camp 5, their highest, at 7560m. From there Lt. M. J. Assadi (Iran) and J. Kagayama (Jap) reached the summit October 12. (18)

1977 German pre-monsoon expedition, leader G. Lenser, made a bid for the summit but abandoned the climb on account of adverse weather and the risk of avalanches; three camps had been established. (19)

1977 A small French expedition failed in its attempt on the mountain.

MANASLU

Principal Source References:

(1) Tilman Nepal Himalaya

(2) Hagen "Das Gebirge Nepals: Die Shisha Pangma-Gruppe" Les Alpes 1956 pp. 165-166

(3) Takagi "Manaslu: Japanese Expeditions 1952 and 1953" MW 1954 pp. 63-70

(4) Muraki "Uprising of the Faithful" MW 1955 pp. 129-132

(5) Maki & Imanishi "The Ascent of Manaslu" HJ 20 pp. 12-13

(6) Maki & Imanishi "The Ascent of Manaslu" HJ 20 pp. 13-25 (5 and 6 are reprinted with some additional notes on equipment used in MW 1958/59 pp. 176-190)

(7) Takahashi "Manaslu West Wall, 1971" HJ 31 pp. 138-144

(8) G. O. Dyhrenfurth "Chroniques Himalayennes" Les Alpes 1972/4 p. 236

(9) G. O. Dyhrenfurth "Chroniques Himalayennes" Les Alpes 1973/4 p. 222

(10) Messner Sturm am Manaslu

(11) G. O. Dyhrenfurth "Chroniques Himalayennes" Les Alpes 1973/4 pp. 222-223

(12) AAJ 1973 pp. 484-485

(13) AAJ 1974 p. 205

(14) HJ 33 p. 200

(15) Sato, Nakaseko & Kuroishi "Manaslu, 1974" HJ 33 pp. 37-41

(16) AAJ 1976 pp. 518-519

(17) AAJ 1977 p. 240

(18) AAJ 1977 p. 239

(19) M 56 p. 11 (brief note only)

Additional books relevant to Manaslu, not already listed:

J. A. C.   Manaslu 1952-3

J. A. C.   Manaslu 1954-6

YODA   Ascent of Manaslu in Photographs 1952-1956

ANNAPURNA

ANNAPURNA
EAST 8010   8051   8091

SICKLE

NW. ridge

NE buttress

ANNAPURNA NORTH GL.

Alfonti

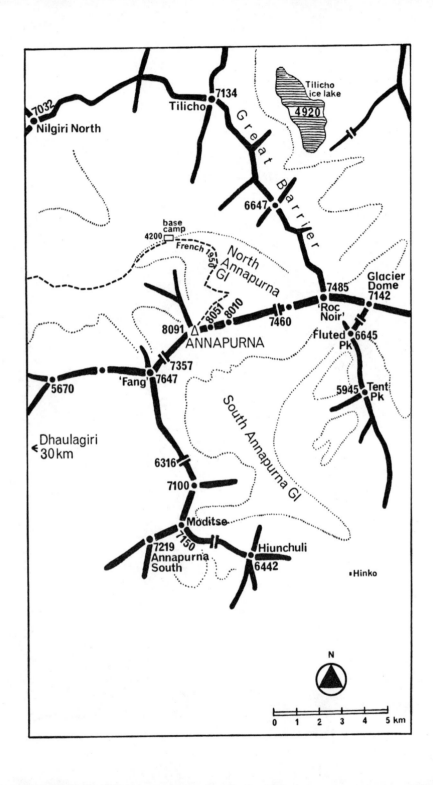

ANNAPURNA 8

Situated: Nepal Himalaya (Gandaki Section) in the Annapurna Himal.

Longitude: 83° 49' 19" E
Latitude: 28° 35' 44" N.

Altitude: Main summit - 8091m.
Central summit - 8051m.
East summit - 8010m.

Early designation No: XXXIX
Name: Previously sometimes called Morshiadi. H. W. Tilman was told (by whom?) that Anna means 'a measure' and Purna means 'heaped-up'. G. O. Dyhrenfurth mentions that the name is a combination of the Sanskrit words Anna meaning 'sustenance' and Purna meaning 'filled with'. Hence the name can be translated as "The Goddess Rich in Sustenance" or more simply as "The Provider".

The Annapurna Himal and the Lamjung Himal stretch from the Kali Gandaki in the west to the Marsyandi in the east, the dividing point being P. 6983 (variously called Siklis-Himal, West Lamjung Spitze, Lamjung Pk.). There are four summits referred to as Annapurna, each followed by a number: Annapurna I - 8091m.; Annapurna III - 7555m.; Annapurna IV - 7525m.; and furthest east Annapurna II - 7937m. Some confusion arises over the name 'Gangapurna'. Herzog was told at Manangbhot that the Triangular Peak dominating the town was called Gangapurna. A small error of translation in the English version of his book <u>Annapurna</u> equates this Triangular Peak with the 'Roc Noir', whereas in the original French version it is written: "C'est de ce fameux sommet rocheux, le Roc Noir dont nous soupçonnions l'importance orographique, ..." not "Sommet Triangulaire". Resulting from this slip the conclusion is drawn that the 'Roc Noir' and Gangapurna are one and the same; they are not. Furthermore, K. Mason, in an article published in HJ 6, attempts an identification of the summits in the Dhaulagiri and Annapurna Himal; basing himself on figures given by Mason, M. Kurz in his <u>Chronique Himalayenne</u> Vol. I page 63 identifies Gangapurna as being Annapurna III; this misconstruction - understandable at the time - is repeated in Vol. II and is shown thus on his map between pages 498 and 499. To-day we know that this complex portion of the Annapurna Himal comprises (west to east): Annapurna I, 'Roc Noir', Glacier Dome, Gangapurna, Annapurna III - and that from Annapurna III a ridge runs south to Muchapuchare. Further observations on this part of the range are to be found in G. Hauser's article "Notes on the Map of the Southern Annapurna Group" to be found in MW 1966/67 pages 63-66.

Annapurna was the first 8000m. peak to be climbed. Its summit has been reached on four occasions - three times from the north and once from the south. Attempts have been made from the west and from the east.

The total height to be ascended from Base Camp on the north side is about 3900m.; from Base Camp on the south side about 3840m.

MAPS - The following modern maps are generally available. Those most recommended are marked with an asterisk (*)

1/506,880 Nepal West Sh. 2nd Ed.-GSGS, 1967. DMS(MoD), London *

1/250,000 Pokhara Sh. NH 44-16, Series U502. 1963. AMS, Washington, D. C. (only fair black & white litho reprint available 1977)

1/250,000 Annapurna & Dhaulagiri Himal. 1970. JGP, New Delhi *

1/126,720 Trekking Map: Pokhara to Jomosom. 1974. Mandara maps, Katmandu (fair dyeline copy of artwork)

CHRONICLE

1949 Though it had been seen from a long distance, little was known about Annapurna until Dr. A. Heim, with the backing of the Swiss Foundation for Alpine Research, had a look at Dhaulagiri and Annapurna from the air, October 18. Unfortunately the Dakota aircraft did not fly high enough for a proper observation or for photographing the Annapurna Himal. (1)

1950 FIRST ASCENT: French expedition, nine members, leader M. Herzog, with Ang Tharkay as Sirdar, left Nautanwa in India and crossed into Nepal via Tansing and Baglung. They based themselves at Tukucha in the Kali Gandaki Valley, April 21. After prolonged exploration of the approaches to Dhaulagiri, with disappointing results, the expedition decided to try for Annapurna instead. Small parties went off to reconnoitre its northern and southern approaches. Those on the northern reconnaissance crossed the West and the East Tilitso Passes (both about 5000m.) and went to Manangbot; but they were unable to see the North Face of Annapurna as their view was blocked by the 'Great Barrier'. The area to the north of Annapurna proved to be different from what was indicated on the old India Survey maps. This induced the expedition to make immediately (May 14) for Annapurna's

North gl., seen earlier, by crossing from Lete a col ('Passage du 27 avril') over the southern end of the Nilgiri then dropping down into the Sanctuary of the upper Miristi Khola above its narrow gorges. A quick tentative ascent of the N. W. Spur was made but abandoned in favour of a route up the glacier to the east of the Spur. Base Camp was advanced to 4600m. May 23, Camp 2 was placed at 5900m.; Camp 3, above a difficult ice-wall, was erected in a snow-filled crevasse at 6600m. May 31; Camp 4, just above the wall of the "Sickle", at 7150m.; and Camp 5, the final camp, at 7300m. June 2. (The altitudes of some camps vary by as much as 200m. in the various accounts written by Herzog and therefore must be regarded as merely approximate). The following morning, June 3, Herzog and L. Lachenal left for the summit, without oxygen; about eight hours later they stood on the top of the first 8000m. peak to be climbed. The weather, fine until then, began to change; they hurried to descend and Herzog dropped his gloves .... the first of a chain of accidents that were to transform dramatically a victorious descent into a desperate and epic fight for survival not only by the summit team, both of whom suffered terrible frostbite, but also by the supporting team of G. Rébuffat and L. Terray and by their rescuers J. Couzy and M. Schatz with Sirdar Ang Tharkay and Sherpas Aila, Pansy and Sarki on whose determination the lives of all four depended. No words of praise can be too high for the steadfast courage and devotion of the Sherpas and porters who carried the injured victims off the mountain during the full monsoon and thence to Butwal where lorries were waiting (July 6). (2)

1953 B. R. Goodfellow and F. Yates (Br) flew to Pokhara from where they travelled (March 17) up the Seti Khola to Bharbhare and beyond to a viewpoint at about 4250m.

They were rewarded with a magnificent panorama of most of the south side of the Annapurna Himal. Then they crossed eastward to the Madi Khola and went to Siklis; from a high point (about 4500m.) on the main ridge west of the village they enjoyed another splendid view of the range. One observation made during this fortnight's trip was that the 1/4 inch Survey of India map was inaccurate south as well as north of the range in the area of Annapurna I. (3)

1956 Lt. Col. J. O. M. Roberts (Br), accompanied by the faithful Ang Nyima, in the course of his reconnaissance for the 1957 Machapuchare expedition, penetrated the Sanctuary at the head of the Modi Khola contained within Hiunchuli (6442m.), the ridge of Tent Peak (5945m.) and the Annapurna range to the north - the first outsider to have entered this sanctuary. (4)

1965 German expedition, eight members, leader G. Hauser, achieved the FIRST and SECOND ASCENTS of Gangapurna (7555m.) on May 6 and 8. They then made the SECOND ASCENT of Glacier Dome (7142m.) on May 29. From the latter the climbers were able to study the S. E. Face of Annapurna and a possible route to its summit along the East Ridge continuing on over the 'Roc Noir' (7485m.). But neither time nor resources available permitted them even to try this tempting proposition. (5)

1969 Second German expedition, nine members, leader L. Greissl, with Ang Temba as Sirdar, left Pokhara March 26 and established their Base Camp at 4300m. April 2. The plan was to climb Annapurna I by its 7.5 km. long E. Ridge. They reached the summit of Glacier Dome - THIRD ASCENT - May 5 and the top of 'Roc Noir' - FIRST ASCENT - (7485m.) May 9. Two camps were placed further along the ridge: Camp 5 at 7100m. and Camp 6 at 7320m. Their advance along the ridge petered out

May 19, defeated by gale force winds from the west. (6)

1970 SECOND ASCENT: British Army expedition, ten members including two from the Royal Nepalese Army, Expedition Commander B. M. Nivens and Climbing Leader Capt. M. W. H. Day, flew into Pokhara March 20. Following the French route of twenty years previously, they crossed the 'Passage du 27 avril' - properly Thulobugin - over the Nilgiris and into the Sanctuary of the upper Miristi Khola; Advance Base (Camp 2) was set up at about 6100m. April 16. They found, as had the French, that the north face of Annapurna is prone to avalanches and Camp 2 was in fact swept away by one on April 24. Capt. G. F. Owens and Lt. R. A. Summerton, who were preparing breakfast at the time, escaped unscathed; the camp was resited two days later. The party first attempted to reach the snow slope above the "Sickle" by a route up the N. E. Buttress - this to avoid the avalanche threat along the French approach - but this route had to be abandoned. They decided to follow more or less in the steps of Herzog's party but with a diversion more to the west when climbing up to the Sickle Bowl. Camp 4 was pitched on the upper ice-field (7300m.) May 18 and Camp 5 (7900m.) was erected the following day. (The altitudes given for most camps vary considerably in the accounts: Owens' figures (in feet) are invariably less than those of Day (in metres), Camp 5 by nearly 1600 ft. or 500m.). May 20, Day and Owens, using oxygen, reached the summit. By ill luck Owens, after returning to Advanced Base, fell down a crevasse and broke some ribs. At the start of the expedition one member had had to be evacuated on account of pneumonia and a little later Summerton fell 15m. and also broke some ribs. The expedition was hampered generally by unwilling and uncooperative Sherpas. (7) (8)

1970 THIRD ASCENT: At the same time as the British Army team was tackling Annapurna from the north, another British expedition of 11 members (including T. Frost of America) led by C. J. S. Bonington was attacking the mountain from the south: by the redoubtable South Face. Base Camp was established in the Sanctuary of the S. Annapurna gl. at about 4250m. towards the end of March. Six camps in all were placed up the face, the highest at 7300m., May 19. May 27 D. Haston and D. D. Whillans reached the summit. Oxygen was used above Camp 5 (6950m.). There had been a small hope that a north-south traverse might be possible with the Army expedition, each party using the other expedition's camps on the descent but, if for no other reason, the two summit parties did not coincide. M. Burke and T. Frost went up to Camp 6 on May 28 and the following day Frost, alone, made a bid for the summit but turned back when at about 7620m. As the expedition was withdrawing off the mountain May 30, I. S. Clough was killed by a falling tower of ice below Camp 2; M. Thompson who was with him escaped. (9)

1973 Japanese expedition of 11 members, leaders S. Tsukamoto and Y. Asawa, made an attempt by the N. E. Buttress during May. One Japanese and a Sherpa failed to reach the summit, being forced back by strong winds and exhaustion when within 50m. of the top. A second bid failed too. Four Japanese and a Sherpa were killed in an avalanche, May 18, while descending from Camp 3. (10)

1973 Italian expedition, 11 members, leader G. Machetto. After leaving Pokhara, August 21, they followed the French route as far as Camp 2, 5750m. Then they climbed a new route up the N. W. Spur. Camp 4 was placed at 6900m. on September 21. Two days later the lead climber reached a high point of 7050m. before turning back. During the night of September 26 an enormous avalanche of rock and ice obliterated Camp 2 in which were L. Cerruti and M. Rava. The expedition was abandoned. (11)

1974 ANNAPURNA EAST - FIRST ASCENT: Spanish expedition, nine members with J. M. Anglada as leader, crossed the Thulobugin Pass from Choya into the Miristi Khola basin and established Base Camp April 4. From Camp 2 (5900m.) they followed the North Ridge of Annapurna East. Camp 5 was pitched, on the ridge, at 7490m. April 29 Anglada, E. Civis and J. Pons continued up the ridge and attained the summit; it was nine o'clock in the evening and the descent was done mostly by moonlight. (12)

1975 Austrian expedition, nine members, leader G. Gantner, attempted to reach the summit by a route leading over Fang (7647m.) during April. Base Camp was set up at 4200m. March 24. Camp 3 was placed at 6150m. Shortly after midnight April 16, Camp 2 (5500m.) was buried by an avalanche and F. Tegischer met his death. The expedition was abandoned. High point reached was about 6400m. Earlier all the Sherpas, disgruntled, had left the expedition. (13)

1977 FOURTH ASCENT: Dutch expedition, 11 members, leader M. van Rajswick. Two members reached the summit October 13 from the north.

ANNAPURNA

Principal Source References:

(1) Heim "In den Zentralen Nepal-Himalaya 1949" BdW 1950 pp. 107-114

(2) Herzog Annapurna

(3) Goodfellow "North of Pokhara" HJ 18 pp. 81-86

(4) Noyce Climbing the Fish's Tail pp. 8-17

(5) Hauser "The German Himalayan Expedition, 1965" AJ 71 pp. 89-97

(6) AJ 75 pp. 197-198

(7) Day "Annapurna - North Face Route" AJ 76 pp. 88-98

(8) Owens "Annapurna I, 1970" HJ 30 pp. 106-111

(9) Bonington Annapurna South Face

(10) AAJ 1974 p. 206

(11) AAJ 1974 pp. 207-208

(12) Anglada "Spanish Annapurna Expedition, 1974" HJ 33 pp. 203-204

(13) AAJ 1976 pp. 519-520

Additional books relevant to Annapurna I, not already listed. (The dates in brackets refer to the expedition written about).

BONINGTON   The Next Horizon (S. Face 1970, part)

HASTON   In High Places (S. Face 1970, 1 chapter)

HERZOG & ICHAC   Regards vers l'Annapurna (1950)

NORTON   Memoires d'un Sherpa (Ang Tharkay)

TERRAY   Conquistadors of the Useless (part, 1950)

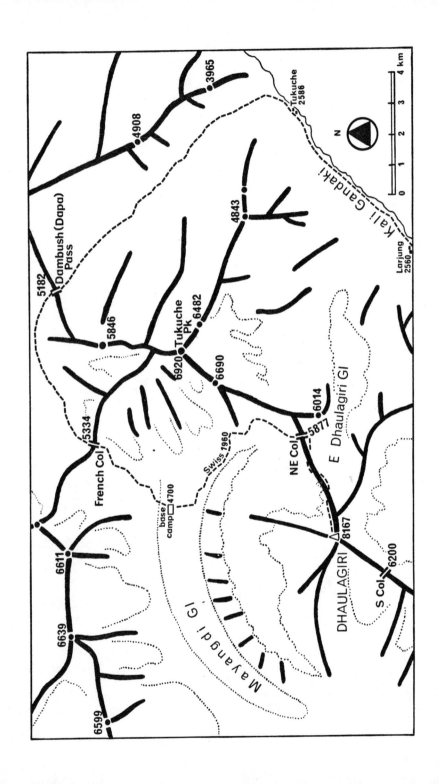

DHAULAGIRI 9

Situated: Nepal Himalaya (Karnali Section) in the Dhaulagiri
Himal

Longitude: 83° 29' 42" E.
Latitude: 28° 41' 48" N.

Altitude: 8167m.

Early designation No: XLII
Name: Dhaulagiri stems from the Sanskrit name Devanagari;
it is a contraction of Dhavalagiri where Dhavala means 'white'
and Giri means 'mountain'. Hence "The White Mountain".

The Annapurna Himal lies to the east of the Kali (or Krishna)
Gandaki, which rises within twenty miles of the mighty Tsangpo.
The Kali Gandaki valley is an ancient trade route to Tibet and
a pilgrims' way as far as Muktinath. To the west of the deep
gorges carved by the river lies the Dhaulagiri Himal, until
recently virtually unexplored. This Himal lies south of the
border with Tibet and the culminating high point at its eastern
end is Dhaulagiri I, the highest mountain entirely within Nepal.
Dhaulagiri I however is situated about 8 km. south of the main
axis of its Himal.
There are five other peaks all classified under the name
Dhaulagiri, followed by an appropriate number; they are all
under 8000m. and are situated to the west of the main Dhaulagiri summit. Perhaps in the near future each of these will be

given its own appropriate native name. Dhaulagiri II is also known as Mula Kang; R. Schatz, in his article in Mountain World 1954, mentions the existence of local names such as Naula Dhaulagiri III?), Sherbong and Jeyre Meyre.

Dhaulagiri I is buttressed by five ridges; four of these have been attempted but only one, the N. E. Ridge, has been climbed. The total height to be ascended from the Mayangdi gl. Base Camp is about 4500m., from the foot of the N. W. Face about 3500m., from the N. E. Col about 2300m., and from the start of the S. Ridge about 4600m.

MAPS - The following modern maps are generally available. Those most recommended are marked with an asterisk (*).

1/506,880 Nepal West Sh. 2nd Ed. -GSGS, 1967. DMS(MoD), London *

1/250,000 Pokhara Sh. NH 44-16, Series U502. 1963. AMS Washington, D. C. (only fair black & white litho reprint available 1977)

1/250,000 Annapurna & Dhaulagiri Himal. 1970. JGP, New Dehli *

1/250,000 Trekking Map: Jomosom to Jumla. 1974. Mandara maps, Katmandu (fair dyeline copy of artwork)

1/100,000 Dhaulagiri Himal. 1971. YYJ, Tokyo *

CHRONICLE

1808 Lt. W. S. Webb, accompanied by Capt. F. V. Raper and
1810 Hyder Young Hearsey, explored the upper Bhagirathi and the Alaknanda rivers - tributaries of the Ganges and joining it west and east of Srinagar. Webb made observations of some of the high peaks. In 1809-1810 he made further observations of the position and height of Dhaulagiri from four different survey stations; he calculated

its height as 26,862 ft. (8187m.), causing incredulity among geographers in the west who were convinced that Chimborazo, in the Andes, was the highest mountain in the world. Webb, though the first to measure 'Dhawala Giri', was not the first person to have seen it.

1814
1816 Lt. James Herbert, who accompanied one of the columns that advanced into Nepal during the Nepalese War, was engaged in survey work and observed some of the high peaks of Nepal; he calculated the height of Dhaulagiri to be 27,000 ft. (8229m.).

1873 Hari Ram, one of the Hindu pundits, undertook a journey from Kumaun into Nepal, traversing northern Nepal eastward to the Kali Gandaki near Muktinath. He then headed north to the Tsangpo and to Tradom where he was able to connect his survey with the traverse of Nain Singh (a Bhotia from Milam) made in 1865-1866. Hari Ram then followed the Kali Gandaki southward back to India.

1949 Dr. A. Heim, with the support of the Swiss Foundation for Alpine Research, visited Nepal travelling by air, train, bus and mule to Katmandu. On October 18 he was taken for a flight towards the Dhaulagiri Himal following up the course of the Kali Gandaki. Heim was able to obtain from an altitude of 4500m. the first photographs of this all but unknown region of the Himalaya. (1)

1950 A French expedition was organized to climb either Dhaulagiri or Annapurna - neither of which had been approached closely on foot before. The nine members, led by M. Herzog, crossed into Nepal and arrived at Tukucha in the Kali Gandaki valley April 21. But their first view of Dhaulagiri - the south Face - was from Baglung, April 17, and it was not encouraging, nor was that of the S. E. Ridge seen later. From Base Camp at Tukucha reconnaissance parties were sent out to examine the S. E. Ridge and the East Dhaulagiri gl. The former party - L. Lachenal,

165

F. de Noyelle and G. Rébuffat - climbed 'White Peak' (about 5500m.) on the ridge May 4, and Rébuffat reported that they found the ridge to be incredibly long and technically very difficult: "there's absolutely no question of going _that_ way". The latter party - in fact three parties in all - found the East gl. approach difficult and dangerous and the risks far too great. A possible approach from the north-east was explored also but the route shown on the map proved illusory for northward from Tukucha Pk. another high ridge ran right across the valley. Eventually a pass (the Dambush or Dapa Pass, 5182m.) on this ridge was reached but beyond lay another valley opening northward, the 'Hidden Valley', with yet another ridge between it and Dhaulagiri. On this ridge was a further pass (French Col, 5334m.); from there J. Oudot and L. Terray at last saw the northern basin of Dhaulagiri and the mountain's northern aspect. It was unprepossessing. They decided to try for Annapurna instead. (2)

1952 A small British expedition, leader O. Polunin, was sent by the British Museum to explore the valleys on the north side of the Dhaulagiri Himal for botanical research. In addition to the botanical information obtained, the party brought back much valuable information of a topographical nature about this unknown side of the range. (3)

1953 A Swiss expedition, seven members, leader Major B. Lauterburg, deputy leader A. Roch, and Ang Tharkay as Sirdar, left Pokhara April 15 and followed up the Kali Gandaki then continued north-west up the main tributary, the Mayangdi Khola, to the tongue of the Mayangdi gl. where Base Camp was set up (3600m.) May 3. Camp 1 was erected at the foot of the N. W. Face (4500m.), Camp 5 at 6500m. (May 26) on the difficult slopes beneath the 'Pear' from where it was hoped to reach the W. Ridge and thence the summit. May 29 P. Braun and R. Schatz very nearly reached the ridge before turning back (at about 7400m.). June 3 Lauterburg with R. Pfisterer and Yila Tensing ascended the Mayangdi gl. and crossed the N. E. Col (space enough on this glacier plateau to land an aeroplane, they noted), having a good look at the E. Ridge before retracing their steps. Lauterburg and Pfisterer then made a circuitous return journey over French Col and Dambush Pass to Tukucha, linking up with the main expedition at Beni. Some of the other members had gone up to the South Col (6200m.) during this time. (4)

1954 Argentinian expedition, 11 members, leader Lt. F. G. Ibañez, with Pasang Dawa Lama as Sirdar. Base Camp was set up on the site of the Swiss one but one month earlier (April 4). The Swiss route was followed and Camp 5 was pitched 200m. below the 'Pear'; with the help of explosives (!) the Argentinians levelled a site for Camp 6 near the top of the 'Pear' at 7200m. Camp 7 was placed just off the W. Ridge at about 7500m. June 1, G. Watzl with Pasang Dawa Lama and Dr. A. E. Magnani with Ang Nyima (Ibañez, unwell, remained behind) left Camp 7 to follow the delicate and difficult ridge, on its south side; they reached about 8000m. then had to bivouac. The following day threatening weather obliged them to turn back for Camp 7 even though the summit was within their grasp. The next day Ibañez could not find his crampons but managed to descend to Camp 6; he could go no further (his feet were already frozen) and said he would wait there until someone could bring him another pair. This help reached him June 7 but by then he was far gone; wrapped in some canvas, he had to be lowered down the steep face by a rope, this only the start of a long and painful journey. Sherpa Sarki, who had assisted Herzog off Annapurna, was among the helpers. At Beni Ibañez had his toes amputated, at Pokhara (June 28) part of his left foot. Two days later he died in hospital at Katmandu. (5) (6)

1955 German-Swiss expedition of ten members, leader M. Meier, made an attempt during April but reached only approximately 7600m. before being turned back by bad weather. The expedition suffered to some extent from poor organization. (7)

1956 Second Argentinian expedition, leader E. Huerta, made an attempt during May but reached only a little higher than the 1955 expedition before being repulsed by the early onset of the monsoon. (8)

1958 Second Swiss expedition, leader W. Stäuble, Sirdar Dawa Tensing, during May attempted the mountain yet again by the 'Pear' route. Camp 5 was placed at about 7000m. May 17 and a higher Camp 6 on the ridge the following day. The climbers reached much the same height as the previous two expeditions before bad weather forced them off the mountain. Camp 4 (6550m.) had been engulfed by an avalanche; M. Eiselin and Sherpa Pasang Sona were buried in their ice grotto but dug themselves out. (9)

1959 Austrian expedition, eight members, leader F. Moravec, Sirdar Pasang Dawa Lama (his third Dhaulagiri expedition), made an attempt by a new route: the N. E. Ridge. Base Camp was established April 3 by the Mayangdi gl. A reconnaissance of the N. E. Ridge quickly showed that this was the right way up to the summit. Camp 4 was set up at 6500m. April 24. Despite adverse weather the site of Camp 5 (7000m.) was reached May 21; Camp 6 (7375m.) was the final camp. From there, May 25, K. Prein and Pasang Dawa Lama made a bid for the summit: they reached 7800m. before turning back. They made two more attempts but each time the gale-force winds and intense cold proved too much; tents torn and camps destroyed added to their difficulties. Earlier, April 29, H. Roiss had fallen into a deep crevasse near Camp 2 and was killed. (10) (11)

1960 FIRST & SECOND ASCENTS: Third Swiss expedition, 13 members including K. Diemberger (Aus), P. Diener (G), N. G. Dyhrenfurth (Am), and G. Hajdukiewicz and A. Skoczylas (both Poles by origin); leader M. Eiselin, and Sirdar Ang Dawa. In addition there were the pilot, E. Saxer, and the co-pilot, E. Wick, for the Pilatus-Porter aircraft (named Yeti) that was to fly from Switzerland to Pokhara and be used for ferrying men and equipment to the N. E. Col, as well as being put at the disposal of T. Hagen for his geological reconnaissances. First an acclimatization camp was air-lifted to the Dapa Col (Dambush Pass) March 28; then activities were switched to the N. E. Col and the N. E. Ridge. April 3 Yeti landed on the N. E. Col (5877m.) where advance Base Camp (Camp 2) was established. Between April 15 and May 12 four more camps were put up along the N. E. Ridge, the highest at 7800m. May 13 six members reached the summit, without oxygen: Diemberger, A. Schelbert and Nawang Dorje, then E. Forrer with Nima Dorje, and finally Diener. Ten days later M. Vaucher and H. Weber repeated the climb. In the meanwhile, May 5, Yeti crashed near the Dambush Pass; both pilots escaped, luckily uninjured, and made their way back to Tukucha. The expedition withdrew to Pokhara on foot. (12)

1969 American expedition, 11 members, leader B. N. Everett, with Phu Dorje II as Sirdar, attempted the mountain by the S. E. Ridge. Leaving Pokhara April 16, they established Base Camp (Camp 2) at 4550m. on the snout of the East Dhaulagiri gl. about April 20. The next few days were occupied in evacuating A. Read (deputy leader), struck by pulmonary oedema, after which probes up the

East gl. were made to an altitude of about 5350m. (a route earlier rejected by the French) from where it was intended to cut left up a spur of rock and ice to the main ridge itself. On April 28 six Americans and two Sherpas returned to this spot with logs for bridging a large crevasse that cut right across the glacier; while they were lowering the log bridge into position a tremendous fall of ice thundered down upon them and swept all but one - L. F. Reichardt - to oblivion. The victims were Everett, P. Gerhard, J. V. Hoeman, W. Ross, D. Seidman, Sherpa Pema Phutar and Sherpa Panboche Tensing. (13)

1970 THIRD ASCENT: Japanese expedition led by T. Ota succeeded in climbing the mountain by the Swiss 1960 route. Camp 6 was set up at 7800m. and from there T. Kawada and Sherpa Lhakpa Tensing reached the summit October 20. (14)

1971 T. Bech (Am) and his wife during the spring surveyed the approaches to the N. E. and S. E. Ridges to try and see a way that would avoid the East Dhaulagiri gl. (referred to as the S. E. gl. in Reichardt's account); they went without Sherpas and managed to reach a height of about 7600m. on the N. E. Ridge (or Spur). They were able to make use of some oxygen bottles abandoned by the Japanese the previous year. Valuable photos of the S. E. Ridge were obtained. (15)

1973 FOURTH ASCENT: American expedition, 16 members, leader Dr. J. Morrissey, Sonam Girmi as Sirdar, set off with the dual objectives of reaching the summit by the N. E. Ridge (or Spur) and by the S. E. Ridge. Approaching from Tukucha and over the Dambush Pass and French Col, the expedition reached the N. E. Col March 30. Equipment and food had been airdropped by E. Wick (one of the pilots who had crashed in Yeti in 1960) from his Pilatus Porter aircraft at French Col; further drops (equal to 200 porter loads) were airdropped during five days at the N. E. Col (Base Camp). April 3 the attack on the S. E. Ridge began, J. Duenwald (expedition deputy leader) acting as climbing leader; the line went straight up the 'hourglass', a 600m. climb. The crest was reached April 13 but the ridge showed itself to be so narrow and so long as to offer no reasonable prospects for a route. The attempt by the N. E. Ridge began April 12; four Camps were placed in all at 6525m., 7125m., 7450m., and 7775m., the last May 6. From there, May 12, L. F. Reichardt (sole survivor of the 1969 tragedy), J. Roskelley and Sherpa Nawang Samden, without oxygen, reached the summit. A second, hoped for, summit bid could not be realized. (15)

1975 Japanese expedition, 17 members, leader T. Amamiya, made an attempt by the very difficult South Ridge. Base Camp was set up March 1 at 3450m. and Camp 3, March 20 at 5800m. A high point of about 6200m. was attained but on March 26 Camp 1 was struck by an avalanche and two Japanese - T. Imura and Y. Numao - two Sherpas - Pasang Kami and Dakiya Dorje - and one local porter were killed; six others in the camp escaped. The climb was abandoned. (16)

1976 FIFTH ASCENT: Italian expedition, 12 members, leader R. de Bertolis, succeeded in ascending the mountain by the Swiss N. E. Ridge route. They left Pokhara March 5 and established Base Camp (4610m.) on the north side three weeks later. '5 camps were set up, three of them above the N. E. Col and the highest at 7530m., May 3. From there the following day L. Gadenz, S. Simoni and G. Zortea left for the summit; Gadenz was obliged to renounce the climb but the other two reached the top that afternoon. (The original plan had been to do the climb via the W. Ridge). (17)

1977 International expedition, 6 members, leader R. Messner,
     had a close look at Dhaulagiri South Face (an idea pro-
     posed to Messner by P. Habeler when they were on
     Gasherbrum I together in 1975). However the tremendous,
     avalanche-swept face appeared too dangerous to warrant
     the risk. (18)

1977 A Japanese team is reported as having made an attempt
     on the mountain by a very difficult route; the attempt did
     not succeed.

DHAULAGIRI

Principal Source References:

(1) Heim "In den Zentralen Nepal-Himalaya 1949" BdW 1950 pp. 107-114

(2) Herzog Annapurna

(3) Polunin "The 1952 Expedition to Western Nepal" RCAS Journal 41 (1953) pp. 37-43

(4) Schatz "A. A. C. Z. Expedition to Dhaulagiri 1953" MW 1954 pp. 71-81

(5) Magnani Argentinos al Himalaya

(6) Kurz "Himalayan Chronicle 1954" (part) MW 1955 pp. 122-124

(7) Meier "Deutsch/Schweizerische Himalaja-Expedition 1955 zum Dhaulagiri" DAVJ 1956 pp. 74-79

(8) Bertoncelj - Arko Dhaulagiri

(9) Winterhalter Der Letzte Achttausender

(10) Moravec Dhaulagiri; Berg ohne Gnade

(11) Moravec "Last of the Forerunners to Dhaulagiri. Austrian Dhaulagiri Expedition 1959" MW 1960/61 pp. 126-130

(12) Eiselin The Ascent of Dhaulagiri

(13) Read, Morrissey & Reichardt "American Dhaulagiri Expedition - 1969" AAJ 1970 pp. 19-26 (also in HJ 29 pp. 130-138)

(14) Dyhrenfurth "Chroniques Himalayennes" Les Alpes 1971/4 p. 223

(15) Reichardt "Dhaulagiri 1973" AAJ 1974 pp. 1-10 (also in HJ 33 pp. 24-33)

(16) AAJ 1976 pp. 520-521

(17) AAJ 1977 p. 243

(18) M 56 p. 11 (brief note)

Additional books relevant to Dhaulagiri I, not already listed.

DIEMBERGER Summits and Secrets (1959)

SWISS FOUNDATION FOR ALPINE RESEARCH The First 10 Years of the S. F. A. R.

NANGA PARBAT

BAZHIN GAP 8125
FOREPEAK

SILVER CRAG
SILVER SADDLE
7530

RAKHIOT PEAK

E. ridge

5367

RAKHIOT GL.

BC

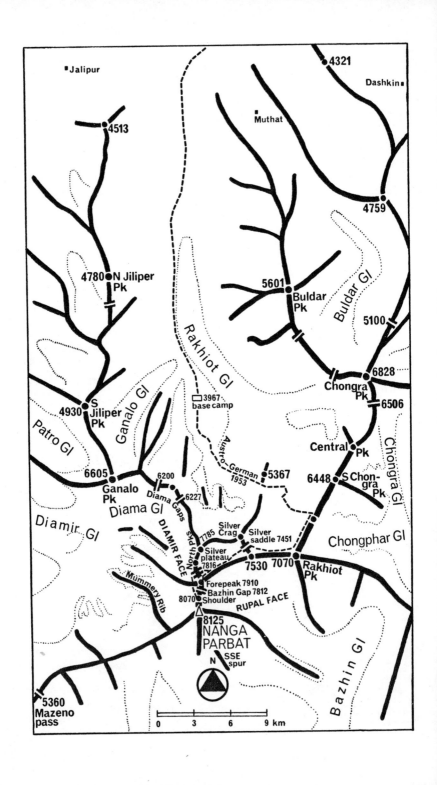

NANGA PARBAT   10

Situated: Punjab Himalaya (Himachal Kashmir Section)

Longitude: 74° 35' 24" E.
Latitude: 35° 14' 21" N.

Altitude: Main summit - 8125m.
           Forepeak - 7910m.

Early designation No: (none)

Name: Nanga Parbat is derived from the Sanskrit words
Nanga Parvata meaning 'Naked Mountain'. Alternative names
used earlier included Deo Mir, Diamir, Diyamir, Dayamur
and other similar variations, all meaning 'King of the Mountains'. Miss E. Knowlton in The Naked Mountain gives the
name as meaning, in Dardi, 'Dwelling Place of the Fairies'
whom legend will have us believe dwell around its summit.
(The Dards inhabit the country between Kashmir and the Hindu
Kush).

NANGA PARBAT is the most westerly of all the 8000m. peaks
and the massif, bounded to the north and west by the Indus
river, is a dazzling culmination of the Western Himalayan
syntaxis which terminates where the range bends south and
drops down towards Baluchistan; it counter-balances, as
though by design, the mountain of Namche Bharwa in the syn-
taxial bend of the Eastern Himalaya where the Tsangpo, flowing

from Tibet, turns south and the Himalayan ranges bend south-
wards too to continue down into Burma. Nanga Parbat stands
in some isolation, separated from its nearest Himalayan 8000m.
peak Dhaulagiri (the more northerly Karakoram excluded) by
nearly 1200 km. Described by many as the most beautiful as
well as the most impressive mountain of all - it towers some
7000m. above the Indus valley in the north and rises almost
sheer for close on 5000m. above the Rupal valley in the south
- it is a mountain reputed nevertheless for inclement weather,
heavy precipitation and ever-threatening avalanches. 35 lives
have been lost on the mountain.
It presents three principal faces: Rakhiot, Diamir and Rupal.
All three have been climbed successfully by German or Austro/
German expeditions, all led by Dr. K. M. Herrligkoffer. There
have been 18 attempts on the mountain - excluding purely reconnaissance expeditions - and eight of these have been led
by Dr. Herrligkoffer.
The total heights to be ascended from Base Camps are 4150m.
on the Rakhiot Face, 4050m. on the Diamir, and 4550m. on
the Rupal.

MAPS - The following modern maps are generally available.
Those most recommended are marked with an asterisk (*)

1/750,000 Karakoram & Nanga Parbat. 2nd Ed. 1971. SSAF,
Zurich *
1/250,000 Gilgit Sh. NI 43-2, Series U502. 1963. AMS, Washington, D. C. (only fair copy of black & white litho reprint
available 1977)

CHRONICLE

1835 G. T. Vigne (Br), an important explorer of the Western
       Himalaya as well as an accomplished artist, obtained

permission to visit Kashmir in June 1835; he stayed five years in that valley 'equal to paradise'. He reached Srinagar for the first time in August. On August 29 he arrived at the foot of the Gurais Pass (probably the Tragbal or Rajidiangan Pass, about 3600m., situated between Bandipur and Gurais village). From the Pass itself a revelation burst upon his sight: "the stupendous peak of Diarmul or Nanga Parbat". He then crossed the Burzil Pass (4200m.) on his way to Skardu with Raja Ahmed Shah. (1)

1856 Between 1854 and 1858 Adolf, Hermann and Robert von Schlagintweit (three brothers of German origin) undertook for the East India Company extensive journeys through the Himalaya. In the autumn of 1856 they passed to the east of Nanga Parbat. Between September 15 and 19 Adolf painted a 150° panorama of the Nanga Parbat massif as seen in the morning light. The Bazhin gl. sweeps round from the Rupal Face into the Rupal valley, and the Chongphar gl. tumbles down from the long snowy ridge stretching northwards from Rakhiot Pk. (7070m.) to abut against the lower hills on the far side of the Chiche valley. The following year Adolf was murdered at Kashgar.

1887 Dr. Arthur Neve (Br), medical missionary and brother of Ernest of Pir Panjal fame, was one of the first Europeans to visit the Rupal valley. Travelling up from Astor he visited the village of Tarshing (2900m.) situated close to the tongue of the Chongphar gl., a village frequently plundered by marauding and murderous tribesmen from Chilas who came over the Mazeno Pass (5360m.) on the West Ridge of Nanga Parbat. Neve was deeply impressed by the "mighty overwhelming magnificence of Diyamir, the Monarch of the Gods". He was to return later in 1906. (2)

1888 During the troubled years of inter-tribal rivalries and
1889 fighting and the subsequent pacification of this remote
corner between Kashmir and Afghanistan, many men of
renown passed in the vicinity of Nanga Parbat on their
way from Srinagar to Gilgit or Skardu. In the summer
of 1888 Col. A. G. Durand and Dr. (later Sir) G. Robertson were sent by Lord Dufferin, Viceroy of India, to
enquire into the causes that had led up to an outbreak of
hostilities between Kashmir and two of its satellite States,
Hunza and Nagar. To reach Gilgit they crossed the Kamri
Pass (about 4000m.) and descended the long valley leading
to the entrance to the Rupal valley. From there, before
skirting round the end of the Chongra S. E. Spur, they
had a view on to the Rupal Face and the snowy ridge con-
necting Nanga Parbat and Rakhiot Pk. They camped later
at Doian - downstream from Dashkin - close to the confluence of the Astor and Indus rivers and at the foot of
the long crest extending north-eastward from Chongra
Pk. (6828m.). Durand and his companion felt over-
powered by the majesty of the mass of Nanga Parbat as
seen from the north. The following year Durand, returning from Skardu, crossed the Banok La (4725m.) to
reach Astor valley; from the top of the pass he enjoyed
a superb view of Nanga Parbat from the east. He was to
return to the Astor valley again in 1891. Also in 1889,
Capt. F. E. Younghusband, returning from his journey to
Hunza and the Pamirs, stopped at Gilgit on his way back
to Srinagar; during December he followed up the Astor
valley, passing Nanga Parbat, and crossed over the Burzil
Pass (a little further east than the Kamri) and the Tragbal Pass. (3)

1891 Travelling from Skardu to Gilgit during July E. F. Knight
(a Times correspondent) crossed the Banok La and descended to Astor. From there he climbed up to various

view points from which to take photographs of Nanga Parbat. He also made a four days trip to the glaciers of Chongphar and Rupal; from the top of a snowy spur (estimated about 1525m.) he beheld the grand spectacle of Nanga Parbat. Knight travelled again through the Astor valley to Gilgit - along the new road then under construction - in September; at Gilgit he met Capt. F. E. Younghusband and Lt. Davison, both of whom had crossed the Pamirs and been 'ordered off' by the Russians. Knight took part in Col. A. G. Durand's expedition against the waring Hunza-Nagas. (4).

1892 W. M. Conway organized and led a British expedition, which included Lt. the Hon. C. G. Bruce, O. Eckenstein, A. D. McCormick (the artist), J. H. Roudebush, M. Zurbriggen (the Swiss guide) and four Gurkha soldiers. Towards the end of April they crossed the Burzil Pass from the south and descended to Astor; on their way they were astounded by the sight of "a great white throne set in heaven: nothing was more sublime" - it was of course Nanga Parbat. During the continuation of their journey to Gilgit Conway had a number of distant views of the massif from the north, particularly from the vicinity of Bunji near the confluence of the Indus and Gilgit rivers. Conway considered that a possible way up the mountain could be by the col west of Pt. 22,360 ft. (6815m. i.e. Chongra Pk.) then round the south side of the shoulder 23,170 ft. (7060m. i.e. Rakhiot Pk.), up an easy snow slope to the east end of the long but gentle, rocky arête leading to the summit. (5)

1895 A British party consisting of Lt. C. G. Bruce (for some of the time), Dr. J. N. Collie, G. Hastings and A. F. Mummery with two Gurkha soldiers, Goman Singh and Raghobir Thapa, undertook the first attempt on Nanga Parbat. Leaving Rawalpindi they crossed the Kamri Pass and set up Base Camp July 16 by the glacier just above Tarshing.

They quickly realized that the South (Rupal) Face offered
no hope and so crossed the Mazeno La into the Diamirai
valley. Several reconnaissances of the glacier, near-by
passes and lesser summits were carried out from a new
Base Camp. A fresh camp was later pitched higher up
the Diamir gl. at 4550m. Several attempts were made
by Mummery and Raghobir Thapa during early August to
force a route up some rock ribs on the N. W. Face; they
reached about 5600m. Mummery and Thapa made a final
attempt, August 18, but the Gurkha became ill at about
6100m. and reluctantly they had to come down. They
decided to make one last bid to climb Nanga Parbat but
from the north where there was probably a snow route
easier than the rock-climbing tried so far. While the
rest of the party went round to the Rakhiot gl. by the long
way Mummery, August 23, accompanied by Goman Singh
and Thapa, set off to reach the glacier by a high snow
pass (the Diama Pass) east of Ganalo Pk. (6605m.). The
night was spent at a 4550m. camp and next morning the
three started off. They were never seen again. The
probability is that an avalanche swept them to their
deaths. (6)

1913 During August and early September E. Candler (Br) with
Longden as companion and Guffara, who had been on the
1892 and 1895 expeditions, as headman completed a tour
of Nanga Parbat. Without any climbing ambitions but
merely for the enjoyment of the trek, they departed from
Woola Lake, north of Srinagar, and arrived at Sopor.
Major C. G. Bruce saw them off from there; their route
was via Shardi, Bunar - where they were joined unexpectedly by Lor Khan, a Chilasi shikari who had climbed
Diamirai Pk, about 5800m., with Collie and Mummery
18 years previously - the Diamirai gl., over 'Red Pass'
on to the Rakhiot gl., Bunji, Astor, Tarshing and back

over the Kamri Pass to Woola Lake. They visited much of the terrain covered by the 1895 expedition and had agreeable views of Nanga Parbat from all sides. (7)

1930
1931 Dr. E. W. Welzenbach (G) planned an attempt on the mountain from the Diamirai side (Mummery's route) but this project had to be postponed. F. S. Smythe (Br) was also planning a reconnaissance of all sides of the mountain for 1932 but yielded to the prior claims of the Germans.

1931 Five Wapiti single-engined biplanes, led by Sqd. Ldr. S. B. Harris, R. A. F., left Risalpur March 30 for Gilgit, flying along the Kaghan valley and over Chilas at about 4900m. The 330 km. journey took 2 hours and 15 minutes. The return by the Indus valley was achieved the following day. Some good aerial photographs of Nanga Parbat were obtained. (8)

1932 A lapse of 37 years occurred between the first and second attempts on the mountain. In this year W. Merkl (G) led a German/American expedition of 9 members (7 Germans, 2 Americans including Miss E. Knowlton, a reporter for the English-speaking Press) to make an ascent from the Rakhiot side. They left Bandapur for Astor May 23 and made a high-level crossing into the Rakhiot valley; Base Camp was there established at 3600m. The attack began June 30; by July 8 Camp 4 was set up at 5800m. and became Advanced Base Camp. July 14 P. Aschenbrenner climbed S. Chongra Pk. (6448m., FIRST ASCENT). July 16 Aschenbrenner and H. Kunigk climbed Rakhiot Pk. (7070m. FIRST ASCENT). July 29 F. Bechtold, Merkl and F. H. Wiessner gained the East Ridge where later at 7000m. Camp 7 was placed. Bad weather then stopped further progress, adding to the problems caused by the poor quality of the Hunza porters (who were inexperienced and untrained in technical mountaineering); only one of

183

them reached Camp 6. Another attempt was made from Base Camp at the end of August but E. R. Herron (Am), Merkl and Wiessner got no further than Camp 4. Great assistance was rendered by Capt. R. N. D. Frier (Br), in charge of coolie-transport; he led four porters up to Camp 5 and there met the party coming down from Camp 7 early August. During the return journey by boat, some of the party visited the pyramids at Giza near Suez; when coming down one of these Herron slipped, fell 100m. and was killed. He was buried that same afternoon, October 13, at Cairo. (The dates given in Miss Knowlton's book - Appendix - and those given in Merkl's article in HJ 5 pp. 65-74 do not always tally). (9)

1934 Second German expedition, ten members, leader W. Merkl, with Capts. R. N. D. Frier and A. N. K. Sangster (Br) acting as transport officers, and with Lewa as Sirdar of the Sherpa and Bhutia porters; there was too a scientific team of three under Dr. R. Finsterwalder, cartographer. Base Camp was set up again by the Rakhiot gl. May 22 at 3967m. The 1932 route was followed though above Camp 5 (6690m.) the line went higher over Rakhiot Pk. Camp 6 was placed at 6955m., Camp 7 at 7050m. and Camp 8 at 7480m. on the Plateau just beyond the Silver Saddle, July 6. A fierce storm broke over the camp and July 8 the occupants decided to descend. There were 16 people in all: P. Aschenbrenner (Aus), W. Merkl, E. Schneider (Aus), W. Welzenbach, U. Wieland and 11 porters. Late that afternoon Aschenbrenner and Schneider managed to reach Camp 4 despite the storm that was raging. The evening of the following day four porters struggled in to Camp 4 frost-bitten and exhausted. Several attempts were made to climb back beyond Camp 5 to help the other climbers and porters but to no avail; the snow storms continued. July 14 one frost-bitten porter,

Angtsering, came down from somewhere above Camp 6; he brought news of tragedy. Wieland had died above Camp 7; Welzenbach had died in Camp 7, and two porters (Dakshi and Nima Nurbu) had perished higher up; Merkl and porter Gaylay had died between Camps 7 and 6; and three porters (Nima Dorji, Nima Tashi and Pinju Norbu) had died shortly before Camp 5. Further rescue attempts had been made but all were repulsed. July 18 Camp 4 was evacuated and the survivors descended to Base Camp. Earlier, June 7, A. Drexel had died of pneumonia after coming down from Camp 3 to Camp 2. In all ten lives were lost. A high point of 7700m. had been reached on the lower slopes of the Forepeak (7910m.). (10) (11)

1937 Third German expedition, nine members, leader Dr. K. Wien, with Lt. D. B. M. Smart (Br) attached as liaison officer, and Nursang as Sirdar. The approach was the same and Camp 1 was placed at 4420m. May 22, Camp 2 at 5380m. May 24. Avalanches were a menace from the beginning and Camp 2 was nearly blown away by one May 26. After a spell of bad weather Camp 3 was established at 5935m. June 5, Camp 4 at 6220m. June 7. More heavy snow fell and Camp 4 was moved June 10 some 50m. higher up to what was judged to be a safer spot. June 12 Camp 5 (6635m.) was reached but not occupied owing to adverse conditions. A despatch dated June 14 from Camp 4 was brought down to Base Camp by Lt. Smart; Camp 4 was occupied by seven climbers and nine porters. June 17 U. Luft went up from Base to join the main party in Camp 4; on arriving at the site the following day, he saw no camp - only a deep scar caused by a gigantic ice avalanche that had hurtled down from some 300m. higher up on the Rakhiot Pk; there were no tents, no survivors at all. P. Bauer, F. Bechtold and K. von Kraus flew out from Munich and with the help of the R. A. F. reached

Base Camp in 12 days. In the meantime Dr. C. Troll had arrived from the Rupal valley where he had been doing research work. With Luft he reached the scene of the disaster July 15 and they were able to find some of the victims who lay buried in their tents beneath 3m. of compacted snow and ice. The accident had occurred probably on the night of June 14 shortly after midnight. There were 16 dead: P. Fankhauser, A. Göttner, H. Hartmann, G. Hepp, P. Müllritter, M. Pfeffer and Dr. K. Wien together with Pasang Norbu (one of the survivors from Camp 8 in 1934), Chong Karma, Karmi, Gyaljen Monjo, Mingma Tsering, Nima Tsering I and II, Ang Tsering II and Tigmay. Ironically, the original site of Camp 4, thought to be unsafe, was untouched by the avalanche. (12) (13)

1938 Fourth German expedition, 12 members including F. Bechtold and U. Luft, leader P. Bauer, with Major K. Hadow and Flt. Lt. McKenna (both Br) attached, and with Nursang again as Sirdar (he had been on Kangchenjunga with Bauer in 1929). They returned to the Rakhiot Face from Srinagar, approaching up the Kaghan valley, over the Babusar Pass (4170m.), then to Bunar from where the usual Base Camp site was occupied June 1. Supplies were dropped there from a Junkers 52 - originally flown out from Germany - by A. Thoenes (Kangchenjunga 1929 also). Avalanches between Camps 1 and 4 were again a danger. Camp 4 (6185m.) was occupied June 22 and more supplies were dropped there by Thoenes. Bad weather intervened again and Camp 5 (6690m.) was pitched only July 16. The 1932 line was followed to the ridge and Camp 6 set up. Little further progress could be made owing to bad weather and after a high point of about 7250m. had been gained, July 24, the mountain was evacuated. A fourth attempt was made and Camp 5 was re-occupied August 3; again the expedition had to withdraw. During July the bodies of Pinju Norbu. W. Merkl and Sherpa Gaylay were found. In Merkl's pocket was a letter written in Camp 7 July 10 1934 by Merkl and Welzenbach begging for help. U. Luft and S. Zuck on the way home visited the Diamir side of the mountain and took many valuable photographs. Other pictures were obtained during the return flight. (14) (15) (16)

1939 German Reconnaissance expedition of only four members, leader P. Aufschnaiter (Aus). As a preliminary to a further attempt under U. Luft during 1940 the party investigated the possibility of establishing a route up the shorter but steeper Diamir Face of Nanga Parbat. The approach to Bunar was as in 1938; then they went up the Bunar valley and established Base Camp June 1 at 3850m. on the right bank of the Diamirai gl. June 13 L. Chicken and H. Lobenhoffer climbed Mummery's supposed route up one of the ribs leading to the North Peak (7816m.); on the way up, at about 5500m., they found a piece of wood approximately 25 cm. long: probably a relic from a Mummery bivouac. Another of the rock ribs to the north-east was attempted too and during July H. Harrer and Lobenhoffer reached a high point of about 6100m., Camp 4. In their opinion a practicable route could exist though Aufschnaiter thought that another 5 camps might be required before the summit could be reached. June 29 Aufschnaiter and Chicken, with Sherpas Pasang and Sonam, climbed Diamirai Pk. (5570m.) ascended by J. N. Collie and A. F. Mummery in 1895. The expedition left Srinagar August 24 for Karachi to catch their boat home but it never arrived; so they tried to reach Persia (Iran) by land but were stopped at Quetta August 28. War broke out and they were interned at Ahmadnagar where they were joined later by L. Schmaderer and H. Paidar who had been with E. Grob (Sw) on Tent Peak in Sikkim. They were all sent to Dehra Dun in 1941. (In April 1944 Aufschnaiter and Harrer managed to escape from the camp and headed for Tibet - see under Shisha Pangma, 1945. Schmaderer and Paidar also escaped from Dehra Dun in March 1945 and reached Tibet; Schmaderer was in all probability murdered in the village of Tabu in Spiti. Paidar returned to India and gave himself up; he returned to Dehra Dun in September 1945 but the war was over). (17) (18)

1950 Three British - J. W. Thornley, W. H. Crace and R. M. W. Marsh - their plans for spending a year in the northern Karakoram thwarted by the Pakistani Government within three weeks of their getting there, opted to undertake a winter reconnaissance of Nanga Parbat instead. They went with four Sherpas, Tenzing (who had been with Thornley to the Zemu gl. in 1946) acting as Sirdar. Base Camp was established November 11 at 3800m. alongside the Rakhiot gl. Camp 1 was set up the following day at 4465m. The Sherpas preferred not to go beyond Camp 1 so the other three continued on their own. Marsh had to return to Base November 18 as he was suffering from frostbite; the other two went on. They could be seen until December 1 carrying loads up to 5500m. at which point a tent was pitched. The tent was still visible three days later but there was no sighting of the two climbers. A heavy snow storm then occurred and the tent was not seen again either. Marsh tried to reach the camp with Tenzing and Ajiba but was not successful. An air search also was of no avail. (19)

1953 FIRST ASCENT: Austro-German expedition, ten members, leader Dr. K. M. Herrligkoffer (step-brother of W. Merkl) arrived at Gilgit by air May 6. They continued to the Indus river and followed down it as far as the

Rakhiot Bridge where they turned south. Base Camp was installed May 24. The route and camps followed much on the lines of earlier expeditions with the exception that Camp 3 was placed on the site of the earlier Camp 4, Camp 4 on that of the previous Camp 5, and Camp 5 (the final one) at 6900m. between the previous Camps 6 and 7 (July 2). The next day H. Buhl (Aus) and O. Kempter left Camp 5 for the summit bid. Kempter, following well behind Buhl, was overcome by lethargy and found it impossible to go on; he waited for Buhl's return. By 5 that afternoon Buhl had not come back so Kempter returned to Camp 5 alone. Buhl in the meantime continued up the Silver Plateau, rounded the north side of the Forepeak (7910m.), reached the Bazhin Gap (7812m.) and attained the summit at 7 that evening. He decided not to return along the North Ridge but to descend by the snow face down to the Diamir Gap. Overtaken by night, he bivouacked - standing all night on a large rock; he had neither food nor spare pullover nor sleeping bag but luckily the weather remained fine and next morning Buhl set off for the Gap and the Silver Plateau. That evening he reached Camp 5 again after his amazing solo ascent. This great success was somewhat marred by porter difficulties and by dissention between the climbers. (20) (21)

1961 Dr. K. M. Herrligkoffer led a German reconnaissance expedition of ten members to the Diamir Face. Gilgit was reached May 17. The Diamir valley was approached via the Indus and Bunar valleys and Base Camp was set up May 24 on the right lateral moraine of the Diamir gl. (4080m.). They climbed up an ice-couloir between Mummery's 1895 route and Aufschnaiter's 1939 route to the 'Eagle's Eyrie' above which Camp 2 was placed (6000m.) June 12. Camp 3 was sited at 6600m. a week later. From there T. Kinshofer, G. Lehne and S. Löw reached the Bazhin hollow June 20 and bivouacked (7100m.) in the hope that the next day they could make an early dash for the top. However a blizzard blew up during the night and they were forced to retreat. The expedition was abandoned. (22)

1962 SECOND ASCENT: Dr. K. M. Herrligkoffer returned with a party of ten including a woman medical assistant, and with Isa Khan as Sirdar of the Hunza porters, to complete if possible the previous year's work. They left Gilgit May 24 and Base Camp was re-occupied May 28. The line of ascent followed that of 1961 with a variation between Camps 2 and 3; a cable-hoist and some 300m. of steel cable were installed to facilitate the provisioning of Camp 2. M. Anderl, Kinshofer, Löw, A. Mannhardt and M. Sturm left Camp 3 June 20 for a summit bid; they pitched Camp 4 at 7150m. on the edge of the Bazhin hollow. There they were delayed for 24 hours by a thunderstorm but in the early hours of June 22 the weather cleared and all except Anderl set off. Soon Sturm was obliged to turn back. It took the remaining three nearly eight hours to reach the Bazhin Gap - they had greatly underestimated the distances. They climbed up the ridge to the Shoulder (8070m.), taking another seven hours, and reached the summit after 5 o'clock. They were obliged to bivouac in a crevasse only 70m. below the top and this without any protection or food. Next morning when coming unroped down a snow gully leading to the Bazhin hollow Löw, suffering from frost-bitten feet and the after-effects of too much dope, fell and was fatally injured. Kinshofer remained beside his dying companion while Mannhardt descended to Camp 3 for help; later Kinshofer, completely exhausted, managed to come down on his own. (Probably owing to a printing omission, Löw's name is not mentioned among the summit party in the Mountain World account - page 122 - but is included in a similar account in HJ 25, p. 126). (23)

1963 Another German reconnaissance, led by Dr. K. M. Herrligkoffer; the team of four wished to examine the Rupal Face of Nanga Parbat - a face that soars precipitously up for more than 4500m. They flew into Gilgit June 6 and travelled via Bunji, Astor, Tarshing and Rupal (3155m.). Base Camp was installed higher up the valley at 3560m. directly south of the summit. Various probes were made to spy out the most favourable route. G. Haller and T. Kinshofer climbed Rupal Pk. (5595m. FIRST ASCENT) on the south side of the Rupal valley, from which distance a better perspective of the immense south face of Nanga Parbat can be obtained. Finally two possible routes presented themselves: a classic approach by the S. W. Ridge (the 'Kinshofer Way') or a direct line up the S. S. E. Spur. (24)

1964 German expedition of nine members, leader Dr. K. M. Herrligkoffer, made a winter attempt on the Rupal Face via the S. S. E. Spur which terminates at the South Shoulder (8042m.). Leaving Munich January 31 and Gilgit February 23, they travelled again via Bunji and the Astor valley; they entered the snow-covered Rupal Valley and established Base Camp February 28. Camp 1 was placed at 4600m. March 1, and re-occupied later after an incident when four climbers had been carried 500m. down the mountain by an avalanche but not injured. Camp 2 was placed at 5400m. March 21. The high point reached was 5800m., well on the way to Camp 3 planned for 6000m. But the weather changed, there were heavy snow falls followed by avalanches. The Pakistani liaison office then made difficulties and caused their permit to be cancelled prematurely. (25)

1968 The German Rupal Face expedition planned for 1965

having been postponed as a result of the political situation, another German expedition of 12 members, leader Dr. K. M. Herrligkoffer, flew into Gilgit from Rawalpindi June 1. 15 Jeeps transported the expedition as far as Rampur and Base Camp was re-established June 7. Camp 3 (5900m.) was placed June 25 high up the S.S.E. Spur. Despite intermittent spells of bad weather Camp 4 was pitched early in July at about 6600m. July 9 K. Golikow, P. Scholz and W. Scholz left Camp 4 and started climbing up towards the 'Merkl Couloir'; Golikow, unwell, returned to the tent. The other two continued up to 7100m. where they bivouacked. Next morning they returned to Camp 4. That same morning G. Strobel broke his leg and the resulting disorganization contributed to the withdrawal of the expedition from the mountain. (26)

1969 A Czechoslovakian expedition, 13 members in all, leader I. Galfy, set off to climb the mountain from the Rakhiot side. Some of the team drove the 8000 km. from Smokovec to Islamabad with the gear, leaving April 2; from Islamabad they all flew into Gilgit, April 24, and continued by lorry to the Rakhiot Bridge. Base Camp was established on the old site May 9. By May 30 Camp 3 had been set up at 6100m., below Rakhiot Pk. Ten days of snowy weather followed before the other camps could be pitched: Camp 4 at 6700m. (placed June 16) and Camp 5 scheduled to be placed close to the 'Mohrenkopf' (6955m.) on June 19. The attempt on the summit was planned for June 21 but bad weather arrived the day before and the threat of avalanches put a stop to it. The mountain was evacuated July 1 and the expedition drove home, arriving back in the High Tatra August 7. (27)

1970 THIRD ASCENT (FIRST TRAVERSE) & FOURTH ASCENT: Another Austro-German expedition to the Rupal Face, 18 members, leader Dr. K. M. Herrligkoffer. They left

Munich April 8 and drove the 7500 km. to Rawalpindi with all the gear, arriving April 26. Then, via Gilgit, to Base Camp in the upper Rupal valley. Following the previous line of ascent, Camp 1 was set up at 4700m. on the S. S. E. Spur May 17; Camp 4 was pitched at 6700m. June 23; and Camp 5, the highest, was placed at 7350m. June 26 by F. Kuen and P. Scholz. It was occupied that evening by G. Baur (cameraman) and the Messner brothers, Günther and Reinhold, whose first expedition to the Himalaya this was.

As Camp 5 was not in radio communication with Base Camp, it had been arranged with Reinhold - before they left Camp 4 - that the report of the weather forecast would be signalled to them by means of a coloured rocket: blue - fine weather; in which case the occupants of Camp 5 would next morning fix ropes in the 'Merkl Couloir' above the camp so that on June 28, together with Kuen and Scholz coming up from Camp 4, a summit bid could be made. Red - bad weather, in which case stay in Camp 5 or come down. Blue and red - uncertain weather, in which case any decision would be left to the Camp 5 occupants; Reinhold is reported to have said that in that event he would at least seek to reach as high as possible up the 'Merkl Couloir' and return to the tent the same day. The weather report from Peshawar was good. By an error - whatever the circumstances - the rocket sent up proved to be red. Camp 5, where the signal was received with scepticism, could not be informed of this error.

Early next morning (June 27) Reinhold ascended the couloir taking neither rope nor any proper equipment with him; Baur and Günther assured the lower half of the couloir with ropes. Günther suddenly went off (also without a rope) to follow his brother, leaving Baur who returned to the tent. As no activity could be seen around Camp 5 during the day, Base Camp assumed that the three, taking advantage of the weather, had departed for the summit; but that evening one person was seen leaving Camp 5 in the direction of Camp 4. It was Baur; Base waited for his radio report. In the meantime Kuen and Scholz had climbed up to Camp 5 ready for the planned summit bid. W. Haim, G. Mändl and H. Saler climbed up from Camp 3 to Camp 5 in support. Late that night Kuen and Scholz set off for the summit, expecting to meet up with the other two who had gone ahead.

At 6 in the morning, June 28, Kuen and Scholz were at the top of the couloir when they heard shouting and calls for help (heard also by Mändl, fixing ropes lower down). A little higher up they saw Reinhold, 80 to 100m. above them, and a shouted conversation ensued. It was 10 o'clock. Apparently the two brothers had been already to the summit, getting there late the previous afternoon, and had come down a different way to the gap above the vertical ending of the 'Merkl Couloir', (avoided by a traverse to the right during ascent). To a direct question from Kuen, concerned by the earlier cries for help, Reinhold replied that all was well and that they would descend by another route and return to Base Camp. Neither help nor rope was asked for during this shouted exchange. Kuen states that he did not see Günther during this time; that the conversation over, Reinhold gave a wave then bent down to pick something up, from his movements something such as a heavy rucksack, and disappeared up the arête. But their rucksack had been left behind in Camp 5.

Kuen and Scholz continued up, rounding the west side of the South Shoulder to reach the summit late that afternoon. Nothing had been seen of the Messner brothers nor were Kuen's calls answered; the pair wondered by which way the brothers had descended and had supposed that they had taken the most likely route down the 'Kinshofer Way' via the West Saddle. Coming down, the pair bivouacked by the S. Shoulder and next day (June 29) returned to Camp 5, where there was no news about the Messners. June 30 they returned to Base Camp; the Messners were not there as they had said they would be. What had happened? Parties were sent up the Rupal Valley to search the 'Kinshofer Way' but there were no signs of the missing two. Lest the pair may have descended by the Diamir side, the authorities in Astor were informed and they arranged for a search of the Diamir valley to be organized from Chilas but by July 3 no positive information was forthcoming. A rescue party stood by, the help of a helicopter was provided. Finally, further searches on the Rupal side having proved abortive, the expedition evacuated Base and made a speedy return to the north side of the massif. When at Bunji, they were informed that an injured person, a stranger, had been brought by Jeep to the hospital in Gilgit; one injured person, not two. Which of the Messners could it be? They met up with Reinhold that evening and he told them his story.

After spending an hour on the summit they had descended by a different way to a niche in the gap and there bivouacked. During the night Günther became semi-delirious and next morning Reinhold, worried by his brother's condition, realized that a traverse from the gap to their route of ascent without a rope would be too risky. Reinhold said he had been shouting for a rope. Also that during the shouted conversation he proposed to the other two that they should climb up to him and then continue to the summit by their (Messners) route of descent which was quicker and easier; he did not ask for help or for a rope; he replied in the affirmative when asked if everything was in order. Then an hour later Reinhold decided to descend the Diamir side by the Mummery route. At

midnight they bivouacked about half way down and next
morning (June 29) they continued down the glacier. Reinhold hurried ahead of his brother; he looked back but
his brother was not following; he continued, looked back
again, but no Günther. Reinhold stopped at a spring and
waited. After an hour he began calling and looking for
his brother; he climbed back up the glacier, searching
and calling until nightfall. He saw the débris of an avalanche lying across a route Günther may have followed.
Next morning Reinhold searched again but to no avail;
he decided to wait and went to sleep. The following
morning (July 1) he descended the valley and found some
men felling trees; they took him to their hut and gave
him sustenance. Next morning he made his painful way
to Diamir and thence to Bunar Bridge and his meeting up
with the expedition (July 3).

The accusations and counter-accusations, the arguments
and conflicting stories, by spoken word and in print became a cause célèbre and ended with writs and libel
actions by the leader. Reinhold Messner in interviews,
in articles, in his book and during subsequent court cases
accused Herrligkoffer of a variety of misdemeanours.
The Bavarian High Court however was unable to find
sufficient proof to substantiate any of Messner's accusations and so forbade him to continue his line of action by
word or in print. His book was withdrawn from publication and Herrligkoffer subsequently won his actions
against a number of German journals.

It is beyond the purpose of this chronicle to do more than
report as factually and fairly as possible the events of
this tragic episode, in so far as the known facts permit.
Nevertheless the impression remains that not all has yet
been explained - in particular what exactly occurred at
the gap in the early morning of June 28 and why a descent
down the Diamir Face was made. It seems that, with

Günther so poorly and unable to descend the 'Merkl Couloir' without a rope, Reinhold could have simply climbed back to the South Shoulder to meet Kuen and Scholz who, together with the support party of three already in the couloir, could have provided all the assistance required. There may have been reasons against this but they do not appear to have been explained.

Nevertheless, whatever the circumstances, the traverse of Nanga Parbat was a remarkable achievement. (28) (29)

1971 FIFTH ASCENT: A second Czechoslovakian expedition, 16 members, leader I. Galfy, approached the mountain again from the Rakhiot side. They drove from Islamabad to Gilgit then to the Rakhiot Bridge. Base Camp was established May 18. They followed the 1953 route and six camps were erected, the last July 9 at about 7600m. July 11 two climbers, I. Fiala and M. Orolin, reached the summit. The third member of the assault team, L. Zahornasky, failed to get much beyond 8000m. Three other members also climbed the Forepeak (7910m. FIRST ASCENT). (30) (31)

1975 A combined German/Austrian/Swiss expedition, leader Dr. K. M. Herrligkoffer, attempted to climb the mountain pre-monsoon by its S. W. Ridge - the 'Kinshofer Way' first reconnoitered in 1963. Camp 2 was at 5900m., Camp 3 at 7000m. and Camp 4 at 7400m. But continual bad weather prevented much further progress; the high point reached by Beyerlein and Hillmaier was 7550m. A group reconnoitered the S. E. buttress and reached 5600m. Another reconnaissance, further east, was made and 3 camps were set up, the third at 6400m. just below Rakhiot Peak. (32).

1976 SIXTH ASCENT: An Austrian expedition of only four members, leader H. Schell, succeeded in climbing up by the 'Kinshofer Way' (via the S. W. Ridge). Base Camp was established July 11. Camp 1 was erected at 5100m., Camp 2 at 6095m., Camp 3 at 7010m. and the final Camp 4 at 7470m. Two further bivouacs proved necessary before the four men - the leader, S. Gimpel, R. Schauer and H. Sturm - were able to set foot on the summit, August 11. They reported this to be the easiest route up Nanga Parbat. (33)

1976 Japanese expedition, nine members, leader H. Kato, attempted the mountain by the German 1961-62 route. Base Camp was established by the Diamir gl. July 23. Camp 1 (5000m.) was set up July 30 after a depot had been made at 4250m. Above this camp the expedition suffered from frequent stonefalls; above the 'Eagle's Eyrie' they made use of the winch installed by the Germans in 1962 to lift supplies up to Camp 2, pitched at 6000m. August 19. This, however, took up a great deal of time. Camp 3 was placed at 6600m. August 25, above the 'Kinshofer ice-field'. A high point of 7100m. was reached before the attempt had to be abandoned. (34) (Some of the dates and the altitude of Camp 2 recorded in AAJ 1977 differ from the above, reported to the author by the expedition leader).

1976 A third expedition during this year: International expedition of eight members (3 German, 2 Austrian, 3 Poles), leader Dr. K. M. Herrligkoffer, attempted the mountain by the 'Kinshofer Way'. Unfortunately, September 26, W. Arnold (Aus) suffered a fall when at 6150m. and was killed. The attempt was abandoned. (35)

1977 American expedition, 14 members, leader J. Hellman, arrived at Rawalpindi June 28 to climb the mountain by the Diamir Face. They suffered from avalanches due to early monsoon and G. Bogel and R. Broughton were killed; several other members were injured.

NANGA PARBAT

Principal Source References:

(1) Vigne Travels in Kashmir, Ladakh, Iskado etc.

(2) Neve Thirty Years in Kashmir

(3) Durand The Making of a Frontier

(4) Knight Where Three Empires Meet

(5) Conway Climbing & Exploration in the Karakoram-Himalaya

(6) Collie Climbing on the Himalaya & Other Mountain Ranges

(7) Candler On the Edge of the World

(8) HJ 5 pp. 184-185. Frontispiece also.

(9) Knowlton The Naked Mountain

(10) Bechtold Nanga Parbat Adventure

(11) Finsterwalder Forschung am Nanga Parbat (includes the 1/50,000 map, and Schlagintweit's panorama in colour as Frontispiece)

(12) Bauer Himalayan Quest

(13) AJ 49 "The Disaster on Nanga Parbat, 1937" pp. 210-227

(14) Bauer The Siege of Nanga Parbat

(15) Bechtold "Nanga Parbat, 1938" AJ 51 pp. 70-78

(16) Dyhrenfurth To the Third Pole plates 31 to 35

(17) Kurz "Himalaya 1939-1946" (part) Montagnes du Monde II 1947, pp. 161-168

(18) Aufschnaiter "Diamir side of Nanga Parbat, Reconnaissance 1939" HJ 14 pp. 110-115

(19) AJ 58 "Nanga Parbat: the Accident in December 1950" pp. 130-131

(20) Herrligkoffer Nanga Parbat (Bibl. No. 132)

(21) Buhl Nanga Parbat Pilgrimage

(22) Herrligkoffer "Nanga Parbat by the Diamir Flank" (part) MW 1962/3 pp. 102-116

(23) Ibid. pp. 116-126

(24) Herrligkoffer Nanga Parbat (Bibl. No. 134) pp. 166-171

(25) Ibid. pp. 172-192

(26) Herrligkoffer Kampf u. Sieg am Nanga Parbat pp. 38-54

(27) Galfy "The Tatra Climbers' Himalayan Expedition, 1969" HJ 30 pp. 249-253

(28) Herrligkoffer Kampf u. Sieg am Nanga Parbat pp. 55-137

(29) Messner Die Rote Rakete am Nanga Parbat

(30) Puskas & Urbanovic Nanga Parbat 8125m.

(31) Orolin "The Second Czechoslovac Tatra Expedition to the Himalaya - Nanga Parbat (8125m.)" HJ 31 pp. 267-274

(32) AAJ 1976 p. 545

(33) AAJ 1977 pp. 274-275

(34) AAJ 1977 p. 274

(35) AAJ 1977 p. 275

Additional books relevant to Nanga Parbat, not already listed.
(The dates in brackets refer to the expeditions written about)

BRUCE   Twenty Years in the Himalaya (1892, 1895)

BRUCE   Himalayan Wanderer (1892, 1895)

CLARK   Six Great Mountaineers   (includes Mummery and Collie, 1895)

DYHRENFURTH   Das Buch vom Nanga Parbat 1895-1953

IRVING   Ten Great Mountains (one chapter)

McCORMICK   An Artist in the Himalayas (1892)

MEADE   Approach to the Hills (one chapter, 1934)

MUMMERY   My Climbs in the Alps & Caucasus (2nd edn. 4th imp. July 1908 contains Frontispiece portrait, an Appreciation and extracts from his last letters. Also in most later books)

SCHLAGINTWEIT   Reisen in Indien u. Hoch Asien Vol. II (1856)

SNAITH   At Grips with Everest (one chapter, 1934)

STYLES   First on the Summits (one chapter)

ULLMAN   Man of Everest (one chapter, 1950)

UNSWORTH   Tiger in the Snow

Karakoram: Baltoro glacier

Four 8000m. peaks - Gasherbrum I and II, Broad Pk., K2 - all lie very close together at the N.E. end of the Baltoro glacier, which itself is situated fairly centrally in the Karakoram Range. This glacier is 58 km. long and contains ten of the world's 30 highest peaks. The early probings and explorations of the glacier are common to all four 8000m. summits and for convenience are chronicled in this preliminary section. The actual mountaineering expeditions follow in their respective sections.

The Karakoram, extending for over 350 km. on a W.N.W.- E.S.E. axis, form the watershed for the rivers draining northward into Central Asia and southward into the Indian Ocean. The Range is highly glaciated: 28-50% as against 8-12% in the Himalaya proper. It is bounded in the north by the Shaksgam river which flows into the Yarkand river, in the south by the Lower Shyok and by the Indus into which it flows and by the Gilgit, in the west by the Ishkuman and its tributary the Karumbar, and in the east by the Upper Shyok. The Range comprises the Great (or Outer) Karakoram and the Little (or Inner) Karakoram and is divided into eleven Mustaghs or Ranges:

Great Karakoram - Batura Mustagh, Hispar, Panmah, Baltoro, Siachen, Rimo and Saser Mustagh.
Little Karakoram - Rakaposhi Range, Haramosh, Masherbrum and Saltoro Ranges.

(Also included in the Little Karakoram are two mountain systems north of the Great Karakoram, in Hunza territory: Lupghar group and Ghujerab mountains).

The four remaining 8000m. peaks are all within the Baltoro Mustagh.

The name Karakoram derives from the Pass (5575m.) a little to the east, once thought to be on the main divide of the north and south drainage systems. Karakoram is said to mean 'black earth' or 'black gravel' in Turki. 'Kara' is common in both Turkish and Mongolian: in Mongolian the range is called Khara-Kherem meaning 'black barrier' (the Great Wall of China is called Tsagaan-Kherem meaning 'white barrier'). The name has been spelt in a variety of ways: Lt. MacCartney in 1808 gave Mooztagh or Kurrakooram on his map; G. T. Vigne spelt it Kara-Kurum in 1842; R. Shaw adopted the old form Karakoorum, not dissimilar from the alternative and more modern form of Karakorum. Opinions remain divided as to whether the 'a' (now officially accepted) or the 'u' is the correct rendering. The old capital of the Mogul Turks in Mongolia is spelt Karakorum and other passes further north, in the Kuen Lun range, are named for example Takta-Korum or Ak-Korum, also denoting the colour of the soil.

The name Mustagh or Muztagh is one commonly given by Turki traders to snow or ice-covered mountains, rather like 'Mont Blanc' or 'Dhaulagiri'; 'Muz' means 'ice' and 'Tagh' means 'mountain'.

W. M. Conway in a letter sent to the R. G. S. from Abbottabad November 2, 1892, writes that after they had left Askole, O. Eckenstein (who did not go with them) found a man who drew for him a rough map of the Baltoro gl. in the sand; he put in correctly both the Mustagh Passes, the Mustagh Pk., K2, Gasherbrum and Masherbrum. The man stated that 'Skinmang' was the local name for the Mustagh Pk. and 'Chiring' that for K2. Conway's communication does not quite tally with Eckenstein who, in his book (1896), merely states that this "geographical old native", who claimed to have been over both Mustagh passes, drew a plan of "the upper valley" (above Chongo?); from his description it seemed to Eckenstein that the proper name for K2 was 'Skinmang' or 'Dapsang'.

Many personal and foreign names are still used at present but these are not acceptable on principle and doubtless they will be replaced on some future occasion.

CHRONICLE

1760 The Portuguese Jesuit, D'Espinaha, is reported as having crossed the Mustagh Pass.

1835 The discovery of the Karakoram system as a whole is due to G. T. Vigne (Br) who showed that north of the Himalayan Range in Kashmir there lay yet another mountain system: the Tibetan Himalaya or Karakoram. He arrived in Skardu in September whence he sought during the years 1835-1838 to penetrate and cross the heavily glaciated range. He undertook four journeys in all. The exact chronology for his journeys is uncertain. For the second he headed north from Skardu up the Shighar and Basho valleys and reached the snout of the Chogo Lungma gl. He attempted to cross the Hispar gl. so as to reach Hunza and he considered the possibility of travelling from Shigar to Yarkand over the Mustagh Pass. But these undertakings, he realized, were quite beyond his experience and capabilities. In 1838 he ascended the Saltoro valley from Khapalu in search of the Saltoro Pass. (1)

1856 The Schlagintweit brothers (Ger) - Hermann, Robert and Adolph - were taken on by the Honourable East India Company to complete a magnetic survey of India but the work they achieved was much more extensive. They arrived in Bombay in 1854. Adolf was in all probability the first European to penetrate the Baltoro area (August 1856); from Askole he tried to cross one or other of the Mustagh passes. He was also probably the first European to traverse the Skoro La (about 5120m.). Hermann and Robert were the first Europeans known to have crossed the Karakoram Pass, in 1856. The Jesuit, Ippolito Desideri of Pistoia, may have crossed with a colleague in 1715 during his journey from Kashmir to Lhasa; it had been ascended by Dr. T. Thompson (Br) in 1848; the claim by A. Gardiner (Am) to have crossed it in 1828 is in some doubt. Adolph crossed the pass the following year (1857) on his way to Yarkand. (2)

1856 The Great Trigonometrical Survey was extended to Kashmir in 1855. In September of the following year Lt. T. G. Montgomerie (organizer of this series) arrived at W. H. Johnson's station set up on or near the top of Mount Haramukh (about 4900m.) and from there, looking towards the north, he saw two fine peaks rising prominently above the general Karakoram range and these he designated K1 and K2. He took bearings on these two mountains and made quick drawings of their outlines. During 1857 and 1858 Brownlow and G. Shelverton intersected the peaks from other stations and from all these observations the altitudes of K1 and K2 were computed as 25,600 ft. (7803m.) and 28,287 ft. (8621m.) respectively. The former was found to be known locally as Masherbrum; the higher peak apparently had no name. The final quarter-inch (1/253,440) map, Jammu, Kashmir & Adjacent Countries, was completed early in 1861. (3) (4)

1861 Lt. H. H. Godwin-Austen joined Montgomerie at Manganwar in 1857 - the turbulent and critical year of the Indian Mutiny that brought about the demise of the old Hon.

Company and the assumption of its responsibilities by the British Crown. In August 1861 Godwin-Austen crossed the Skoro La into the Braldu valley and explored and mapped the complex of glaciers comprising the Chogo Lungma, Kero Lungma, Biafo, Panmah and Baltoro; he discovered the Hispar gl. from the top of the Nushik La but he failed in his attempt to cross the Mustagh Pass from the Panmah gl., being turned back by bad weather when within 150m. from the top. He was the first to ascend nearly all these glaciers and the first to discover the approach to K2 by the Baltoro gl. A day's march took him from Paiju to around Urdokas (a grazing ground on the left bank of the Baltoro) then he continued to the Yermanendu gl. On his return he climbed about 600m. above Urdokas to view K2. Apart from his descriptions of the area and his sketches, he also produced a map (the first of this hitherto unknown area), scale 1/513,510. (5)

Note: There were two Mustagh Passes, an old and a new, both leading across to the Sarpo Laggo gl. Some confusion can arise from the contradictory reports appearing in various works of reference. The old pass was closed by increased glacial activity during the first half of the 19th century and so a new pass was sought; this new pass became impassable too on account of changes in the glaciers. One (about 5400m.) is at the head of the Panmah gl., the other (about 5422m.) is a few kilometres further east at the head of the Mustagh gl. The contradictions arise over which is which. In 1903 A. C. Ferber and E. Honigmann (both Ger.) went to the eastern pass and found near the Mustagh gl. the ruins of an old village. This discovery left little doubt that the eastern pass was the original crossing on the route from Askole to Yarkand in Turkestan (now Sinkiang). Vigne probably planned to cross the old pass (according to him it was still open under Rajah Ahmed Shah); there is doubt as to which one Schlagintweit attempted (probably the new); and Godwin-Austen tried to reach the new pass.

1887 Towards the end of his epic journey from Peking to Rawalpindi across the Gobi Desert, Lt. F. Younghusband reached Yarkand and decided to cross into Kashmir by the Mustagh Pass. He had with him as guide Wali, a Balti native of Askole who had crossed the pass 25 years previously. Younghusband and his party left Yarkand September 8, followed up the Yarkand river, crossed the Aghil Pass (4780m.) to the Shaksgam river, then ascended the Sarpo Laggo gl. to the (old) Mustagh Pass. Thanks to Wali's determination and despite the great dangers the Pass was crossed. Younghusband was the first to see K2, "a peak of appalling height", and Gasherbrum from the north. No sooner had Younghusband reached Askole than he determined to return over the (new) Mustagh Pass to see if it was really as impracticable as had been reported. He was unable to reach it owing to an immense ice-slip onto the Panmah gl. (6)

1889 In June the Foreign Office in Simla asked Younghusband to undertake an exploration on the northern frontier of Kashmir. As explained to him by Sir M. Durand, the Foreign Secretary, he was required to explore all the Himalayan passes from the north into the State of Hunza. From Leh Younghusband travelled north over the Karakoram Pass to, Shahidula thence westward to the Aghil Pass. His idea was to explore the unknown Saltoro and Shimshal Passes (about 5550m. and 4735m. respectively) before proceeding on to the Pamir and down to Gilgit. He followed the Shaksgam (Oprang) river to a glacier on the east side of Gasherbrum, which he named the Urdok gl. (he had also discovered the Gasherbrum gl.). He ascended the Urdok towards what he assumed must be the Saltoro Pass but he never reached the top of it on account of avalanches. His measurements however indicated that his pass (now called Indira Col, 5775m.) lay about 35 km. N. N. W. of the one fixed by the Indian Survey from the south; but the Survey did not accept Younghusband's calculations. Twenty years later Dr. T. Longstaff set off to resolve this discrepency and with Dr. Arthur Neve and A. M. Slingsby (nephew of Cecil Slingsby of Norway fame) crossed the Saltoro Pass from the south. Young-husband had been right; they were not one and the same pass and between them flowed the Siachen glacier. (6) (7)

1892 W. M. Conway (Br) led the first climbing expedition (though exploration was the primary object) to the Kara-koram glaciers - Hispar, Biafo and Baltoro. After passing round Nanga Parbat on the way to Gilgit the expedition proceeded, having explored and mapped the first two glaciers during July, to Askole and Paiju. At Askole, July 27, it was decided that because of disagreement Eckenstein should leave the expedition. They ascended the full length of the Baltoro gl. and from Pool Camp (on the right bank between Gore and Concordia) they climbed the South summit of Crystal Pk. (5913m.), August 10. They then continued up the upper Baltoro gl., discovering the Godwin-Austen and Vigne glaciers, and finally placed their Upper Plateau Camp at 6100m. From there, August 25, an attempt to climb 'Golden Throne' (Baltoro Kangri, 7312m. or 7350m.) was made. Climbing by the S.W. Spur, the party reached the top of a subsidiary summit (about 6970m.) which they called 'Pioneer Peak'; they could go no further for between them and the true summit lay a very deep depression. The return journey was along the left bank of the Baltoro. From Corner Camp the Stachikyungme (Yermanendu) gl. on the west side of Biarchedi (6759m.) and leading up to Masherbrum was explored, September 2. Conway's map, published in two sheets, scale 1/126,720, remained for many years the definitive map of the Baltoro gl. region. Pristi, Bruce's dog, reached Lower Plateau Camp, 5790m. (8)

1899 Mrs. Fanny Bullock Workman and Dr. William Hunter
1912 Workman (Am) carried out much useful and original ex-ploration and topographical survey in the Karakoram. They did not penetrate the Baltoro gl. area. In 1899 they

were active in the Biafo gl. and around Skoro La. In 1911 they were first in the Saltoro Range; afterwards they explored the glaciers south of the Baltoro: Aling, Masherbrum, Gondokhoro and Chogolisa. They sought in vain a practicable way over onto the Baltoro. In 1912, accompanied by C. G. Peterkin (a British surveyor), three guides and 3 porters from Courmayeur in Italy, they were busy at the head of the Siachen gl. where they discovered the Sia La (5702m.) south of 'Queen Mary Peak' (now called Sia Kangri, about 7600m.); also the way over to the Kondus gl. south of Conway Saddle (5974m.) and of the Baltoro Kangri. In addition to the information gained, they brought back many invaluable photographs, not least of Masherbrum from the S. W. and S. E. (9)

1902 O. Eckenstein's K2 expedition travelled up the Baltoro gl. and the Godwin-Austen gl. to its source. This first exploration of the glacier contributed a great deal of information to the existing knowledge of this part of the Baltoro Mustagh. Five camps were set up along this section of the journey; the highest, Camp 12 at about 6294m., was claimed to be the highest ever known camp. H. Pfannl and V. Wesseley (both Aus) reached 'Windy Gap' (Skyang La, 6233m.) and later hoped to climb 'Staircase Peak' (Skyang Kangri, 7544m.) from the pass; their proposal however was not taken up. A preliminary sortie on K2 was made. While in Camp 12 Pfannl developed pulmonary oedema (July 15) and had quickly to be taken down to Rdokas (Urdokas, about 4055m.) on a sledge improvised from skis. Bad weather then settled in and the expedition returned to Askole. (10) (11)

1903 Setting out from Askole and via Urdokas and Lobsang Brangsa, A. C. Ferber and E. Honigmann (both Ger) visited the old Mustagh Pass in September and found evidence that this abandoned pass - too difficult for their loaded porters - had been used in earlier times. (12)

1909 The Abruzzi expedition to K2. Though the main object of this large enterprise was the mountain, an extensive exploration and survey were made during June and July of the whole region not only of K2 but also of the Broad Peak, Gasherbrum and Chogolisa groups. The topographer was M. F. Negrotto whose 1/100,000 map was a great improvement on earlier ones. V. Sella produced an outstanding collection of very fine photographs. (13)

1928 A large Italian expedition under H. R. H. the Duke of
1929 Spoleto (and including Prof. A. Desio) was active in the Baltoro region for scientific and exploratory purposes. Headquarters was established at Urdokas during May 1929. One party, under the Duke, continued up the Baltoro to Concordia. They explored the Godwin-Austen gl. to below the Sella Saddle (6159m.) then went to the head of the Abruzzi gl. seeking a way over the main watershed to the Urdok gl.; they reached Conway Saddle (already first reached by Desio and E. Croux May 28) but found that it led over to either the Kondus or the Siachen gls. At the same time Dr. U. Balestreri and G. Chiardola had crossed the (old) Mustagh Pass from Baltoro; Karpho Gang (5931m.) to the immediate west of the pass was climbed June 7. Two days later a party under Balestreri descended the Sarpo Laggo gl. - some on skis - and began a fresh survey of the Shaksgam area on the north side of K2. They reached the Gasherbrum gl. June 18, crossed the saddle over to the Urdok gl. at the head of which is Indira Col discovered by Younghusband forty years previously. Balestreri tried to cross this col with the intention of finding a way over into the Upper Baltoro in the area of Sia Kangri - by the Conway Saddle - but bad weather prevented them from doing this. Some members returned over the Mustagh Pass while Balestreri

with Desio and eight porters continued eastward up the Shaksgam valley to the glaciers north of the Siachen Mustagh as far as the Kyagar gl., explored by K. Mason in 1926. During their return journey the head of the Sarpo Laggo gl. was re-surveyed and its saddle (5685m.) was ascended; the (new) Mustagh Pass was also sketched in on the survey. In addition Desio ascended the Trango gl. (which flows into the lower Baltoro gl. from the N.W.) and reported that the way up to the Sarpo Laggo Saddle from the south side also would go. They got back to Urdokas July 13. A map, scale 1/75,000 was published in three sheets. (14) (15)

1934 International expedition, 14 climbing members (including the leader's wife), leader G.O. Dyhrenfurth (Sw), visited the upper Baltoro gl. There were two groups, one for mountaineering and one for filming. Unfortunately M. Kurz (Sw), the topographer, had had a riding accident during his outward journey and so no actual survey could be undertaken. Nevertheless various reconnaissances - frequently on ski - were carried out from the Base Camp established on a moraine of the Abruzzi gl. June 23, not far from where Conway had placed his Footstool Camp; these included the southern approach to Gasherbrum I, the South Gasherbrum gl. round to G.I's N.W. side, Conway Saddle and the approach to Chogolisa Saddle. August 3 J. Belaieff (Fr), P. Ghiglione (It), A. Roch (Sw) and Dr. H. Winzeler (Sw) climbed the eastern summit of Baltoro Kangri (about 7250m.) from below the Conway Saddle and via the summit's N.W. Ridge. At the same time another party put up a Camp 7 at 6800m. beyond this saddle. August 3 Dyhrenfurth, his wife, H. Ertl, A. Höcht (Ger), coolies Raji and Hakim Beg reached the Central and West summits of Sia Kangri. August 12 Ertl and Höcht climbed the Central, East and Main summits of Sia Kangri. Much subsequent discussion arose over the exact heights of these summits; Dyhrenfurth, basing himself on corrected aneroid readings, remained convinced that the height of the Main summit of Sia Kangri is about 7600m. - higher than the estimates of V. D. B. Collins (1911 Siachen gl. survey), Peterkin and the Duke of Spoleto. (16) (17) (18)

1936 Dr. Ph. C. Visser and his wife (Dutch) during their fourth expedition to the Karakoram were again accompanied by Dr. R. Wyss (geologist) and by Afraz Gul Khan (who had been with Sir Aurel Stein in Central Asia and also with K. Mason in 1926) and Muhammad Akram, both surveyors. They went to the head of the Shaksgam; their survey embraced the side glaciers coming down from the high mountains, including the Urdok, Gasherbrum and Skyang Lungpa (previously 'Windy Gap gl.'). In addition Muhammad Akram formed the opinion that the Zug Shaksgam - whose valley was partly explored by Mason accompanied by Major H. D. Minchinton in 1926 - must flow northward to join the Yarkand river and not southward to the Shaksgam as supposed; nevertheless this region still remained rather blank. (19)

1937 British expedition, leader E. E. Shipton, with J. B. Auden (geologist), M. Spender (surveyor, also to the 1935 Everest expedition), and H. W. Tilman, with seven Sherpas from Darjeeling, set off to survey the blank area remaining in the middle of the Shaksgam area: as far upstream as Durbin Jangal, the region lying to the north of K2, and the country traversed by F. Younghusband during his crossing of the Aghil Pass in 1889. From Srinagar they travelled to Skardu and Askole (May 24); then the party headed for Paiju from where it ascended the Trango gl. , crossed over the Sarpo Laggo Saddle and descended the glacier of the same name as far as Suget Jangal near

213

which Base Camp was established. From the Aghil Pass
(June 19) Shipton and Tilman with two Sherpas crossed
over into the Zug Shaksgam, linked up with K. Mason's
1926 survey and resolved the problem: the river flows
north to join the Surukwat, which in turn joins the Yarkand
a little further on its course. During July Auden, Shipton and Tilman with two Sherpas explored the glaciers
coming down from the northern flanks of K2 and Skyang
Kangri (previously 'Staircase Pk.', 7544m.). They ascended the K2 gl. right up to the great amphitheatre at
the foot of K2; on the way Shipton and Tilman had climbed
Peak 6350 on the east side of the glacier where a side
glacier joins it. From this peak's summit their view
dominated all the north side of the Baltoro Mustagh and
looked down onto the Skyang gl., which is linked to the
K2 gl. by the side glacier and a small col. Tilman
crossed the col during the next couple of days and descended the Skyang gl. After ascending Crevasse gl. the
expedition split up into small groups: Auden to the Panmah gl., Tilman to 'Snow Lake', and Shipton and Spender
over the Shimshal Pass (4735m.) to Gilgit. The highly
successful exploration of this region of the Great Karakoram and of the Aghil Mountains resulted in a map,
scale 1/250,000. (20)

KARAKORAM : BALTORO GLACIER

Principal Source References:

(1) Vigne Travels in Kashmir, Ladak, Iskardo, etc.

(2) Schlagintweit Results of a Scientific Mission to India and High Asia etc.

(3) Phillimore "Survey of Kashmir and Jammu, 1855 to 1865" HJ 22 pp. 95-102

(4) Keay When Men and Mountains Meet pp. 192-193

(5) Godwin-Austen "On the Glaciers of the Mustakh Range" JRGS 34 pp. 19-56

(6) Younghusband The Heart of a Continent

(7) Longstaff This My Voyage

(8) Conway Climbing & Exploration in the Karakoram-Himalayas

(9) Workman Two Summers in the Ice Wilds of Eastern Karakoram

(10) Jacot-Guillarmod Six Mois dans l'Himalaya

(11) Pfannl "Eine Belagerung des Tschogo-Ri (K2) in der Mustaghkette des Hindukusch (8720m.)" DOAVZ Vol. 35 (1904) pp. 88-104

(12) Ferber "An Exploration of the Muztagh Pass in the Karakoram Himalayas" GJ 30 pp. 630-643

(13) de Filippi Karakoram & Western Himalaya 1909

(14) Spoleto & Desio La Spedizione Geografica Italiana al Karakoram

(15) "The Italian Expedition to the Karakoram, 1929" HJ 3 pp. 102-107

(16) Dyhrenfurth Dämon Himalaya

(17) Dyhrenfurth Baltoro

(18) (Dyhrenfurth) "The Karakoram" HJ 7 pp. 142-148

(19) Mason Abode of Snow pp. 242-244

(20) Shipton Blank on the Map

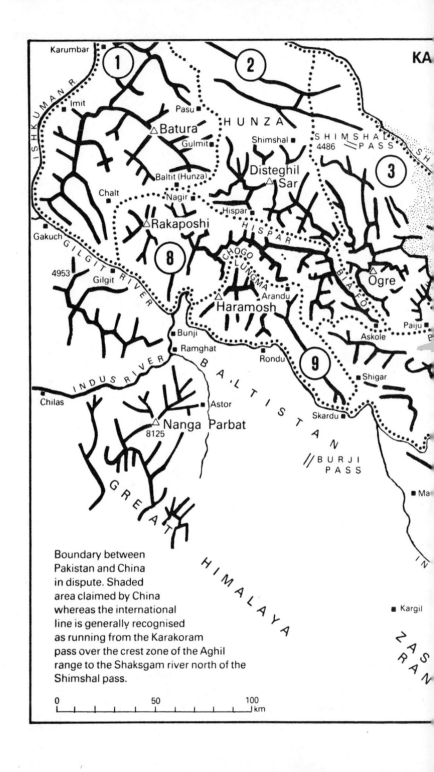

Boundary between
Pakistan and China
in dispute. Shaded
area claimed by China
whereas the international
line is generally recognised
as running from the Karakoram
pass over the crest zone of the Aghil
range to the Shaksgam river north of the
Shimshal pass.

)RAM RANGE main zones of the mountain system

GREAT (OUTER) KARAKORAM
1. Batura Mustagh (7785m)   2 Hispar Mustagh, Disteghil Sar (7885m)
3. Panmah Mustagh, The Ogre (Baintha Brakk, 7285m), The Crown (7265m)
4. Baltoro Mustagh, K2 (8611/8760m)
5. Siachen Mustagh, Teram Kangri (7463m)
6. Rimo Mustagh (7385m)   7 Saser Mustagh, Saser Kangri (7672m)

LITTLE (INNER) KARAKORAM
8. Rakaposhi Range (7788m)
9. Haramosh Range (7406m)
10. Masherbrum Range (7821m)
11. Saltoro Range (7742m)

GASHERBRUM I

8068

7784

7504

7069

N

MARGANG GL.

ABRUZZI GL.   BC=I

Alfondi
m

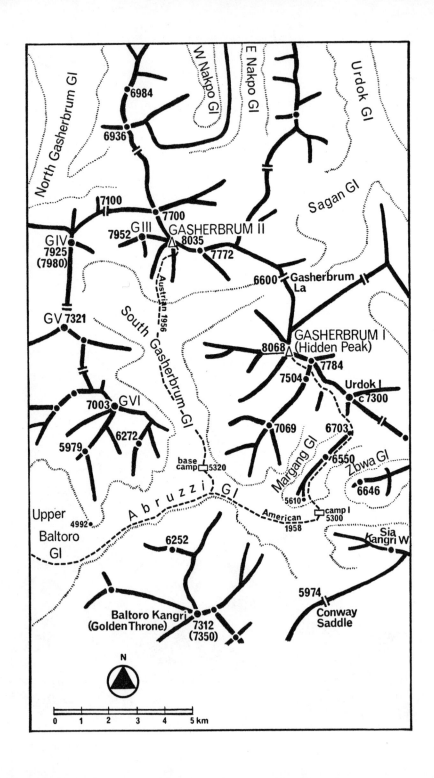

GASHERBRUM I 11
(Hidden Peak)

Situated: Great Karakoram, Baltoro Mustagh

Longitude: 76° 41' 48" E.

Latitude: 35° 43' 30" N.

Altitude: 8068m.

Early Designation No: K5

Name: Originally called 'Hidden Peak' by W. M. Conway as it is screened from general view by other mountains until the traveller reaches the Abruzzi gl. It had been referred to in an early Alpine Journal (August 1888) as Gusher-Brum which, according to Col. Godwin-Austen, is equivalent to 'Peak of Sunset'. G. O. Dyhrenfurth, in To the Third Pole, mentions that he had been told in the Baltoro region that the meaning was 'Shining Wall' but that he had some doubts about this. The present name derives from two Balti words (Balti, the westernmost of the Tibetan dialects, but not a written language): Rgasha meaning 'beautiful' and Brum meaning 'mountain'.

•

The GASHERBRUM group, at the eastern end of the Baltoro basin, forms a semi-circle round the South Gasherbrum glacier. The easternmost summit is the highest - Gasherbrum I, 8068m. Then follow in an anti-clockwise direction G. II 8035m., G. III 7952m., G. IV 7925m. (perhaps 7980m.), G. V 7321m. and G. VI 7003m. The territory north and east of G. I and G. II is in dispute between Pakistan and China.

The total height to be ascended from the foot of the (1934) ridge is about 2765m., from above the second ice-fall of the S. Gasherbrum gl. about 2165m.

MAPS - The following modern maps are generally available. Those most recommended are marked with an asterisk (*)

1/750,000 Karakorum & Nanga Parbat. 2nd ed. 1971. SSAF, Zurich *
1/250,000 Karakorum. 1971. WALA, Warsaw *
1/250,000 Chuling Sh. NI 43-2, Series U502. 1963. AMS, Washington, D. C. (only fair copy of black & white litho reprint available 1977) *
1/200,000 Karakorum Sh. 3 Baltoto region. 1977. ITY, Tokyo*
1/200,000 Karakorum Sh. 4 Siachen region. 1977. ITY, Tokyo*
1/100,000 Ghiacciaio Baltoro. 1969. IGM, Florence*

CHRONICLE

1861 Lt. H. H. Godwin-Austen probably saw the top of Gasherbrum I from the Baltoro gl.

1887 Lt. F. Younghusband saw Gasherbrum from the north.

1889 Younghusband, September 2, had a view of the Gasherbrum peaks from the Oprang (Shaksgam) river and the following day passed round the end of Gasherbrum gl. first seen from the Aghil Pass. He then ascended the Urdok gl. towards the supposed Saltoro Pass, travelling to the east of the Gasherbrum group. (1)

1892 W. M. Conway had placed Junction (or Concordia) Camp where the Vigne gl. joins the Baltoro. What is to-day known as Concordia, Conway had referred to as the 'Place de la Concorde'. As the expedition moved towards Footstcol Camp, at the foot of the 'Golden Throne's' (Baltoro

Kangri's) W. Ridge, they saw 'Hidden Peak' (Gasherbrum I) come into view. (2)

1928 In the course of the photogrammetric survey carried out
1929 by the Duke of Spoleto's expedition (It), one party was active in the Abruzzi gl. south of the mountain. Another party travelled up the Urdok gl. to the east of the mountain. (3)

1934 G. O. Dyhrenfurth's International expedition to the Baltoro carried out an important reconnaissance of Gasherbrum I (which they had hoped to climb). H. Ertl (Ger), A. Roch (Sw) and 3 porters set off to reconnoitre the mountain from the south, June 26, from Camp 5 on the Abruzzi gl. Ertl and Roch climbed up the S. W. Ridge that comes down from Urdok I and reached Pt. 6550; above them was Pt. 6703 beyond which a large snow basin led up towards the main summit. Given the support of a small number of high-level porters, they reckoned they could do the climb in three days; but this support was not forthcoming. An optimistic alternative of gaining the summit from Conway Saddle (12 km. of ridge!) was planned by Dyhrenfurth but the project was never realized. Next, they decided to examine the west side of the mountain from the S. Gasherbrum gl. , never visited before. Dyhrenfurth and Roch left Base Camp June 30 but they experienced some difficulty in ascending the heavily-crevassed glacier whose basin is enclosed by the six Gasherbrum summits. They kept to the true left side of the glacier and proceeded to just beyond the end of Gasherbrum I's West Ridge, to an estimated height of 6250m. Some 250m. above them and to their right they could see Gasherbrum La and gain a fore-shortened impression of Gasherbrum I's steep N. N. W. Ridge. On their way back they had to bivouac unexpectedly on the glacier; they had no sleeping bags or anything. (4) (5)

1936 French expedition, ten members, leader H. de Ségogne, with Capt. N. R. Streatfield (Br) attached as transportation officer. 35 Sherpas were engaged from Darjeeling; the porters were local Balti. From Srinagar (April 17) the expedition followed the usual route via Zoji-La (about 3530m.), Skardu and Askole, up the Baltoro gl. to where it is joined by the Abruzzi; there Base Camp was established (5000m.) May 26. Camp I was placed near a small lake at the base of the long ridge pointing S. W. and coming down from the E. S. E. Shoulder (7784m.) through the subsidiary summits 7504 and 7069. An attempt was made up this route; four further camps were erected along the difficult lower buttress leading up to Pt. 7069, the last of which (Camp 5) was pitched June 20 at 6550m. by P. Allain and J. Leininger. June 21, joined by L. Neltner, they pushed on a little further but were prevented from placing Camp 6 on Pt. 7069 by appalling weather. The onset of the monsoon necessitated the evacuation of the mountain. June 19 Dr. J. Arlaud and M. Ichac reached the Kondus Saddle (about 6550m.) on skis for nearly all the way. Two Sherpas, descending to Camp 2 July 1, slipped and started an avalanche. They were swept 600m. down the mountain ("passing Camp 2 like meteors") and ended up at the bottom of a big couloir, well on the way to Camp 1. Luckily Ichac happened to be filming in the vicinity and so aid was quickly available. Neither Sherpa was killed. (6)

1958 FIRST ASCENT: An American expedition of six members, 'director' N. B. Clinch and leader P. K. Schoening, with Capts. Mohd. Akram and S. T. H. Rizvi (Pakistan) attached, flew into Skardu May 18. Base Camp was set up near the confluence of the S. Gasherbrum and Abruzzi gls., June 6, and from there parties went north and east to prospect the west and south sides of the mountain.

Base had to be moved later to near the Italian (Gasherbrum IV) Base owing to deterioration of the glacier surface. Camp 1 was erected about 8 km. due east, June 13, near the foot of the 1934 expedition's S. W. Ridge at 5300m., this route having been decided on in preference to the shorter but steeper N. W. Ridge terminating below Gasherbrum La. Camp 3 was placed above the ice-dome (high point reached in 1934) at about 6600m. approximately June 22. Two further camps were pitched - Camp 5, an overnight camp at about 7300m. on the plateau immediately west of Urdok I summit, July 4. The following day, with Clinch, Dr. T. O. Nevison, and R. L. Swift in support at Camp 4 (6850m.), A. J. Kauffman and Schoening, using oxygen, reached the top about 4 km. distant through deep, floundering snow for most of the way. Skis, as suggested by Dyhrenfurth many years previously may have proved useful on this high snow plateau. (7) (8)

1975 SECOND ASCENT: A daring and rapid alpine-style ascent was achieved by P. Habeler and R. Messner (Aus) by a new route on the N. W. Face. They left Skardu July 13 with 12 porters and a liaison officer and established Base Camp July 25 at 5100m. After three reconnaissances, during which they carried up supplies, up the glacier between Gasherbrum I and II to an altitude of about 6700m., the two climbers left Base Camp August 8 and ascended to their Camp 1 at 5900m. The following day they overcame many hours of difficult climbing and bivouacked on the shoulder at 7100m. They reached the summit August 10 after a further six hours climbing. (9)

1975 THIRD ASCENT: An Austro-German expedition of six members (one of whom was the leader's wife), leader H. Schell, originally intended to climb Baltoro Kangri but decided instead to try the 1958 American route up Gasherbrum I. They arrived at Skardu July 2 and established Base Camp on the S. Gasherbrum gl. at 5180m. July 13. Four camps were placed along the route, the highest at 7300m. From Camp 3 (about 6800m.) five climbers made the FIRST ASCENT of Urdok I (about 7300m.), August 4. R. Schauer, H. Schell and H. Zefferer reached the summit of Gasherbrum I on August 11. (10)

1976 French expedition of two climbers - L. Audoubert and M. Batard - attempted to climb the mountain by the 1936 route (over Pts. 7069 and 7504) in alpine-style. Base Camp was established June 6 at 5150m. They reached 6500m. June 9 and there made a depot of equipment. Then it snowed for two days but June 14 the two climbers were able to continue up to about 7000m. Another ten days of snow obliged them to retreat and June 25 they were back in Urdokas. However the weather brightened and so June 28 they returned to their Base Camp. June 30 they climbed back to 6500m. only to find that their dump had been swept by avalanches. They returned to Skardu. (11) (12)

1977 FOURTH ASCENT: Yugoslavian expedition, eight members, leader J. Loncar. The ascent was made from the S. Gasherbrum gl. by a new route up the S.W. (W. ?) Ridge. Two climbers reached the summit July 8: A. Stremfelj and N. Zaplotnik. A third climber, D. Bregar, hoped to achieve a subsequent solo ascent but all contact with him was lost and finally, July 19, the expedition was obliged to leave. (13)

GASHERBRUM I

Principal Source References:

(1) Younghusband The Heart of a Continent

(2) Conway Climbing & Exploration in the Karakoram-Himalayas

(3) Spoleto & Desio La Spedizione Geografica Italiana al Karakoram

(4) Dyhrenfurth Baltoro

(5) Roch Karakoram Himalaya

(6) de Ségogne (and others) Himalayan Assault

(7) Schoening "Ascent of Hidden Peak" AAJ 1959 pp.165-172

(8) McCormack "The Ascent of Gasherbrum I" HJ 21 pp.46-54

(9) Messner The Challenge

(10) AAJ 1976 p. 542

(11) M & A 1976/3 p. 364

(12) AAJ 1977 pp. 268-269

(13) M 58 p. 12

Situated: Great Karakoram, Baltoro Mustagh

Longitude: 76° 39' 15" E.

Latitude: 35° 45' 31" N.

Altitude: 8035m.

Early Designation No: K4

Name: The origins are as for Gasherbrum I. One can only hope that one day, as also for the Annapurna and Dhaulagiri summits, each peak in this group will be given its own proper name instead of the present uninspiring numeration.

•

The total height to be ascended from above the second ice-fall of the S. Gasherbrum glacier is about 2035m., from Base Camp area at the confluence of the S. Gasherbrum gl. and the Abruzzi, it is about 2700m.

MAPS - As for Gasherbrum I.

CHRONICLE

1892 W. M. Conway's expedition enjoyed a good perspective of the Gasherbrum group from the top of 'Pioneer Peak' though its clouded head - as those of Broad Peak and K2 also - was not very striking from this viewpoint. The mountain appears on Conway's map as Pk. 26,360 ft. (8034m.). (1)

1909 The Duke of Abruzzi's expedition obtained a view onto the northern flanks of Gasherbrum I, II and III from the Sella Pass (6159m.). Another good sighting was from near the top of 'Bride Peak' (Chogolisa, 7654m.), July 18, when the Duke with Emil and Henri Brocherel and J. Petigax reached about 7400m. in their attempt on its summit. Abruzzi noticed that Gasherbrum II seemed to be connected with 'Hidden Peak' by a high crest thus forming an unbroken chain from 'Hidden Peak' to Broad Peak. He also surmised that there was in all probability no crest intervening between Pk. 22,139 (a subsidiary summit immediately north of Gasherbrum V) and 'Hidden Peak' and that therefore a large glaciated valley must lie between them. V. Sella obtained some excellent photographs of the Gasherbrum group (particularly his Panorama F). (2)

1934 Dyhrenfurth's International expedition made a reconnaissance up the S. Gasherbrum gl. - the one guessed at by the Duke of Abruzzi - and they were able to examine Gasherbrum II from close by. Falling directly towards them was a ridge, so tempting that for a moment Dyhrenfurth was ready to switch his whole expedition to climbing this mountain. For experienced climbers the route was clear, direct, middling difficult and avalanche free; however he realized that the climb would be beyond the capabilities of his Balti porters. An excellent panorama (C) embracing all the group, from G. VI in the west to G. I in the east, was obtained from the upper section of the glacier. (3)

1956 FIRST ASCENT: Austrian expedition, eight members, leader F. Moravec. They left Skardu May 3 and set up Base Camp May 25 at the junction of the S. Gasherbrum and Abruzzi gls. (5320m.). June 5 saw the start of the reconnaissance to establish a route up the 11 km. glacier to the foot of Gasherbrum II; Camp 1 was placed there at 6000m. June 11. Despite long spells of bad weather and Camp 1 being struck by an avalanche (June 30), with the loss of much equipment and stores, the attack pressed on. The line of ascent followed the S. W. Ridge on which Camp 2 (6700m.) and Camp 3 (7150m.) were pitched July 3 and July 6 respectively. The plan was to have no further camps but to allow for one high bivouac before the summit bid. S. Larch, Moravec and H. Willenpart continued the ascent and bivouacked at 7500m. Next morning, July 7, the three traversed the base of the summit pyramid, passed over the top of the S. E. Ridge and climbed up the E. Ridge to the summit. They were back at Base July 11. (4) (5)

1975 SECOND ASCENT: French expedition, 15 members, leader J-P. Frésafond climbed the mountain by its S. E. Ridge. M. Batard and Y. Seigneur reached the top June 18 without oxygen. A second attempt was made June 19 but ended in tragedy. From their high-altitude bivouac (7650m.) L. Audoubert and B. Villaret de Chauvigny set off for the summit but very soon Villaret turned back; Audoubert continued alone but was forced to retreat owing to high winds when only some 100m. from the top. He returned utterly exhausted to the tent. By next morning, with the storm unabated, their very survival was at stake; Villaret was unable or unwilling to leave the tent despite all Audoubert's exhortations. Finally Audoubert was forced to descend on his own, Villaret having said he would follow later. From Base Camp Villaret was seen to leave the tent, take a few steps and go back again; he never came down. The storm continued in increasing violence for eight days; he was beyond rescue. (6) (7)

1975 THIRD ASCENT (FIRST TRAVERSE), FOURTH & FIFTH
ASCENTS: A dual Polish expedition of seven men (leader
J. Onyszkiewicz) and nine women (leader W. Rutkiewicz)
arrived at Skardu May 26 and reached their Base Camp
June 16. Camp 1 was placed above the second ice-fall of
the S. Gasherbrum gl. at 6000m., June 19. Camps 2
and 3, similar to the 1956 Austrian route, were set up by
July 9. Further progress was halted by bad weather
despite many sorties by both the women's and the men's
teams in efforts to climb back to Camp 3 and to push on
to Camp 4. At last, July 31, five climbers were able to
re-occupy Camp 3 (7350m.) at the foot of the summit
pyramid. Next day, August 1, both teams crossed to the
col between Gasherbrum II and III (7550m.). From the
col the men's team - L. Cichy, Onyszkiewicz and K.
Zdzitowiecki - decided to ascend the N. W. Face of
Gasherbrum II (less difficult than the W. Ridge) and they
reached the summit the same day; they descended by the
East Ridge. The two women - H. Krueger-Syrokomska
and Rutkiewicz - failed to reach the summit of Gasherbrum III by its E. Ridge. August 4 M. Janas, A. Lapinski
and W. L. Wozniak (all men) set off to climb Gasherbrum
II by the Austrian route; they reached the summit August
9. At the same time two other mixed teams of four each
set off on a final bid for Gasherbrum III. The outcome
of this rather complex operation was that Onyszkiewicz,
his English-born wife Alison, Rutkiewicz and Zdzitowiecki
achieved the FIRST ASCENT of Gasherbrum III (7952m.)
by its E. Face, August 11; while Krueger-Syrokomska
and A. Okopinska (both women) climbed Gasherbrum II,
again by the Austrian route, and reached the top August
12. (8)

1976 Japanese expedition, 13 members, leader H. Aoki, approached the mountain from the south. Camp 1 was

erected at 5180m., May 21, and Camp 2 was placed at 5790m. five days later. Two climbers - Y. Hiramatsu and T. Miyamoto - fell down a crevasse near Camp 2, May 27, and were killed. A third member, O. Matsuura, died from exhaustion and altitude, June 1, as a result of helping in the rescue of the first two victims. The expedition was abandoned. (It may be assumed from the altitudes of the camps that the accident occurred during the approach march from the Abruzzi gl. up the S. Gasherbrum gl., probably in the vicinity of the second ice-fall). (9)

GASHERBRUM II

Principal Source References:

(1) Conway Climbing & Exploration in the Karakoram-Himal-ayas

(2) de Filippi Karakoram & Western Himalaya 1909

(3) Dyhrenfurth Baltoro

(4) Moravec Weisse Berge - Schwarze Menschen

(5) Moravec "Gasherbrum II" MW 1958/59 pp. 112-125

(6) Frésafond & Audoubert "Des Français au Karakorum en 1975" M & A 1976/1 pp. 236-244

(7) Audoubert "My Escape from Gasherbrum II" HJ 34 pp. 97-104

(8) Onyszkiewicz "Polish Ascents of Gasherbrum II and Gasherbrum III, 1975" HJ 34 pp. 93-96

(9) AAJ 1977 p. 269

8000 8047 **BROAD PEAK**

PLATEAU

GODWIN-AUSTEN GL   BC

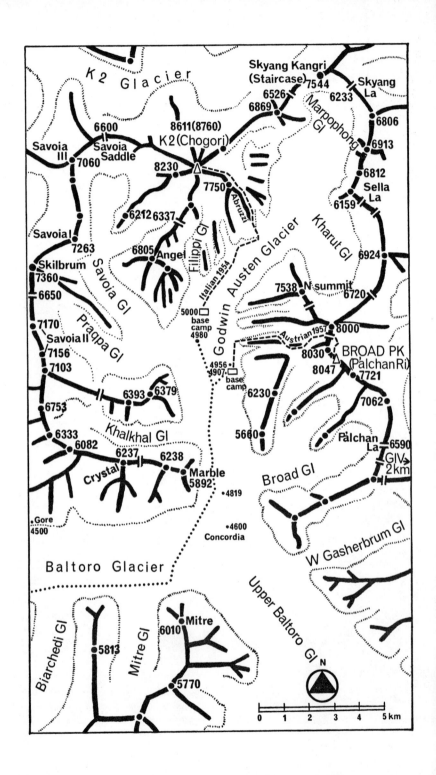

BROAD PEAK 13

Situated: Great Karakoram, Baltoro Mustagh

Longitude: 76° 34' 25" E.
Latitude: 35° 48' 35" N.

Altitude: Main summit - 8047m.
         Central summit - c. 8000m.
         North summit - 7538m.
Early designation No: Nil

Name: "Broad Peak" was bestowed by W. M. Conway. The literal translation into Balti, Phalchan Kangri (sometimes erronously spelt Falchan and more correctly spelt P'alchan according to M. Kurz in Chronique Himalayenne p. 392 - the sound of 'f' being unknown in Tibetan and in Balti), has no acceptance among the Baltis (H. A. Carter, AAJ 1975 p. 53). But W. Kick (MW 1956/57 p. 198) writes that P'al-chen-ri, according to Col. Atta Ullah, is used by the natives. The Main and North summits have been referred to on occasions as Broad Peak I and Broad Peak II respectively.

The sheer bulk of the mountain, so aptly named by Conway, is what seems to have impressed most travellers. It dominates the left bank of the Godwin-Austen gl. for most of the latter's length. Its three summits are linked by a long, tortuous crest, steep and heavily corniced. The Main summit has been ascended twice and the Central summit only once to date. The

mountain has not been attempted from the east.
The total height to be ascended from Base Camp on the Godwin-Austen gl. is about 3135m. and from Broad gl. about 3345m.

MAPS - As for Gasherbrum I.

CHRONICLE

1892 The British expedition led by W. M. Conway left Fan Camp (on the right bank of the Baltoro, downstream from Concordia) August 12; Lt. C. G. Bruce and M. Zurbriggen (Sw) continued up the glacier, Conway and A. D. McCormick climbed up to the Fan Pass (5715m.). To the right of the view from the top of the col there was "a fine breadth of mountain splendour displaying itself - a huge Breithorn, as it were, filling the space between K2 and the hidden Gusherbrum". An illustration of this vista of Broad Peak, as Conway called the mountain, was sketched by McCormick and appears in Conway's book. The expedition passed to the south of the mountain on its way to 'Golden Throne'; its altitude appears not to have been measured. (1)

1902 O. Eckenstein's expedition, when ascending the Godwin-Austen gl., passed along the west side of Broad Pk. Camp 10 was sited close to the foot of the mountain's north westerly ridge, and all three summits were seen end-on from Camp 11 sited higher up the glacier. The altitude of Broad Peak was estimated simply as "more than 8500m." (2)

1909 The Duke of Abruzzi's expedition to K2 likewise ascended the full length of the Godwin-Austen gl. whose left wall, in its lower reaches, was "formed largely by a low screen of black rock which detaches itself from the western crest of Broad Peak and runs southward". Behind this screen is the "heavy and massive outline" of Broad Pk. The summit was measured by M. F. Negrotto and calculated surprisingly as 8270m., this result making it the sixth highest mountain in the world. The northern aspects of the mountain were examined too; enormous ice-avalanches were seen crashing down from its formidable north wall. Some excellent photographs were taken by V. Sella (particularly his panorama C which includes Broad Pk. seen from the S. W.). (3)

1926 Major K. Mason led a small British survey party for the S. O. I. to the Shaksgam; the other members were Capt. F. O. Cave, Major R. C. Clifford, Afraz Gul Khan (who had been with the Vissers in Hunza the year previously), and Major H. D. Minchinton. From the Aghil Range they enjoyed magnificent views of K2, Broad Pk. and the Gasherbrum mountains, particularly from above the Kyagar gl. and from Tatar La. Fresh bearings taken from these stations resulted in a substantial downgrading of Broad Peak's height (from 8270m. to 8047m.). (4) (5)

1929 The Duke of Spoleto's expedition was active also in the Shaksgam valley area. Dr. U. Balestreri led a group over the old Mustagh Pass and travelled as far as the Kyagar gl. He made new measurements of Broad Pk. and of other mountains and confirmed Mason's findings; the altitude of 8047m. made the peak thirteenth in order of height. (6)

1954 German expedition of 12 members (including two Austrians but not including L. Terray (Fr) who had been invited but had had to withdraw at the last moment or W. Kick who went off to survey in the Chogo Lungma area), leader Dr. K. M. Herrligkoffer, not able to go for K2, received permission for an autumn attempt on Broad Pk. instead. (Before receiving this permit Herrligkoffer had considered

239

the possibility of climbing Gasherbrum I from the Siachen gl. side). The leader was delayed in Germany for a long time so the expedition did not reach Askole until the end of September. Base Camp was set up at Concordia, 4700m., mid-October. The projected route on Broad Pk.'s west side was considered too difficult for the Hunza porters; instead they decided to go up the west side of the more northerly of the two glaciers that join the Broad gl. opposite Marble Peak (5892m.) - sometimes referred to as Broad Pk. gl. This route, on the east side of Abruzzi's "screen of black rock", leads up to a high snow terrace (the Plateau) from the top of which a small col (about 7800m.) between the Central summit (about 8000m.) and the Foresummit (8030m.) can be reached. October 22 T. Messner and two companions went by ski to reconnoitre the glacier. Later Camp 1 was placed at 5300m., Camp 2 at 6000m. (probably overestimated); above Camp 2 a dangerous 300m. couloir - an avalanche trap they called "Kanonenrohr" (the gun barrel) - led up to a large snow shoulder north of Pt. 6230; there Camp 3 was pitched. Camp 4 had been planned for 6900m. or 7000m. but November 5, with the wind turning bitterly cold, M. Anderl and E. Senn were forced to turn back after reaching 7200m. (probably 6900m., the various heights having been rather overestimated). (7)

1957 FIRST ASCENT: Austrian expedition, 4 members, leader M. Schmuck, left Skardu April 18. Their porters left rather hurriedly and the climbers were obliged to ferry the loads for the last few kilometres to Base Camp, positioned on the true left side of the Godwin-Austen gl. a little beyond Pt. 6230 at 4910m. The line of ascent was to be directly up the avalanche free West Ridge leading to the snow Plateau, thence up a hanging glacier to the small col and along the crest to the actual summit. They set off May 13; three camps were placed along the West Ridge, the third on May 28 at 6950m. after they had been back in Base Camp for a few days rest. Early next morning, May 29, the four climbers (H. Buhl, K. Diemberger, Schmuck and F. Wintersteller) left for the summit; they reached the col at 3 p.m. and continued on along the ridge until they thought they had at last reached the top. But it was not so for there was another summit, only some 15m. to 20m. higher than theirs, rising beyond a shallow dip and about one hour away; it was too late to go any further so they turned back. After a few more days rest in Base Camp the team set off again, June 7; they reached Camp 2 (6350m.) in one day and were able to leave Camp 4 very early on June 9. Schmuck and Wintersteller were the first pair to reach the summit (all without oxygen); Buhl, troubled by fierce pains in his right foot (he had lost two toes as a result of frostbite on Nanga Parbat), finally gave up when still below the subsidiary summit; Diemberger continued alone and reached the top at about 6 p.m. just as the first pair were leaving. On his return Diemberger met Buhl who, refusing to be beaten, had struggled up to the subsidiary summit. Without stopping, Buhl went on, plodding slowly for the goal. Diemberger paused, turned round and followed after Buhl. They reached the summit together. It was half past midnight when they got back to Camp 3. (8)

(Diemberger followed by Buhl, June 27, after turning back when within striking distance of the summit of Chogolisa (7654m.), were groping their way back along the precipitous and heavily corniced S. E. Ridge when suddenly one of the cornices broke off and Buhl plunged to his death).

1974 Japanese expedition, 8 members, leader T. Arioka had

intended to climb K12 but unexpectedly the Pakistan Government gave them a permit for the more difficult Broad Pk. shortly before they were due to leave Japan. They did not have time to plan an assault on this peak but decided to attempt its North summit instead. Base Camp was established at Concordia June 30, and Camp 1 on the Godwin-Austen gl. at 4875m. They were unable to find a way up the West Ridge so turned their attention to the north. They are reported as having tried to reach the summit along the N. E. Ridge from Sella La (6159m.) but found it too long and had to turn back after reaching 6300m. Reports mention the attempt as being on "the 8000m. North Peak". It is the Central Summit which is 8000m. and it seems that it must have been this summit that Arioka was aiming for and not the North Summit (7538m.): this would make an approach from the Sella La more understandable. (9)

1975 CENTRAL SUMMIT - FIRST ASCENT: Polish expedition, 14 members, leader J. Ferenski, landed at Skardu June 13 and reached Concordia June 29 with the intention of climbing Central Summit. Base Camp was placed on the middle moraine of the Godwin-Austen gl. at 4950m. The line of ascent was much the same as for the 1957 Austrian climb and again three camps were set up, the last at 7200m., July 13. A summit team of six - R. Bebak, K. Glazek, M. Kesicki, J. Kulis, B. Nowaczyk and A. Sikorski - left Camp 3 early in the morning of July 28, and reached the small col after $12\frac{1}{2}$ hours climbing; Bebak was obliged to turn back just short of the col. The other five reached the summit at 7.30 p.m. - $16\frac{1}{2}$ hours from Camp 3. The height quoted by the Poles is 8016m. On the way back to the col, in a raging snow storm, Nowaczyk disappeared down the east side of the ridge. The others were obliged to bivouac on the col and next morning the search for Nowaczyk continued but to no avail. A second bivouac lower down became necessary but just before this Kesicki, Kulis and Sikorski slipped and fell; Kesicki and Sikorski were both killed. The two survivors reached Base Camp, with the help of their colleagues, August 1. (10)

1976 A small French expedition of four (B. Mellet, J-C. Mosca and Y. Seigneur with Dr. D. Mennesson in support) set off with the intention of climbing the Central and Main summits in alpine-style, without the help of porters beyond Base Camp. The line followed was that of the Austrian 1957 ascent. They were dogged by exceptionally bad weather and despite four attempts - the last one to beyond the small col on the way to the Main summit - they were forced to give up in the face of terrific winds and intense cold. High point reached was about 7850m., June 30. (11) (12)

1977 SECOND ASCENT: Japanese expedition, 14 members, leader M. Yuasa. The route followed was that of the Austrians in 1957. Three climbers reached the summit August 8. (13)

BROAD PEAK

Principal Source References:

(1) Conway Climbing & Exploration in the Karakoram-Himalayas

(2) Jacot-Guillarmod Six Mois dans l'Himalaya

(3) de Filippi Karakoram & Western Himalaya 1909

(4) Mason "The Shaksgam Valley and Aghil Range" GJ 69 pp. 289-332 with 1/250,000 map

(5) Minchinton "With the Shaksgam Survey Party - 1926" AJ 39 pp. 209-240 with 1/250,000 map

(6) Spoleto & Desio La Spedizione Geografica Italiana al Karakoram

(7) Herrligkoffer Deutsche am Broad Peak

(8) Diemberger "Broad Peak" MW 1958/59 pp. 126-141

(9) AAJ 1975 pp. 212-213

(10) Glazek & Ferenski "Victory and Tragedy on Broad Peak" AJ 82 pp. 129-133

(11) M & A 1976/3 p. 363

(12) AAJ 1977 p. 268

(13) M 58 p. 12

K2   14

Situated: Great Karakoram, Baltoro Mustagh

Longitude: 76° 30' 51" E.

Latitude: 35° 52' 55" N.

Altitude: 8611m. (8760m.)

Early Designation No: K2

Name: The mountain, not visible from any inhabited place, has no known local name. By usage it has retained its original designation number bestowed on it by Lt. T.G. Montgomerie in 1856. Several native names have been attributed to the mountain but none has been authenticated. The most commonly used alternative is Chogori, more properly Ch'ogo Ri (Balti for 'Great Mountain'); Mch'og is Tibetan for 'elevated'. This name was obtained by the 1902 expedition (see Freshfield Round Kangchenjunga p.201 note) but it has no local acceptance (H.A. Carter "Balti Place Names in the Karakoram" AAJ 1975 p.53). Dr. J. Jacot-Guillarmod also reported that in 1902 the name Dapsang had been sometimes heard   O. Eckenstein mentioned in his book The Karakorams and Kashmir that the names Skinmang and Dapsang had been intimated to him by a native;   W.M. Conway, in a letter to the R.G.S., 1892, reported on this information but quoted the name for K2 as Chiring. Other supposed native names have been Lanfafahad and Lamba Pahar. The most popular occidental name (sometimes still used) has been Mt. Godwin-Austen, a name proposed rather on impulse by General J.T. Walker (a former Surveyor

General of India) at a meeting of the R. G. S. in London in 1888; the suggestion was not accepted. Earlier the name Mount Waugh had been put forward (Sir A. Waugh had succeeded Sir G. Everest as Surveyor General of India in 1843); Mount Albert (after the Prince Consort, Queen Victoria's husband) had been also proposed; Mount Montgomerie, too. None of these was acceptable. Occasionally the mountain is now referred to locally as Ketu, Kechu, Kechu Kangri and similar adaptations of the original designation number K2.

K2, the most westerly of the Karakoram 8000m. giants, stands centrally at the head of an all but enclosed cirque formed, in the west, by the range running from Marble Pk. through Skilbrum to the Savoia Saddle and, in the east, by the range of Broad Pk. northward to Skyang Kangri. It has dominated the area both physically and in man's imagination since it was first observed (by Westerners) 120 years ago. It has been a magnet for many expeditions, and has been climbed three times. Situated 1500 km. from the sea - more than twice as far as is Mount Everest - K2 is not subjected to the regular monsoons as are the mountains of Nepal; nevertheless it suffers vagaries of weather that alternate from fine spells of hot weather to frequently long spells of bitter cold and raging blizzards. From all aspects it is a formidable mountain and its seven ridges all rise steeply from the surrounding glaciers to unite in the final summit pyramid whose top attains 8611m. - or may be 8760m. if the latest pronouncement by the Pakistan Survey proves correct. The territory to the north of K2 is in dispute between Pakistan and China.
The total height to be ascended from the base of the Abruzzi Ridge is about 3210m. and from Base Camp lower down the glacier, about 3610m. - assuming 8611m. to be still the accepted altitude.

MAPS - The following modern maps are generally available. Those most recommended are marked with an asterisk (*)

1/250,000 Mundik Sh. NI 43-3, Series U502, 2nd Ed. 1963. AMS, Washington, D. C. (only fair black & white litho reprint available 1977)

1/12,500 K2. 1954. IGM, Florence*

CHRONICLE

1856 Lt. T.G. Montgomerie in September observed a number of high peaks in the Karakoram from Mount Haramukh, east of the Wular (Woola) Lake in Kashmir. One of these he entered in his book as K2. The officially accepted height of 28,250 ft. (8611m.) was obtained from the mean of readings observed subsequently from nine separate stations.

1861 Lt. H.H. Godwin-Austen saw K2 from above Urdokas, on the true left bank of the Baltoro gl.; he was at a distance of about 27 km. from the mountain which he then sketched. A copy of this sketch appeared in The Illustrated London News of February 27, 1892

1887 Lt. F. Younghusband was the first European to see K2 from the north. Before crossing the (old) Mustagh Pass he ascended the Sarpo Laggo river towards Suget Jangal. Suddenly he saw K2 "rising in an almost perfect cone but to an inconceivable height". He was about 18 km. distant from the mountain. (1)

1902 An expedition comprising O. Eckenstein (Br) as leader, A. Crowley (Br), Dr. J. Jacot-Guillarmod (Sw), G. Knowles (Br), H. Pfannl (Aus) and V. Wessely (Aus) set off optimistically to climb K2. An incident took place at the start of the journey that has given rise to much speculation. They left Rawalpindi March 29 for Srinagar and stopped overnight at Treet. The next morning a messenger, sent by the Governor of Rawalpindi, arrived with an order (it is said) from the Viceroy, Lord Curzon, for Eckenstein to return to Rawalpindi and to hold himself at the Viceroy's disposal. No reasons were given for this constraint. The notorious Crowley suggested that it was due to the scheming of W. M. Conway because of a clash of opinion ten years earlier resulting in Eckenstein's leaving the Conway expedition when at Askole. Knowles' opinion inclined towards that of Crowley, though for no stated reasons. Crowley's view is possible, none the less it does seem a little unlikely and pointless - Conway was no Coolidge. Of greater significance is the brief report in the Friend of India (May 1, 1902) to the effect that Eckenstein's intention was to climb Mount Everest. At that time Curzon was involved in delicate negotiations with the Government of Nepal for an official British expedition to Everest; the gate-crashing of Nepal or Tibet by an unauthorized party would have had severe repercussions. Although the report was without substance, the rumour may also have reached Curzon's ear - hence the need to recall Eckenstein and to obtain clarification of his real intentions. In any event Eckenstein rejoined the expedition three weeks later (April 22) at Srinagar. Crowley waxed indignant over the affair; Jacot-Guillarmod and Pfannl mention it but briefly.

The expedition approached the Baltoro via Skardu and Askole, then ascended the glacier's left bank as far as Rdokass (Urdokas). They crossed to the other side, rounded Marble Peak (5892m.) and, with K2 before their eyes, went up the Godwin-Austen gl. on which they pitched their camps 8, 9 and 10. The last was sited on Conway's "Possible Saddle" (beyond which he had been unable to see) mid-way between K2's S. E. Ridge and Broad Peak's N. W. Ridge, at 5715m., June 20. An ascent of the S. E. Ridge, June 28, was put off because of strong winds; instead they decided to place a Camp 11 in the hitherto unknown upper section of the glacier at the foot of a short spur coming down from Pt. 6869 and at 5925m. July 10 Jacot-Guillarmod and Wessely set off to climb the longer spur; though hampered by deep snow they got as high as about 6525m. then came down again. It was decided to wait a few days to allow the snow to compact. In the meantime Pfannl and Wessely went off to establish Camp 12 from which they hoped to reach the col between Pt. 6869 and Skyang Kangri (7544m.). Pfannl was taken ill and had to be evacuated; no further attempts on K2 were made. The expedition suffered from lack of effective direction, bad weather, ill-health, and friction between the participants. (The map at the end of Jacot-Guillarmod's book, based on Conway's map and drawn by W. Brendel, has a more professional appearance than Pfannl's sketch map but the latter gives a truer impression of the upper section of the Godwin-Austen gl. and its heights are less inaccurate than the former's). (2) (3) (4)

1909 The Duke of Abruzzi led a large Italian expedition of 13 members for a further exploration of the Baltoro and a reconnaissance of (and possibly an attempt on) K2. Leaving Srinagar April 24, the same approach was followed as in 1902 and Camp 3, their second Base Camp, was established at the entrance to the De Filippi gl. (named after the party's geographer) at 5030m., May 24. Realizing quickly that an ascent from the south or south-west was impracticable and that the N. E. Ridge was out of the question, the Duke decided to attempt the S. E. Ridge - the only route that appeared to offer any hope. For logistical reasons the Duke decided he would go alone so, with the three Courmayeur guides (A. Brocherel, H. Brocherel and J. Pettigax), the four porters (also from Courmayeur) and some coolies, he set off for the attack; Camp 4 was set up at 5560m. and the same day, while the Duke remained in camp, the guides continued up to about 5860m. before returning to the tents. The following day, May 31, the guides climbed up to about 6095m. - well above the small couloir negotiated the day before - then came down again reporting that, though there appeared to be no serious obstacles higher up, the ascent would take much longer than imagined. Next morning the guides and porters went up again to a point beyond that reached the previous day, to about 6250m. During the climb they came to realize that the difficulties were greater than anticipated and that without fixing ropes all the way for the loaded porters (the route would be unthinkable for coolies), it would be useless to continue with the attempt. Next day, June 2, they all went back to Base Camp. Then followed extensive reconnaissances of the Godwin-Austen gl. - Sella Pass (6159m.) and 'Windy Gap' (Skyang La, 6233m.) were reached, a Camp 8 was placed above 'Windy Gap', and a high point of 6600m. was achieved on the ridge leading up to 'Staircase Peak' (Skyang Kangri, 7544m.), June 25. The Savoia gl. was explored too and the Duke with three guides attained Savoia Saddle (6600m.) June 7. The expedition finally headed south to the Abruzzi gl.

(The initials of the guides and porters can create puzzlement. Courmayeur is in Aosta in Italy; because Aosta was formerly a part of the kingdom of France, French is still spoken there. The christian or first name of Petigax, father, was Joseph; in Italian this is Guiseppe. One of the two Brocherel guides (they were brothers) was named Henri; in Italian this is Enrico - not to be confused with the porter <u>E</u>mil or <u>E</u>milio Brocherel. For clarity, the initials of the christian names in French have been used in this chronicle.) (5)

1928 In the course of the Duke of Spoleto's expedition, a party
1929 under Dr. U. Balestreri crossed the (old) Mustagh Pass and made its way round into the Shaksgam valley towards Suget Jangal during mid-June 1929. From there they, like Younghusband more than 40 years earlier, enjoyed glorious views of the north side of K2; alas, not one good photograph of that side of the mountain was taken. (6)

1937 During E.E. Shipton's expedition in the Shaksgam area, J.B. Auden, Shipton and H.W. Tilman explored the glaciers on the north side of K2 and ascended the K2 glacier as far as the great amphitheatre at the foot of the mountain. Several photographs of the north side of K2 and of its glacier were obtained. (7)

1938 American expedition, six members including Capt. N.R. Streatfeild (Indian Army) as liaison officer, leader C.S. Houston, with six Sherpas from Darjeeling selected by H.W. Tilman, Pasang Kikuli as Sirdar. Having departed from Srinagar May 12 to make the first determined attempt on K2, they established Base Camp a little below where Abruzzi had placed his Camp 3, June 12. First they reconnoitered the west side to investigate the W.N.W. Ridge but were unable to reach the Savoia Saddle on account of the steep ice-wall, then the east side as far as Skyang La to inspect the N.E. Ridge which was found to be not promising. So they decided to reconnoitre the Abruzzi Ridge; it proved discouraging. After examining again the Savoia Saddle and the long N.E. Ridge, they finally decided to try the Abruzzi Ridge. Camp 1 was placed at its base, July 1, Camp 2 at about 5880m.; Camp 3, 6320m., was occupied July 10; Camp 4 was pitched at the top of a high gendarme at about 6550m.; Camp 5, at 6700m., was above a very difficult and almost vertical chimney 45m. high forced by R. H. Bates and W. P. House; and Camp 6 was placed at 7100m. (July 18). Next day Houston and P. K. Petzoldt climbed to about 7620m., above the top of the Black Pyramid, and returned to Camp 6 where Bates and House were by then ensconced. They decided to site one more camp then for two men to push as high as possible and return to camp the same day, this because time was short and a break-up of the weather was feared. July 20 Bates, House and Pasang Kikuli carried loads to above the Pyramid, Houston and Petzoldt finally erecting their Camp 7 a little beyond at 7525m. On the morrow the two reached an estimated high point of 7925m. before turning back. The descent from Camp 7 to Camp 4 was achieved in one day. The bad weather did not materialize. (8)

1939 Second American expedition of six members, leader F. H. Wiessner, with Lt. G. S. C. Trench (Br) as Transport Officer and nine Sherpas under Pasang Kikuli, Sirdar. They left Srinagar May 2 and established Base Camp at the foot of K2 at about 5400m. The route and camps were to be similar to those of 1938. Despite bad weather Camp 6, 7100m., was occupied July 5. By July 11, owing to illness and other factors, only three climbers and seven Sherpas remained available for the push to the summit; the three climbers were J. Durrance, Wiessner and D. E. Wolfe. During July 13 and 14 Wiessner and Wolfe with one Sherpa (Pasang Lama) climbed up to Camp 7, 7525m., then to Camp 8, about 7711m.; Durrance, taken ill on the way to Camp 7, had had to return to Camp 6 then came down to Camp 2 with the Sirdar and one porter. The other porters went up and down between camps, ferrying loads. After a couple of days of bad weather

Wiessner, Wolfe and Pasang Lama climbed up through deep snow to Camp 9, estimated at 7940m., but Wolfe was too exhausted to make it and returned to Camp 8. Two days later (July 19) Wiessner and Pasang Lama made a bid for the summit and reached an estimated 8365m. before retracing their steps back to Camp 9. July 21 the summit pair made a second unsuccessful attempt and returned to Camp 9. They went down to Camp 8 the following morning, leaving most of their gear at the top camp in the expectation of being able to make yet another attempt; Wolfe told them that no one had come up with supplies since July 17. In theory all the lower camps were well provisioned and supported; the leader was unaware that Durrance and Sirdar Pasang Kikuli had in the meanwhile returned to Base and that their support and lines of communication were therefore no more than tenuous. The three went down to Camp 7 that they themselves had stocked; during the descent Wolfe slipped and lost his sleeping bag. To their astonishment they found the camp deserted and the tent in disarray and virtually empty. After a most uncomfortable night, the summit pair continued (July 23) down to Camp 6 to fetch supplies; Wolfe preferred to stay where he was and await their return. To Wiessner's amazement Camp 6 was deserted and empty too; so were Camps 5, 4 and 2 (Camp 3 had been only a depot). Next day, July 24, the pair, now utterly exhausted, left Camp 2 and reached Base Camp. Wolfe, alone, remained on the mountain.

It appears that owing to a possible error of judgement by Durrance and to the other porters being left without supervision (there were no climbers or Sirdar on the mountain at all after the 19th) all the fully-provisioned camps (numbers 7, 6, 4, and 2) had been stripped of their sleeping bags, food and stoves between July 19 and 23, the day when the last of the porters, loaded with gear, arrived down at Base and reported that they thought a fatal avalanche accident must have overwhelmed the summit team of three.

Durrance set off July 25 with a rescue team of three porters but was taken ill again at Camp 4 and had to return, leaving two porters at the camp. July 28 Pasang Kikuli and Sherpa Tsering went from Base Camp to Camp 6 - some 1700m. - in one day, picking up the other two porters (Pasang Kitar and Phinsoo) during their amazing ascent. The following day Pasang Kikuli, Pasang Kitar and Phinsoo went up to Camp 7 to bring down Wolfe, by now in a terribly weakened condition. Wolfe was unable and unwilling to make the descent and asked them to return the next day. But next day a storm blew up. So it was not until July 31 that the three were able to go up once more. They were never seen again; nor was Wolfe. Tsering, alone on the mountain, waited until August 2 then returned to Base, all the way down that long and difficult ridge by himself.

One last rescue attempt was made by Wiessner accompanied by Dawa and Tsering on August 3. All three were by now in a poor condition and when in Camp 2 a storm started and raged until the 7th; the three were obliged to go back to Base. (9) (10) (11) (12) (13)

1953 Third American expedition, seven members, leader C. S. Houston, with Capt. H. R. A. Streather (Br) as Transport Officer, Col. M. Atta Ullah (Pak), and six Hunza porters, set up Base Camp at about 5000m. near the foot of K2's South Ridge. The expedition was to follow the previous line on the Abruzzi Ridge. Camp 3, the limit to which the Hunza porters were allowed to carry, was pitched at 6250m. July 6 and Camp 5 was pitched at 7100m. about three weeks later. It was at this site that they found the

remains of two tents from 1939 with the rolled sleeping
bags and personal belongings of the brave Sherpas -
Pasang Kikuli, Pasang Kitar and Phinsoo - still waiting
for their return. Camp 7, a small one-tent cache, was
placed at the foot of the snow shoulder at about 7465m.
and Camp 8, a little higher near the top of the shoulder
at 7770m. August 1. By the following evening the entire
team was at Camp 8, provisioned with food and fuel for
ten days: R. H. Bates, G. Bell, R. Craig, Houston, D.
Molenaar, P. K. Schoening, A. Gilkey and Streather; the
Colonel and the six Hunzas were at Base. All was set
for the summit attempt. However the storm that had
started up that evening increased in intensity during the
night and continued to rage until August 7. As the members prepared some to go down to Camp 7 to bring up
more supplies, others to reconnoitre a route up to Camp
9, Gilkey complained of a pain in a leg, then collapsed;
it was thrombophlebitis. They had to get him down immediately. But bad weather blew up again and finally,
August 10, they were obliged despite the storm to start
dragging and lowering Gilkey down the mountain. When
almost abreast of Camp 7 one of the climbers slipped and
five people were pulled off the ice-slope, falling a distance of up to 90m. By good fortune their several ropes
became intermingled and Schoening, the only one well
belayed, was able to hold them all. Shocked, concussed,
injured, frost-bitten, somehow they managed to help each
other across to the tiny platform where stood the single
tent of Camp 7 cache, leaving Gilkey anchored to two
ice-axes on the slope. When they went back for him, he
was gone - swept away by an avalanche. After a miserable
night in Camp 7, the survivors proceeded down to Camp
2; it took four days of grim determination. There the
Hunza porters came to meet and help them; next day,
August 15, they arrived at Base Camp. G. Bell, suffering

serious frost-bite, had to be transported all the way back to Skardu on a stretcher. (14)

1953 Professor A. Desio made a preliminary journey to K2 during the autumn. He and R. Cassin left Italy August 20 and when at Rawalpindi met Houston's American expedition returning from their attempt on the mountain. They reached K2 during September, did a reconnaissance below the Abruzzi Ridge, then returned to Skardu and home.

1954 After his 1953 expedition to Nanga Parbat Dr. K. M. Herrligkoffer left most of his equipment in Gilgit, hoping to be able to tackle K2 the following year. However the Italians had already made an application for this mountain and Herrligkoffer conceded their priority. Instead he led an expedition to Broad Peak.

1954 FIRST ASCENT: Italian expedition of two parties: a scientific group and a climbing group of 12 members under the overall leadership of Prof. A. Desio, with Col. M. Atta Ullah (Pak), three Pakistan Army Transport Officers and one assistant topographer (also from Pakistan). Almost every contingency had been catered for in the planning: the entire route of the Abruzzi Ridge to above the shoulder was to be fitted with pegs and fixed ropes, all camps were to be kept always stocked with food and equipment; windlasses and rope pulleys were to be used for lifting loads up the ridge; nothing seemed left to chance. From Skardu, April 30, a reconnaissance flight over K2 was carried out. 500 coolies were organized to carry 500 loads to Base Camp; 700 men marched up the Baltoro gl. Porter trouble delayed the setting up of Base Camp at the confluence of the De Filippi and the Godwin-Austen gls., about 5000m., but by the end of May Base Camp and Camp 1 were erected; Camp 4 was in position June 16. During another ten day spell of bad weather, M. Puchoz, taken ill while descending from

Camp 4, died from pneumonia in Camp 2 (June 21). He was buried six days later near the monument built to the memory of A. Gilkey, the victim of the 1953 tragedy. C. Floreanini fell 240m. without being seriously hurt after some fixed ropes from 1953 became detached as he was using them. Camp 7 was pitched on the site of the 1953 Camp 8 (7500m. according to Desio) and Camp 8 at 7770m. three days later. The last Camp, No. 9, was set up at 8060m. by A. Compagnoni and L. Lacedelli July 30; the same day A. Bonatti and the Hunza porter Mahdi tried to reach Camp 9 with extra oxygen equipment for the summit pair but could not quite make it and were forced to spend the night in a snow hole at 7990m. The following day, July 31, Compagnoni and Lacedelli succeeded in reaching the top even though their oxygen had been used up before they got there. (15)

Note: not too much reliance should be placed on the altitudes quoted in these last expeditions; they are relative rather than accurate. For example the 1939 Camp 8 was probably, based on the 1954 I.G.M. data, 7627m. but as this would make it only 100m. above the Camp 7, the altitudes of the lower camps can be assumed to be over-estimated too. Five different heights are to be found for the 1939 Camp 9, varying between 7727m. in Ref. (10) to 8610m. (!) in Ref. (15) - the latter in fact gives three different heights. The 1953 Camp 8 is given as 7711m. in Ref. (15) p. 129 and as 7818m. on the preceding illustration. The 1954 Camp 7 was placed on the site of this 1953 Camp 8; in Fantin's I Quattordici "8000" p. 124 L. Serra's account "Il gran monte" gives the height as 7345m. while on p. 128 A. Desio's account "Sul K2" gives it as 7500m. M. Kurz in Chronique Himalayenne gives 7345m. (probably the correct altitude) which accords with 7627m. for the 1954 Camp 8 placed on the same spot as the 1939 Camp 8. And so forth. If the 1954 I.G.M. calculations are correct (they were obtained from the photogrammetric survey carried out by Capt. F. Lombard of the scientific group of Desio's expedition) then most of the earlier estimates are too high. On the other hand if the new height for K2 - 8760m. instead of 8611m. - proves to be correct, then a complete revision of all figures will become necessary.

1960 An American-German expedition, leader Major W. D. Hackett, attempted to climb K2 by the Abruzzi Ridge but failed mainly as a result of bad weather. The climbers were unable to get higher than 7260m. L. Greissl, G. Jähr and H. Wünsche (all Ger) remained stormbound for ten days on the ridge. (16)

1974 Permission was granted to Poland to send an expedition to K2 but in the short time available to them they were unable to get a team together.

1975 Another American expedition, ten members, leader J. Whittaker, with Ghulam Rasul as Sirdar, failed in their attempt to climb the mountain by a new route up the North West (W. N. W.) Ridge reconnoitred in 1938. The expedition suffered from the usual porter trouble during the approach up the Baltoro; Base Camp was positioned on the Savoia gl. at 5365m., June 5. Two days later Camp 1 was set up at 5760m. They climbed up to the Savoia Saddle (6600m.) and placed Camp 2 just below the pass on its north side. Several attempts were then made to force a route along the pinnacled and corniced ridge leading up towards the summit. Though several members were ill and the weather was stormy, four climbers pushed on but finally, early July, when at 6700m. they conceded defeat - the ridge from the pass was not a feasible proposition. (17)

1976 Polish expedition, 19 members, leader J. Kurczab, failed in its attempt to climb K2 by its N.E. Ridge, the intended route of Dr. J. Jacot-Guillarmod and V. Wessely in 1902, a route also inspected by a Japanese team in 1975 but judged to be not feasible, a conclusion arrived at too by the American 1938 expedition. No porters were used beyond Base Camp established on the Godwin-Austen gl. June 26. Camp 3 was pitched at 6750m. July 7; beyond it lay a pinnacled and heavily corniced ridge at the end of which Camp 4 was placed July 17. Bad weather intervened and the return traverse from Camp 4 to Camp 3 proved particularly arduous. It was not until August 6 that the climbers, stormbound at Base, were able to resume their attack. They found the tents erected earlier were all flattened and buried beneath the new snow but these difficulties were overcome and Camp 5 was erected at 7700m., August 12. Camp 6, at the foot of the steep rock rib, 8000m. was set up August 13. The following day L. Cichy and J. Holnicki made the first bid for the summit; they got as far as the second ice-wall. August 15 E. Chrobak and W. Wroz made a second attempt; they reached 8400m. before turning back. Because of shortages of food and fuel and because K. Glazek (one of the three, including the doctor, who had remained in support in Camp 5) had been stricken with paralysis, an immediate retreat down the mountain became imperative in spite of blizzard conditions prevailing. Glazek was sufficiently recovered to be able to walk and two days later a rescue team came to their help. A third attempt was mounted but because of bad weather it got no further than Camp 3; the final retreat began September 4. (18)

1976 Japanese Reconnaissance expedition, six members, investigated the Abruzzi Ridge. Base Camp was established at 4875m. July 11 and Camp 3 was placed at 6700m. July 28. The weather then changed for the worse but August 7 three climbers managed to get as high as about 7160m. (19)

1977 SECOND and THIRD ASCENTS: Japanese expedition, 50 members, leader I. Yoshizawa. Base Camp was established on the Godwin-Austen gl. early June. Camp 6 was set up late July, high on the Abruzzi Ridge. Finally August 8 three Japanese reached the summit: S. Shigehiro, T. Shigehiro, T. Takatsuka. The following day a second team of four reached the summit: A. Aman (Pak), M. Hiroshima, M. Onodera and H. Yamamoto.

K2

Principal Source References:

(1) Younghusband The Heart of a Continent

(2) Jacot-Guillarmod Six Mois dans l'Himalaya

(3) Pfannl "Eine Belagerung des Tschogo-Ri (K2) in der Mus-
    taghkette des Hindukusch (8720m.)" DOAVZ Vol. 35 (1904)
    pp. 88-104

(4) Blakeney & Dangar "Oskar Eckenstein, 1859-1921" AJ
    60 pp. 62-79

(5) de Filippi Karakoram & Western Himalaya 1909

(6) Spoleto & Desio La Spedizione Geografica Italiana al
    Karakoram

(7) Shipton Blank on the Map

(8) Bates & others Five Miles High

(9) Wiessner & Cranmer "The Second American Expedition to
    K2" AAJ 1940 pp. 9-19

(10) (Mason) "The American Expedition to K2, 1939" HJ 12
    pp. 123-128 and Note pp. 138-140

(11) Dyhrenfurth To the Third Pole pp. 84-91

(12) Wiessner K2, Tragödien und Sieg am Zweithöchsten Berge
    der Erde

(13) Dornan "An Interview with Fritz Wiessner" Ascent 1969
    pp. 15-19

(14) Houston & Bates K2 The Savage Mountain

(15) Desio Ascent of K2

(16) DOAVZ Vol. 86 (1961) pp. 127-134

(17) Wickwire "The Northwest Ridge of K2" AAJ 1976 pp. 359-
    367

(18) Onyszkiewicz & Chrobak "The Polish K2 Expedition" M
    56 pp. 16-21

(19) AAJ 1977 p. 265

Additional books and articles relevant to the Baltoro Glacier, Gasherbrum I and II, Broad Peak and K2. (The dates in brackets refer to the expeditions written about).

AJ 47 pp. 155-156   Review of the film "Dämon Himalaya"

HJ 10 pp. 86-125   Mason "Karakoram Nomenclature and Conference Report, 1936-1937"

BONATTI   On the Heights (K2 1954)

BRUCE   Himalayan Wanderer

BRUCE   Twenty Years in the Himalaya

CLARK   The Splendid Hills (part)

CONWAY   Autobiography of a Mountain Climber

CONWAY   Mountain Memories

DIEMBERGER   Summits and Secrets (Broad Peak 1957, part)

ECKENSTEIN   The Karakorams & Kashmir

EVANS   The Conways

FEATHERSTONE   An Unexplored Pass

McCORMICK   An Artist in the Himalayas

MARAINI   Karakoram

MASON   The Exploration of the Shaksgam Valley & Aghil Ranges 1926

MIDDLETON   Victorian Lady Travellers (includes Mrs. Bullock Workman)

MILLER   On Top of the World (includes Mrs. Bullock Workman)

PETZOLDT   On Top of the World (K2 1938, part)

ROWELL   In the Throne Room of the Mountain Gods (K2 1975)

SCHLAGINTWEIT   Reisen in Indien u. Hoch Asien, Vol. III

SCHOMBERG   Unknown Karakoram

SEAVER   Francis Younghusband

SHIPTON   Upon that Mountain (part)

SHIPTON   That Untravelled World (part)

STYLES   First on the Summits (K2, 1 chapter)

SYMONDS   The Great Beast (Crowley biography, brief mentions)

ULLAH   Citizen of two Worlds (K2 1953, 1954 - part)

UNSWORTH   Because it is There (includes Bruce, Conway, Eckenstein)

VISSER   Karakoram, Vol. II

ZURBRIGGEN   From the Alps to the Andes (1892)

Bibliography

ABBREVIATIONS USED IN BIBLIOGRAPHY

A. C.	The Alpine Club
b/w	black and white, monochrome
c.	(circa) approximately, about
C. A. S.	(Club Alpin Suisse) Swiss Alpine Club
C. B. C.	Companion Book Club
chap.	chapter
col.	colour, coloured
diag.	diagram
d/p.	double-page
drg.	drawing
ed.	editor
edn.	edition
eng.	engraved, engraving
e/p	end-paper
E. P.	Educational Productions
etc.	(et cetera) and so on
fig.	figure
f/map	folding map (also f/chart, etc.)
frp.	frontispiece
ill.	illustration
imp.	impression
inc.	including
intro.	introduction
J. A. C.	Japanese Alpine Club
J. A. S. B.	Journal of the Asiatic Society of Bengal
litho.	lithograph
mono.	monochrome
n. d.	no date

no.	number
p. , pp.	page, pages
pan.	panorama
p/back	paperback
P. B. C.	Popular Book Club
plt.	plate
pubr.	publisher
Q. B. C.	Quality Book Club
q. v.	(quod vide) which see, (in cross reference)
R. G. S.	Royal Geographical Society
repr.	reprinted
R. S.	Reprint Society
R. U.	Readers Union
revd.	revised
S. A. C.	(Schweizer Alpen-Club) Swiss Alpine Club
sk. map	sketch map
S. O. I.	Survey of India
T. B. C.	Travel Book Club
transl.	translator, translation
vol.	volume

4to.	quarto (size). Publications are otherwise 8vo. (octavo) size, or another specified size.

Some months of the year are contracted, thus: Jan. , Feb. , Mar. . . . .

□

□

A.

GENERAL WORKS   Historical, reference, topographical,
dealing in general with the Himalaya and the 8000m. peaks.
Many include useful bibliographies on their particular subjects.

ANONYMOUS, (ADAMS, W. H. D.)	Mountains and Mountain Climbing
ALPINE CLUB, The	Catalogue of the Centenary Exhibition
BELL, C.	Tibet, Past and Present
BLACK, C. E. D.	A Memoir of the Indian Surveys 1875-1890
BURRARD, S. G.	On the Origin of the Himalaya Mountains
BURRARD, S. G.	Exploration in Tibet and Neighbouring Regions
BURRARD, S. G. & HAYDEN, H. H.	A Sketch of the Geography and Geology of the Himalaya Mountains and Tibet
BURRARD, S. G. & HERON, A. M.	A Sketch of the Geography and Geology of the Himalaya Mountains and Tibet
CLARK, R. W.	A Picture History of Mountaineering
CLARK, R. W.	Men, Myths and Mountains
DOUGLAS, J. S.	Summits of Adventure
DYHRENFURTH, G. O.	To the Third Pole
FANTIN, M.	I Quattordici 8000
FANTIN, M.	Sherpa Himalaya Nepal
GANSSER, A.	Geology of the Himalayas
GURUNG, H.	Annapurna to Dhaulagiri
HAGEN, T.	Nepal, the Kingdom in the Himalayas
HINDLEY, G.	The Roof of the World
HUXLEY, A.	Standard Encyclopaedia of the World's Mountains
INDIA, SURVEY OF	Records, Reports, Technical Papers

IRVING, R. L. G.	A History of British Mountaineering
KAZAMI, T.	The Himalayas: A Journey to Nepal
KEAY, J.	When Men & Mountains Meet
KEENLYSIDE, F. H.	Peaks and Pioneers
KURZ, M.	Die Erschliessung des Himalaya
KURZ, M.	Chronique Himalayenne 1940-1945
KURZ, M.	Chronique Himalayenne II
LEIFER, W.	Himalaya, Mountains of Destiny
LUNN, A.	A Century of Mountaineering 1857-1957
MARKHAM, C.	A Memoir on the Indian Surveys 1871-1878
MASON, K.	Abode of Snow
MILL, H. R.	The Record of the Royal Geographical Society 1830-1930
MILNE, M.	Book of Modern Mountaineering
MORDECAI, D.	The Himalayas
MUMM, A. L.	Five Months in the Himalaya
MUMM, A. L.	The Alpine Club Register
NEWBY, E.	Great Ascents
NICOLSON, N.	The Himalayas
NORTHEY, W. B.	The Land of the Gurkhas
NOYCE, C. W. F. & McMORRIN, I.	World Atlas of Mountaineering
PECCHIO, C. O.	La Lunga Strada Agli 8000
PHILLIMORE, R. H.	The Historical Records of the Survey of India
SCHLAGINTWEIT, H. von	Results of a Scientific Mission to India and High Asia undertaken between the years 1854 and 1858
SCHLAGINTWEIT, H. von	Reisen in Indien und Hochasien
SHIPTON, E. E.	Mountain Conquest
SHIRAKAWA, Y.	The Himalayas
SIRCAR, S. J.	The Himalayan Handbook
SMYTHE, F. S.	British Mountaineers
SPENCER, S.	Mountaineering
STYLES, S.	On Top of the World

STYLES, S.	First on the Summits
STYLES, S.	The Forbidden Frontiers
SWISS FOUNDATION FOR ALPINE RESEARCH	The First Ten Years of the S.F.A.R.
TEMPLE, P.	The World at Their Feet
TICHY, H.	Himalaya
ULLMAN, J. R.	High Conquest
ULLMAN, J. R.	The Age of Mountaineering
UNSWORTH, W.	Encyclopaedia of Mountaineering
VERGHESE, B. G.	Himalayan Endeavour
VIGNE, G. T.	Travels in Kashmir, Ladak, Iskardo, etc.
WARD, F. Kingdon	Modern Exploration
WILSON, A.	Abode of Snow
WOOD, Capt. H.	Report on the Identification and Nomenclature of the Himalayan Peaks, etc.
YAMADA, K. & YAKUSHI, Y.	The Himalaya from the Air
YOSHIZAWA, I.	Mountaineering Maps of the World: Himalayas

□

B.
BIBLIOGRAPHIES AND CATALOGUES

ALPINE CLUB, The	Catalogue of Books in the Alpine Club Library
BÜHLER, Dr. H.	Alpine Bibliographie für das Jahr ...
DREYER, A.	Bücherverzeichnis der Alpenvereins-bücherei
HIMALAYAN CLUB	Classified Catalogue of Books
KAMBARA, T.	Nepal Bibliography
KURZ, M.	Bibliographie de l'Himalaya
MERKL, W.	Himalaja Bibliographie (1801-1933)
SURVEY OF INDIA	Map Catalogues
SWISS ALPINE CLUB	Katalog der Zentralbibliothek des S. A. C.
WOOD, H. B.	Nepal Bibliography

(There are other important and general bibliographies of Nepal, Tibet, etc.)

Bibliographies are also to be found in many books, e.g. G.O. Dyhrenfurth, To the Third Pole and Baltoro, ein Himalaja-Buch; D.W. Freshfield, Round Kangchenjunga; M. Kurz, Chronique Himalayenne; etc.

□

C.
BIOGRAPHICAL

ANG THARKAY	See: NORTON, B. P.	Mémoires d'un Sherpa
BAILEY, F. M.	SWINSON, A.	Beyond the Frontiers
BRUCE, The Hon. C. G.	UNSWORTH, W.	Because It Is There
COLLIE, J. N.	CLARK, R. W.	Six Great Mountaineers
"	UNSWORTH, W.	Because It Is There
CONWAY, W. M.	EVANS, J.	The Conways
"	UNSWORTH, W.	Because It Is There
CROWLEY, A.	SYMONS, J.	The Great Beast
ECKENSTEIN, O.	UNSWORTH, W.	Because It Is There
GYATSO, S.	MULLIK, B. N.	The Sky was his Limit
HOOKER, J. D.	HUXLEY, L.	Life & Letters of Sir Joseph Dalton Hooker
HUNT, H. C. J.	CLARK, R. W.	Six Great Mountaineers
MALLORY, G. L.	CLARK, R. W.	Six Great Mountaineers
"	PYE, D.	George Leigh Mallory
"	ROBERTSON, D.	George Mallory
"	STYLES, S.	Mallory of Everest
"	UNSWORTH, W.	Because It Is There
MAZUCHELLI, E. S.	MILLER, L.	On Top of the World
MUMMERY, A. F.	CLARK, R. W.	Six Great Mountaineers
"	UNSWORTH, W.	Tiger in the Snow
"	UNSWORTH, W.	Because It Is There
NEVE, A.	NEVE, E. F.	A Crusader in Kashmir
SMYTHE, F. S.	UNSWORTH, W.	Because It Is There
TENZING NORGAY	BARNES, M.	After Everest

271

TENZING NORGAY	MALARTIC, Y.	Tenzing of Everest
"	ULLMAN, J.R.	Man of Everest
WILSON, M.	ROBERTS, D.	I'll Climb Mount Everest Alone
WORKMAN,F. Bullock	MIDDLETON,D.	Victorian Lady Travellers
"	MILLER, L.	On Top of the World
YOUNGHUSBAND,F.E.	SEAVER, G.	Francis Younghusband

Biographical records of some of the early British mountaineers are to be found in The Alpine Club Register compiled by A.L. MUMM: included are -

Vol. I   - H.H. Godwin Austen

Vol. II - D.W. Freshfield

Vol. III - W.M. Conway, G. Hastings, A.L. Mumm, A.F. Mummery, V. Sella.

□

D.

JOURNALS Most club journals and national magazines contain material, with illustrations and maps, relevant to the 8000m. peaks. Among the principal ones for reference are -

LES ALPES/DIE ALPEN	Swiss Alpine Club
THE ALPINE JOURNAL	Alpine Club
ALPINISMUS	Alpinismus
AMERICAN ALPINE JOURNAL	American Alpine Club
GEOGRAPHICAL JOURNAL	Royal Geographical Society
HIMALAYAN JOURNAL	Himalayan Club
MOUNTAIN	Mountain Magazine Ltd.
NATIONAL GEOGRAPHIC MAGAZINE	National Geographic Magazine Inc.
SANGAKU	Japanese Alpine Club

Other national magazines published in Western Europe and Japan, not generally referred to in compiling this work, include -

DER BERGSTEIGER	Austrian Alpine Club
DEUTSCHER ALPENVEREIN	German Alpine Club
THE IWA TO YUKI	Yama-To-Keikokusha Co. Ltd.

LA MONTAGNE ET ALPINISME   French Alpine Club

ANNALES G. H. M.   Groupe de Haute Montagne

RIVISTA DELLA MONTAGNA   Italian Alpine Club

□

MAIN BIBLIOGRAPHY

ANONYMOUS (ADAMS, W. H. D.)

●1. Mountains and Mountain Climbing, Records of Adventure and Enterprise Among the Famous Mountains of the World. 1883. 415 pp, 33 eng. plts. 1 chap. on the Himalaya.

AHLUWALIA, Major H. P. S.

●2. Higher than Everest, Memoirs of a Mountaineer. Delhi, 1973. x + 188 pp, 16 pp. ills., map, e/p route diag.

ALPINE CLUB, The

●3. Catalogue of Books in the Library of the Alpine Club. 1880 - 36 pp. New edn. 1888 - 111 pp. New edn. 1899 - 223 pp. (Addenda to the Library were printed in most subsequent numbers of the Alpine Journal, the last in No. 283, Vol. 58, May 1951).

●4. Catalogue of the Exhibition of Photographs from the Mount Everest Expedition 1921. (Intro. by A. E. W. Mason). 24 pp, 8 plts.

●5. Catalogue of the Exhibition of Photographs and Paintings from the Mount Everest Expedition 1922. 16 pp, 8 plts.

●6. Catalogue of Paintings and Photographs from the Mount Everest Expedition 1924. (Intro. by Sir F. Younghusband). 23 pp.

●7. Catalogue of the Centenary Exhibition. 32 pp. (The exhibition was held from Nov. 5th to Dec. 10th, 1957).

●8. The Alpine Journal. First published March 1863 and regularly ever since at varying intervals of time - annually since 1969. The 1977 journal was number 326, Vol. 82.

●9. In addition: four Indexes:
Vols. 1-15 (1863-1891) including the preceding three volumes of Peaks, Passes and Glaciers (no Himalayan material in these); ed. R. A. Wallworth. 1892. viii + 111 pp, f/map.
Vols. 16-38 (1892-1926); ed. R. Bicknell. 1929. iv + 89 pp.
Vols. 39-58 (1927-1952); ed. D. F. O. Dangar. 1954. iv + 87 pp.
Vols. 59-73 (1953-1968); ed. D. F. O. Dangar. 1970. vi + 63 pp.

'A LADY PIONEER' The Indian Alps - See MAZUCHELLI, E. S.

ALPINISMUS

● 10. Magazine first published October 1963; issued monthly
in Germany.

AMERICAN ALPINE CLUB

● 11. American Alpine Journal. First published 1929 and
thence annually. The 1977 journal was Vol. 21, Number 1,
Issue 51.

ANDERSON, J. L. R.

● 12. The Ulysees Factor. The Exploring Instinct in Man.
1970. 352 pp, 8 ills. (chaps. on M. Herzog, E. E. Shipton,
H. W. Tilman).

ANG THARKAY

Mémoires d'un Sherpa - See NORTON, B. P.

ASAMI, M.

Makalu 1970 - See HARA, M.

BARNES, M. (ed.)

Mountain World - See SWISS FOUNDATION FOR ALPINE
RESEARCH

BARNES, M.

● 13. After Everest. 1977. 184 pp, 42 ills. (10 in col.).
As told by Tenzing Norgay).

BATES, R. G. (and Burdsall, R; House, W. P.; Houston, C. S.;
Petzoldt, P.; Streatfeild, Capt. N. R.)

● 14. Five Miles High. (New York, 1939). 1940. 319 pp,
31 ills, e/p maps.

BATES, R. G.

K2 The Savage Mountain - See HOUSTON, C. S.

BAUER, P. (transl. AUSTIN, S.)

● 15. Himalayan Campaign. The German attack on Kangchenjunga. (Kampf un dem Himalaja. Munich, 1934). Oct. 1937,
repr. Nov. 1937. xviii + 174 pp, 82 ills, 3 maps, diag.

● 16. (transl. HALL, E. G.) Himalayan Quest. The German
expeditions to Siniolchum and Nanga Parbat. (Auf Kundfahrt
in Himalaja. Munich, 1937). 1938. 4to, xxv + 150 pp,
96 plts, 4 maps.

● 17. Kangchenjunga Challenge (Kampf um den Himalaja.

Munich, 1952). 1955. 202 pp, 12 ills, e/p maps.

●18. (transl. RICKMERS, R. W.) The Seige of Nanga Parbat, 1856-1953. (Das Ringen um den Nanga Parbat. Munich, 1955). 1956. 211 pp, 23 ills, 2 text maps.

BECHTOLD, F. (transl. TYNDALE, H. E. G.)

●19. Nanga Parbat Adventure, A Himalayan Expedition. (Deutsche am Nanga Parbat. Munich, 1935). 1935, repr. Oct. 1935, Nov. 1935, cheap edn. 1938. 4to, xx + 93 pp, and 80 pp. ills, 3 maps.

BELL, Sir C.

●20. Tibet, Past and Present. 1924, cheap edn. 1927, repr. 1968. xiv +326 pp, 92 ills. (3 in col.), 2 f/maps.

BENSON, C. E.

●21. Mountaineering Ventures. N. d. (c. 1928). 224 pp. 17 plts. (1 chap. on Everest).

BERGE DER WELT - See SWISS FOUNDATION FOR ALPINE RESEARCH

BERTONCELJ, D. and ARKO, B.

● 22. Dhaulagiri, Slovenec y Argentinski Odpravi na Himalajo. Buenos Aires, 1956. 165 pp, 58 ills. Text in Slovenian.

BLACK, C. E. D.

● 23. A Memoir on the Indian Surveys 1875-1890. 1891. 4to, vi + 411 pp, frp. , map. (For preceding Memoirs see MARKHAM, C. R.).

BONATTI, W. (transl. EDWARDS, L. F.)

●24. On the Heights. (Le Mie Montagne. Bologna, 1962). 1964. 248 pp, 20 ills.

BONINGTON, C. J. S.

●25. Annapurna South Face. 1971. x + 334 pp, 60 col. ills, 2 maps, f/route plan. B. C. edn. 1972. Penguin p/back edn. 1973, repr. 1973, 1976. 410 pp, 12 pp.col. ills, 2 maps, e/p route plan.

●26. The Next Horizon. 1973. 304 pp, 75 ills. (6 in col.), 15 maps and diags. Arrow p/back edn. 1976.

●27. Everest, South West Face (with contributions from others). 1973. 347 pp, 56 ills. (b/w and col.), 6 maps and diags, f/route plan. P/back edn. 1975, 2nd imp. 1976, 3rd imp. 1977. 368 pp, 16 pp. ills. (b/w and col.). U. S. A. title: The Ultimate Challenge).

● 28.   Everest The Hard Way. 1976, repr. 1977 (3 times).
239 pp, 85 col. ills, photo-diags., charts, etc. Arrow
p/back edn. 1977. 352 pp, 26 pp. ills. (col. and b/w).

BORDET, P. (and others)

● 29.   Recherches Géologiques dans l'Himalaya du Népal,
Région du Makalu. Paris, 1961. 280 pp, 6 f/pans, 9 plts,
diags, etc. Text in French.

BOUSTEAD, Col. Sir H.

● 30.   The Wind of Morning. 1971. 240 pp, 21 ills, 4 maps
in text.

BRAHAM, T.

● 31.   Himalayan Odyssey. 1974. 243 pp, 32 ills, 14 maps,
e/p map.

BRIDGES, T. C. and Tiltman, H. H.

● 32.   More Heroes of Modern Adventure. 1929, repr. Jan.
1931, Oct. 1931, 1932. vi + 266 pp, 32 ills. (1 chap. on
Everest by Brig. Gen. C. G. Bruce, pp. 3-16, 2 ills.).

BROUGHTON, G. (ed.)

● 33.   Climbing Everest. An anthology selected from the
writings of the climbers themselves. 1960, repr. 1963.
158 pp, 11 ills, 2 diags, e/p maps. Paper covers.

BROWN, J.

● 34.   The Hard Years. 1967, repr. 1967, 1969, 1972, 1974.
256 pp, 43 ills. Penguin p/back edn. 1975. 252 pp, 12 pp.
ills.

BRUCE, Maj. The Hon. C. G.

● 35.   Twenty Years in the Himalaya. 1910. 331 pp, 60 ills,
map.

BRUCE, Brig. Gen. The Hon. C. G.

● 36.   (and others) The Assault on Mount Everest, 1922.
1923, repr. 1924. xii + 340 pp, 36 ills, 2 f/maps.

● 37.   Himalayan Wanderer. 1934. 309 pp, 25 ills.

BRYANT, L. V.

● 38.   New Zealanders and Everest. Wellington, 1953. 26 pp,
inc. 16 pp. ills. and map. Paper covers.

BUCHAN, J.

● 39. The Last Secrets, The Final Mysteries of Exploration.
Sept. 1923, 2nd imp. Nov. 1923. 303 pp, 12 plts, 10 maps.
Edinburgh Library edn. 1925, 2nd imp. 1926. 303 pp, 10
maps. (One chap. on Everest).

BUHL, H. (transl. MERRICK, H.)

● 40. Nanga Parbat Pilgrimage. (Achttausend, Drüber und
Drunter. Munich, 1954). 1956. 360 pp, 19 ills, 3 sk. maps.
(U.S.A. title: Lonely Challenge).

BÜHLER, Dr. H.

● 41. Alpine Bibliographie für das Jahr .... Munich, 1931
and annually until 1938 (the last published in 1942). Index for
years 1931-1938 published 1949. 293 pp. Texts in German.

BURRARD, Col. S. G.

● 42. On the Origin of the Himalaya Mountains. S.O.I. Professional Paper No. 12. Calcutta, 1912. 4to, 26 pp, 2 maps.

● 43. Exploration in Tibet and Neighbouring Regions. Records
of the S.O.I., Vol. 8. Dehra Dun, 1915. 2 vols. Part I
1865-1879. xii + pp. 1-213, frp., 12 charts in pocket.
Part II 1879-1892. pp. 214-411, frp., 12 charts in pocket.

● 44. Mount Everest and its Tibetan Names. A Review of Sir
Sven Hedin's book. S.O.I. Professional Paper No. 26.
Dehra Dun, 1931. 18 pp, 2 maps.

● 45. (with HAYDEN, H.H.) A Sketch of the Geography and
Geology of the Himalaya Mountains and Tibet. Calcutta,
1907-8. Parts I-IV, High Peaks of Asia, Principal Mountain
Ranges of Asia, Rivers of Himalaya and Tibet, Geology of
the Himalaya. 4to, xvi + 308 pp; 53 ills, charts and maps
(many folding).

● 46. (with HERON, A.M.) Geography and Geology of the
Himalayan Mountains and Tibet. (Revd. edn. of previous
entry). New Delhi, 1933. Parts I-IV; xx + 360 + xxxii pp;
52 ills, charts and maps (many folding).

CANDLER, E.

● 47. On the Edge of the World. 1919. vii + 278 pp, 35 ills,
map.

CASSIN, R. and NANGERONI, G.

● 48. Lhotse '75. Italy, 1977. 4to, 238 pp, 159 photos, 23
drawings. Text in Italian.

CHARTWELL PRESS

• 49.   Everest, A Guide to the Climb. N. d. (1953). F/chart
showing ascent and details of climb; route diag. , map.

CHEVALLEY, G.

Forerunners to Everest - See DITTERT, R.

CHINA (Publications from)

• 50.   A Photographic Record of the Mount Jolmo Lungma
Scientific Expedition. 1966-1968. Peking, n. d. 4to, 116 pp,
ills. in col. and b/w, pan.
See also: PEOPLE'S PHYSICAL CULTURE PUBLISHING
HOUSE and FOREIGN LANGUAGES PRESS.

CLARK, R. W.

• 51.   The Splendid Hills. The Life and Photographs of Vittorio Sella, 1859-1943. 1948. 4to, x + 38 pp, 3 portraits
and 83 ills.

• 52.   The Victorian Mountaineers. 1953. 232 pp, 45 ills.

53.   An Eccentric in the Alps. The Story of W. A. B. Coolidge, the great Victorian Mountaineer. 1959. 224 pp, 23 ills,
text drgs.

• 54.   Six Great Mountaineers. 1956. 203 pp, 6 ills. (Collie,
Hunt, Mallory, Mummery, Whymper, G. W. Young).

• 55.   A Picture History of Mountaineering. 1956. 4to, 18 pp.
+ 142 pp. with 352 ills. and accompanying text.

• 56.   Men, Myths & Mountains. The Life and Times of Mountaineering. 1976. 4to, viii + 292 pp, many ills. and maps
within text.

CLEARE, J. S.

• 57.   Mountains. 1975. 256 pp. inc. many ills. (col. and
b/w). (2 chaps. on Everest).

CLYDESDALE, Sq. Ldr. Marquess of

The Pilots' Book of Everest - See DOUGLAS and CLYDES-
DALE.

COBHAM, Sir A.

Tight Corners - See LONGLAND, J. L.

COLLIE, J. N.

• 58.   Climbing on the Himalaya and other Mountain Ranges.
1902. xi + 315 pp, 18 ills, 3 maps.

COLLINS, F. A.

- 59. Mountain Climbing. (Toronto, 1923). 1924. vi + 314 pp, 20 ills. (2 chaps. on Himalaya and Everest).

CONWAY, W. M.

- 60. Climbing and Exploration in the Karakoram-Himalayas. 1894. xxviii + 709 pp, 300 ills. by A. D. McCormick, f/map. Supplementary Volume: 1894. Scientific Reports by various contributors. viii + 127 pp, photogravure frp. of the Author (as included in the Limited Edn.); together with 2 maps 1/126, 720 in end pockets.
Edition de Luxe. 1894. Limited to 150 numbered copies signed by the Author (Vol. I). 2 vols: Vol I - xx + pp. 1-360, frp. portrait of the Author. Vol II - xvi + pp. 361-709, frp. as in standard edn. In the two vols. 300 ills. by A. D. McCor-mick; Vol. I contains 22 duplicate proofs of selected ills. on Japan silk tissue, mounted, and the frp. on Japan silk tissue, mounted, only. Vol. II contains 29 similar duplicate proofs. Without f/map.
Supplementary Volumes: 1894. Scientific Reports by various contributors. viii + 127 pp. (without frp.). N. d. (1894).
3 Maps in separate case. F/map of Kashmir of the standard edn. and 2 maps 1/126, 720.
All 4 items bound by Zaehnsdorf. (Contemporary advertise-ments imply that in the Edition de Luxe the Scientific Reports and the Maps are published together as with the standard Supplementary Volume but the present author has never found them thus).

- 61. Mountain Memories, A Pilgrimage of Romance. 1920. 282 pp, 16 plts.

- 62. The Autobiography of a Mountain Climber. 1933. 246 pp. (Travellers' Library revd. edn. of previous entry).

- 63. (as Lord Conway of Allington) Episodes in a Varied Life. 1932. viii + 276 pp, 39 ills.

CREMER, R. W.

- 64. Mount Everest and Other Poems. 1923. 59 pp. Pri-vately printed.

CUNNINGHAM, Major A.

- 65. Ladak, Physical, Statistical and Historical. 1854. xiv + 485 pp, 31 litho plts. (17 in col.), map.

DENMAN, E.

- 66. Alone to Everest. 1954. 255 pp, 13 ills, 4 maps. T. B. C. edn. 1955. 255 pp, 13 ills, 4 maps.

DESIO, Prof. A. (transl. MOORE, D.)

• 67. The Ascent of K2. (La Conquista del K2, Seconda Cima del Mondo. Milan, 1954). 1955. 239 pp, 22 pp. ills, 3 maps, diags. (U.S.A. title: Victory Over K2, Second Highest Peak in the World).

La Spedizione Geografica Italiana al Karakoram - See SPOLETO, Duca di.

DIAS, J.

• 68. The Everest Adventure. Story of the Second Indian Expedition. Delhi, 1965. 4to, 63 pp. + 46 pp. of col. and b/w ills.

DIEMBERGER, K. (transl. MERRICK, H.)

• 69. Summits and Secrets. (Gipfel und Gefährten - zwischen Null und Achttausend). 1971, repr. 1976. 344 pp, 78 ills, 8 maps and sketches.

DITTERT, R., CHEVALLEY, G. and LAMBERT, R. (transl. BARNES, M.)

• 70. Forerunners to Everest: The Story of the Two Swiss Expeditions of 1952. (Avant-Premières à l'Everest. Paris, 1953). 1954. 256 pp, frp. in col, 24 pp. ills, 9 maps and route diags. P/back edn. 1956. 240 pp, 8 ills, map.

DOIG, D.

High in the Thin Cold Air - See HILLARY, Sir. E.P.

DOLBIER, M.

• 71. Nowhere near Everest. New York, 1955. 56 pp. inc. 35 pp. ills. drawn by V.F. Partch.

DONOUGHUE, C.

• 72. The Ascent of Mount Everest. 1975. Wallet containing 10 reproductions of contemporary documents with accompanying explanatory leaflets. 'Jackdaw' No.128, for children.

DOUGLAS and CLYDESDALE, Sq. Ldr. the Marquess of: M'INTYRE, Flt. Lt. D.F.

• 73. The Pilots' Book of Everest. 1936. xvi + 209 pp, 50 ills, f/map, 2 maps, 3 diags.

DOUGLAS, J.S.

• 74. Summits of Adventure. The Story of Famous Mountain Climbs and Mountain Climbers. 1955. xii + 227 pp, 16 ills.

DREYER, Dr. A.

● 75. Bücherverzeichnis der Alpenvereinsbücherei. Munich, 1927. 1358 entries (no page numbers). Supplement to 1930. Munich, 1939. 716 entries. Texts in German.

DURAND, Col. A.

● 76. The Making of a Frontier. 1899, repr. 1900. xvi + 298 pp, frp. portrait of Author, 35 ills, f/map. Nelson ('pocket') Library edn. N. d. (c. 1910). 383 pp, 8 ills, map.

DYHRENFURTH, G. O.

● 77. (and others) Himalaya: Unsere Expedition 1930. Berlin, 1931. 380 pp, 120 ills, pan, geological profile, map. Text in German.

● 78. (and others) Himalaya-Fahrt. Unsere Expeditions 1930. Zurich, 1942. 292 pp, ills, map. Text in German. (New edn. of previous entry).

● 79. (and others) Dämon Himalaya. Bericht der Internationalen Karakorum-Expedition, 1934. Basel, 1935. viii + 112 pp, 123 ills, 3 sketches; f/pan. with 3 maps. Text in German.

● 80. (and others) Baltoro. Ein Himalaya-Buch. Basel, 1939. 196 pp, 202 ills, 3 drawings. 4 pans, 50 outline tracings, f/map (4 maps together) all in separate folder. Text in German. (Revised version of previous entry).

● 81. Zum Dritten Pol. Die Achttausender der Erde. Munich, 1952. 286 pp, 47 ills, 2 route drgs, 8 sk. maps, 2 profiles, e/p maps. Text in German.

● 82. To the Third Pole. The History of the High Himalaya. 1955. xxx + 234 pp, 47 ills, drg, diags, sk. maps. (A revised edn. with Supplement of the above entry; transl. H. Merrick).

● 83. Der Dritte Pol. Die Achttausender und ihre Trabanten. Munich, 1960. 263 pp, 35 ills, 4 drgs, 16 maps, 6 profiles, tables. (An updated and expanded version of Zum Dritten Pol). Text in German.

● 84. Das Buch vom Nanga Parbat. Die Geschichte seiner Besteigung 1895-1953. Munich, 1954. 200 pp, 13 ills, drgs, 2 maps. Text in German.

● 85. Das Buch vom Kantsch. Die Geschichte seiner Besteigung. Munich, 1955. 190 pp, 18 ills, 2 maps. Text in German.

Chroniques Himalayennes. See SWISS ALPINE CLUB - LES ALPES/DIE ALPEN.

Mount Everest. See HAGEN, T.

ECKENSTEIN, O.

●86.   The Karakorams and Kashmir.   An Account of a Journey. 1896. xvi + 253 pp.

EGGLER, A. (transl. MERRICK, H.)

●87.   The Everest-Lhotse Adventure. (Gipfel Über den Wol-
ken. Lhotse und Everest. Bern, 1956). 1957. 224 pp,
frp. in col, 24 pp. ills, drg, 2 maps.

EISELIN, M. (transl. BOWMAN, E. N.)

●88.   The Ascent of Dhaulagiri. (Erfolg am Dhaulagiri.
Zurich, 1960). 1961. xii + 160 pp, 43 ills. (5 in col.), 2
maps.

ENGEL, C. E.

●89.   They Came to the Hills. 1952. 275 pp, 17 ills.

EVANS, J.

●90.   The Conways. A History of Three Generations. 1966.
308 pp, 9 ills.

EVANS, R. C.

●91.   Eye on Everest. A Sketch book from the Great Everest
Expedition. 1955. 4to, 123 pp. of drgs. and text.

●92.   Kangchenjunga the Untrodden Peak. 1956. xx + 187 pp,
37 ills. (5 in col.), 5 diags, 2 maps. T. B. C. edn. 1962.
xv + 187 pp, 8 pp. ills, 5 diags, 2 maps.

FABREGAS, J. M. Montfort

●93.   Makalu. Expedicion Española Himalaya 1976. Man-
resa, 1976. 4to, 16 pp, 15 ills. Text in Spanish.

FANTIN, M.

●94.   K2 Sogno Vissuto. Bologna, 1958. 4to, 246 pp. ills.
with accompanying text, 2 f/maps, charts. Text in Italian.

●95.   I Quattordici "8000". Bologna, 1964. 4to, 302 pp, 48
ills, 28 pp. drawings mostly showing routes, 25 maps,
charts. Also e/p maps. Text in Italian.

●96.   Sherpa Himalaya Nepal. (Bologna, 1971). New Delhi,
1974. 4to, 116 pp, 118 col. ills, 5 pp. maps.

FAUX, R.

Soldiers on Everest - See FLEMING, J.

FEATHERSTONE, Capt. B. K.

●97.   An Unexplored Pass. A Narrative of a Thousand-Mile
Journey to the Kara-Koram Himalaya. N. d. (1926). 295 pp,
25 ills, f/map.

FELLOWES, Air-Commodore P. F. M. (and BLACKER, L. V. S.;
ETHERTON, Col. P. T.; DOUGLAS and CLYDESDALE, Sq. Ldr.
the Marquess of; BARKAS, G.)

●98.   First Over Everest. The Houston-Mount Everest Expedition. Dec. 1933, repr. 1933 (3 times), 5th imp. 1934.
xix + 279 pp, 51 ills, 6 d/p ills, 4 diags, anaglyph (*)
2 f/maps. 2-coloured viewer in back cover. (The list of
Illustrations is corrected in the reprints; and 'Diagram of
Portion of Everest Flight' facing p. 219 in 1st edn. but omitted
from the List is correctly placed and shown in subsequent
reprs. as facing p. 109).
Cheap edn. 1935. xviii + 279 pp, 28 ills, 5 d/p ills, 1 diag.,
e/p diag. and map.
(*) Anaglyph: a composite picture printed in superimposed
complimentary colours so as to appear in stereoscopic relief
when viewed through suitably coloured viewing spectacles.

FILIPPI, F. de (transl. PORTER, H. T.)

●99.   Karakoram and Western Himalaya 1909. An Account
of the Expedition of H. R. H. Prince Luigi Amedeo of Savoy,
Duke of the Abruzzi. (La Spedizione nel Karakoram e nell'
Imalaia Occidentale, 1909. Bologna, 1911). 1912. 2 vols:
Vol. I 4to, xviii + 470 pp, 2 col. plts. , 32 photogravure plts.
and d/page pans, mostly by V. Sella. Many text ills.
Vol. II 4to folder containing 18 pans, 3 maps, also List of
Ills. and Index. A Limited presentation edn. in full vellum
was issued.

●100.   The Italian Expedition to the Himalaya, Karakoram
and Eastern Turkestan (1913-1914). (Storia della Spedizione
Scientifica Italiana nel Himalaia, Caracorum e Turchestan
Cinese, 1913-1914. Bologna, 1923). 1932. (transl. H. T.
Lowe-Porter). 4to, xvi + 528 pp, 2 col. plts. , over 300 full
page and text ills, 7 pans, 2 Orohydrographical maps in col;
8 pans and 2 maps in end pocket.

FINCH, G. I.

●101.   The Making of a Mountaineer. May 1924, 2nd imp.
1924, 2nd edn. 1926, 3rd edn. 1927. 340 pp, 78 ills, 1 drg.,
2 diags.

●102.   (transl. SCHMIDKUNZ, W.) Der Kampf um den Everest. Leipzig, 1925. 207 pp, 90 plts, 2 maps. (No edn. in
English).

●103.   (as Capt. G. I. Finch) Climbing Mount Everest. Philips

"New Prospect" Readers. 1930, 2nd edn. 1931. 72 pp, 23 text ills, map. Stiff paper covers or limp cloth. (An account under the same title appeared in Boys All-Round Book, 1926, pp. 144-160).

FINSTERWALDER, R. (and RAECHL, W; MISCH, P; BECHTOLD, F.)

●104. Forschung am Nanga Parbat. Deutsche Himalaya-Expedition 1934. Hanover, 1935. vi + 143 pp, frp. in col. of A. von Schlagintweit's pan., 58 ills, 23 diags, map; 2 maps, tracing, list of ills. with captions. Text in German.

FLEMING, J. and FAUX, R.

●105. Soldiers on Everest. 1977. xvi + 239 pp, 24 pp. ills. (4 in col.). maps, diags. Paperback.

FOREIGN LANGUAGES PRESS

●106. Another Ascent of the World's Highest Peak - Qomo-langma. Peking, 1975. 120 pp. many ills. (col. and b/w). Stiff paper covers.

FRANCO, J. (transl. MORIN, D.)

●107. Makalu. (Paris, 1955). 1957. 256 pp, 19 ills, 5 maps.

FRASER, J. B.

●108. Journal of a Tour through part of the Snowy Range of the Himālā Mountains and to the Sources of the Rivers Jumna and Ganges. 1820. 4to, xx + 548 pp, f/map.

●109. In addition: Views of the Himālā Mountains. 1820. Folio folder containing Title page and vignette, 20 hand-coloured lithos after Havell.

FRESHFIELD, D. W.

●110. Round Kangchenjunga. 1903. xvi + 367 pp, 41 ills. mostly by V. Sella, pan, 3 maps.

●111. The Conquest of Mount Everest. 1924. 8 pp. (Published by the Mount Everest Committee of the R. G. S. and the A. C.).

FÜRER-HAIMENDORF, C. von

Mount Everest - See HAGEN, T.

●112. Himalayan Traders. Life in Highland Nepal. 1975. xvi + 316 pp, 44 ills, 7 maps.

GANSSER, A.

●113. Geology of the Himalayas. (Regional Geology Series; ed. L. U. de Sitter). 1964. 4to, xvi + 289 pp, 95 ills, 149 diags; 4 f/plts. (tectonic maps, geological sections, pans.) in end pocket.

The Throne of the Gods - See HEIM, A.

GEOGRAPHICAL MAGAZINE

●114. First published May 1935 (incorporating Wide World Magazine). A monthly magazine issued in London. Dec. 1977 was Vol. 50, No. 3.

●115. Special Number, Oct. 1953, Vol. 26, No. 6, containing (i) "Everest, 1953" pp. 298-308, ills. (col. and b/w), maps. (ii) "After Everest" by E. Shipton, pp. 329-331 with supplement of 8 photogravure plates.

GILL, M.

●116. Mountain Midsummer. Climbing in Four Continents. 1969. 220 pp, 70 ills, 10 maps.

GOSWAMI, S. M.

●117. Everest, Is it Conquered? Calcutta, 1954. xvii + 122 pp, 1 ill.

GRAHAM, W. W.

●118. Climbing the Himalayas. Contained in: From the Equator to the Pole by eminent travellers. N. d. (1885?). pp. 53-131, eng. ills.

GREENE, Dr. R.

●119. Moments of Being. Random Recollections. 1974. x + 180 pp, 25 ills.

GREGORY, A.

●120. The Picture of Everest. 1954. 4to, 96 pp. of text and ills. (43 in col.).

GULATEE, B. L.

●121. Mount Everest, Its Name and Height. S. O. I. Technical Paper No. 4. Dehra Dun, 1950. 9 pp, ill, map.

●122. The Height of Mount Everest, a New Determination (1952-54). S. O. I. Technical Paper No. 8. Dehra Dun, 1954.

GURUNG, H. B.

●123. Annapurna to Dhaulagiri: A Decade of Mountaineering in the Nepal Himalaya 1950-1960. Katmandu, 1968.

x + 122 pp, 17 plts. (6 in col.), f/map. Paper covers.

HAGEN, T.

• 124. Nepal, The Kingdom in the Himalayas. (Nepal. Konig-reich am Himalaya. Bern, 1961, repr. 1970, repr. 1971, 1975). (Bern) 1961, repr. 1970, (London) 1972. 4to, 180 pp, 84 plts. (col. and b/w), 24 sk. maps, f/map (loose).

• 125. (with DYHRENFURTH, G.O.; FÜRER-HAIMENDORF, C. von; SCHNEIDER, E.) Mount Everest. Formation, Population and Exploration of the Everest Region. (Mount Everest - Aufbau, Erforschung und Bevölkerung des Everest-Gebietes. Zurich, 1959). 1963. xiv + 195 pp, 31 ills, 25 diags, e/p map; f/map of Chomolongma-Mount Everest 1/25,000 in end pocket.

HARA, M. and ASAMI, M. (transl. OKAMOTO, N.)

• 126. Makalu 1970, The First Ascent by the South-East Ridge. Nagoya, 1971. Text in Japanese: ii + pp. 15-22. Text in English: vi + pp. 1-14. With 12 ills, 2 maps, route diag. Paper covers. (Privately printed by the Tokai Section of the J.A.C.).

HARPER, S.

• 127. Lady Killer Peak. 1965. 124 pp. Consul p/back edn. 1965. 124 pp.

HARRER, H. (transl. GRAVES, R.)

• 128. Seven Years in Tibet. (Sieben Jahre in Tibet. Mein Leben am Hofe des Dalai-Lama. Vienna, 1952). 1953, 2nd imp. 1953, 3rd imp. 1953, 4th imp. (corrected) 1953, 5th imp. 1953, 6th imp. 1954. xvi + 288 pp, frp. in col, 24 pp. ills, map. R.S. edn. 1955. 320 pp, 26 ills, map. P/back edn. 1956. 267 pp, 16 ills, map. 'Adventure Library' edn. 1957, repr. 1966. 320 pp, 26 ills, map.

HASTON, D.

• 129. In High Places. 1972, 2nd imp. Jan. 1973, 3rd imp. Oct. 1973. (vi) + 168 pp, 8 pp. ills.

HAYDEN, H.H.

A Sketch of the Geography and Geology of the Himalaya Mountains and Tibet - See BURRARD, Col. S.G.

HEDIN, S.

• 130. Mount Everest. Leipzig, 1923. 194 pp, diag, 3 pro-files, 7 maps. 2nd edn. (enlarged) 1926. 205 pp, 8 drgs., 5 diags., 9 maps. Text in German.

HEIM, A. and GANSSER, A. (transl. PAUL, E. and C.)

●131. The Throne of the Gods. An Account of the First Swiss Expedition to the Himalayas. (Thron der Götter. Zurich, 1938). 1939. xxvi + 236 pp, 220 ills, 18 text drgs. and diags., 11 musical items, 2 pans; f/map in end pocket.

HERON, A. M.

Geography and Geology of the Himalayan Mountains and Tibet - See BURRARD, Col. S. G.

HERRLIGKOFFER, K. M. (transl. BROCKETT, E. and EHRENZWEIG, A.)

●132. Nanga Parbat. (Nanga Parbat 1953. Munich, 1954). 1954. 254 pp, 9 col. plts, 44 pp. b/w ills, 6 maps and route diags. (The English edn. contains additional material). Panther p/back edn. 1956. Ills.

HERRLIGKOFFER, K. M.

●133. Deutsche am Broad Peak, 8047m. Durch Pakistan zur Wunderwelt des Himalaya. Munich, 1955. 164 pp, 24 ills, map. Text in German.

●134. Nanga Parbat. Sieben Jahrzehnte Gipfelkampf in Sonnenglut und Eis. Berlin, 1967. 208 pp, 16 pp. ills, f/map. Text in German.

●135. Kampf und Sieg am Nanga Parbat. Die Bezwingung der höchsten Steilwand der Erde. Stuttgart, 1971. 4to, 143 pp, 8 pp. col. ills, 32 pp. b/w ills, diags, e/p maps. Text in German.

HERZOG, M. (transl. MORIN, N. and SMITH, J. Adam)

●136. Annapurna. Conquest of the First 8000-metre Peak (26,493 feet). (Annapurna, Premier 8000. Paris, 1951). Nov. 1952, 2nd imp. Nov. 1952, 3rd and 4th imps. 1952, 5th and 6th imps. 1953. 288 pp; frp, d/p ill, and one ill. in col; 24 b/w ills, 3 route diags, 5 maps, f/map and pan. R. S. edn. 1954. 288 pp, frp. in col., 16 ills, 3 route diags, 5 maps, e/p map. P/back edn. 1952. 283 pp, 27 ills, maps.

HERZOG, M. and ICHAC, M.

●137. Regards Vers l'Annapurna. Paris, 1951. 4to, xvi + 98 pp, 9 col. and 76 b/w ills, f/map (loose). Text in French.

HILLARY, Sir E. P.

●138. High Adventure. 1955. 2nd imp. 1955. 225 pp, frp. in col., 31 ills, text drgs. and maps. C. B. C. edn. 1956. 256 pp, 32 pp. ills, text drgs. and maps. P/back edn. 233 pp, 31 ills, maps.

●139. Nothing Ventured, Nothing Win. 1975, 2nd imp. 1975.
319 pp, 17 col. ills, 42 b/w ills, 17 maps. Coronet p/back
edn. 1977. 381 pp, ills. in col. and b/w, diags, maps.

●140. (with DOIG, D.) High in the Thin Cold Air. 1963.
287 pp, 72 ills, e/p map.

●141. (with LOWE, G.) East of Everest. 1956. 4to, 70 pp.
text; 48 pp. ills.

HIMALAYAN CLUB

●142. The Himalayan Journal. First published 1929 then
every 12 to 18 months. Vol. 34 (1974-1975) was published in
1977.

●143. Index to the Himalayan Journal. Vols. I to XXI. (1929-
1958); compiler D. F. O. Dangar. N. d. iv + 22 pp. Paper
covers.

Contents and Index to the Himalayan Journal - (a Japanese
publication) - See SUWATA, E. and YAKUSHI, Y.

●144. Library. Classified Catalogue of Books with Alpha-
betical Index of Authors 1935. Simla & New Delhi, 1936.
iv + 69 pp. Supplements: 1936, iv + 13 pp. 1937, 4 pp.
1938, 2 pp.

HINDLEY, G.

●145. The Roof of the World. (Aldus Encyclopaedia of Discovery and Exploration). 1971. 4to, 191 pp. text and ills.
(col. and b/w), maps.

HOOKER, Sir J. D.

●146. Himalayan Journals; or, Notes of a Naturalist in Bengal, the Sikkim and Nepal Himalayas, the Khasia Mountains,
etc. 1854. 2 vols. xxiii + 408 pp. and xii + 487 pp; 12 col.
litho ills, 80 woodcuts, 2 f/maps.
1885, new edn. revd. and condensed, 2 vols.
Minerva Library edn. 1 vol. 1891, repr. 1892, 1893. xxxii
+ 574 pp, 13 plts, many text woodcuts, 2 f/maps with views
of mountains.
Repr. 1905 (but not in Minerva Library). xxxii + 574 pp, 13
plts, many text woodcuts, 2 f/maps with views of mountains.
A 2-volume edn. was published in New Delhi, 1969. xvi +
348 pp. and xii + 345 pp; ills.

HORNBEIN, T. F.

●147. Everest: The West Ridge. (San Francisco, 1965).
1966. Large 4to, 202 pp, inc. 84 pp. of col. ills, 2 sk. maps.
1971 - 8vo, 181 pp, 20 col. ills. (Ballantine Books, U. S. A.
published an edn. in 1968: 160 pp. inc. col. ills.).

HOUSTON, C.S. and BATES, R.G.

- **148.** K2, the Savage Mountain. (New York, 1954). 1955.
192 pp, 22 ills, 4 diags. and maps.

HOWARD-BURY, Lt. Col. C.K. (and others)

- **149.** Mount Everest: The Reconnaissance, 1921. 1922.
xii + 356 pp, 33 plts, 3 f/maps. Limited Edition, 200 numbered copies, Large Paper. 1922. xii + 356 pp, 12 photogravure plts, 2 f/pans, 33 plts, 3 f/maps.

HUNT, Brig. Sir H.C.J.

- **150.** The Ascent of Everest. Nov. 1953, 2nd imp. Dec.
1953, 3rd imp. Jan. 1954, 4th imp. Apr. 1954, 5th imp. 1956,
6th imp. 1965, 7th imp. 1974. xx + 300 pp. 8 col. plts, 48
pp. b/w ills, text drgs., 3 maps.
R.U. edn. 1955. xiv + 328 pp, 24 pp. ills. (col. and b/w),
maps.
C.B.C. edn. 1954. 320 pp, 8 col. plts, 48 pp. b/w ills,
drgs, maps.
P/back edn. 1953. 291 pp, 48 ills, map. 1973. xii + 300 pp,
8 pp. ills, text drgs. and maps.
University of London school edns, abridged: Senior - N.d.
(1954). 160 pp, 28 ills, many text drgs. and maps. Junior -
1954. 96 pp, text ills, drgs. and sk. maps. (U.S.A. title:
The Conquest of Everest).

- **151.** Our Everest Adventure. 1954. 4to, 128 pp, of illustrated text, inc. diags. and maps.

HUXLEY, A.

- **152.** Standard Encyclopaedia of the World's Mountains.
1962, repr. 1964. 384 pp, 16 col. plts, many other ills.

HUXLEY, L.

- **153.** Life and Letters of Sir Joseph Hooker. Based on mat-
erials collected and arranged by Lady Hooker. July 1918,
repr. Aug. 1918. 2 vols. Vol. I - xii + 546 pp, 4 plts, f/map.
Vol. II - viii + 570 pp, 5 plts.

ICHAC, M.

Regards Vers l'Annapurna - See HERZOG, M.

INDIA, SURVEY OF

- **154.** Catalogue of Maps Published by the Survey of India.
Calcutta, 1921, 1922, 1928, 1931. Foolscap size. Appendices published.

- **155.** Survey of India Map Catalogue. Calcutta, 1945. Dehra
Dun, 1950, 1970. Foolscap size. Addenda published.

INDIAN MOUNTAINEERING FEDERATION

● 156. Indian Mount Everest Expedition 1965. New Delhi, 1965. 43 pp, ill.

IRVING, R. L. G.

● 157. The Romance of Mountaineering. 1935, repr. 1935, 1946. xiv + 320 pp, 41 ills, 2 drgs, 4 diags, 3 maps.

● 158. Ten Great Mountains. 1940, repr. twice 1940, repr. 1942, 1947. xii + 214 pp, 14 plts, d/p ill, 11 diags.

● 159. A History of British Mountaineering. 1955. xvi + 240 pp, 65 ills.

IZZARD, R.

● 160. The Innocent on Everest. Feb. 1955, 2nd imp. Feb. 1955. 256 pp, 44 ills.

JACKSON, J. A.

● 161. More Than Mountains. 213 pp, frp. in col, 48 ills, 2 drgs, 4 maps.

JACOT-GUILLARMOD, Dr. J.

● 162. Six Mois dans l'Himalaya, le Karakorum et l'Hindu-Kush. Neuchâtel, 1904. 363 pp, 10 photogravure plts, 269 text ills, pan, map, 2 f/maps, f/chart. Text in French.

JAPANESE ALPINE CLUB

● 163. Sangaku. Journal first published 1906 then annually. The 1977 issue was Vol. 72. (Frequently contains a brief résumé of contents in English).

● 164. Manaslu 1952-53. Tokyo, 1954. 4to. Text in Japanese: pp. 1-214. Text in English: pp. 215-218 + 18 pp. col. plts, 124 b/w ills, f/map, 2 maps; text ills, drgs, diags.

● 165. Manaslu 1954-56. Tokyo, 1958. 4to. Text in Japanese: pp. 1-353. Text in English: 15 pp. 36 b/w ills, f/map, 2 f/charts; text ills, drgs, diags, maps.

● 166. Ascent of Everest. Tokyo, 1970. 4to, 144 pp. of text and ills. (col. and b/w). Stiff paper covers. Text in Japanese. (Special number of magazine published by the Mainichi Newspaper).
Everest. Tokyo, 1970. 4to, 202 pp. inc. 132 col. plts, map. Text in Japanese. Summary in English. (Similar to above entry but hard cover edn.).

● 167. The Official Report of the Japanese Mount Everest Expedition 1969-1970. Tokyo, 1972. 2 vols. Vol. I, Mountaineering Account. 444 pp. Vol. II, Scientific Reports. 140 pp. Ills, diags, map, tables. Text in Japanese. Summary in English in Vol. I, pp. 117-128.

KAMBARA, T.

●168. Nepal Bibliography 1959. Tokyo, 1959. 121 pp, and 7 pp. of Errata and Addenda. Paper covers. Text in English. Intro. in Japanese.

KAZAMI, T.

●169. The Himalayas: A Journey to Nepal. (Tokyo, 1968). 1969. 154 pp, 111 col. ills, 2 maps.

KEAY, J.

●170. When Men and Mountains Meet. Explorers of the Western Himalaya 1820-75. 1977. 288 pp, 12 pp. ills, 7 drgs, 4 maps.

KEENLYSIDE, F. H.

●171. Peaks and Pioneers. 1975. 4to, 248 pp, 40 col. plts, 220 b/w ills, 4 maps.

KNIGHT, E. F.

●172. Where Three Empires Meet. A Narrative of Recent Travel in Kashmir, Western Tibet, Gilgit, and the Adjoining Countries. March 1893, repr. June 1893. xvi + 496 pp, 54 ills, map.
New cheap edn. Aug. 1893, repr. Jan. 1894, 1897. xv + 528 pp, 54 ills, map.
Colonial Library edn. Feb. 1894, repr. 1895. xv + 528 pp, 54 ills, map.
Silver Library edn. 1903, repr. 1905. xv + 528 pp, 54 ills, map.

KNOWLTON, E.

●173. The Naked Mountain. New York, 1933. x + 335 pp, 28 ills, map.

KOGAN, C.

White Fury - See LAMBERT, R.

KOHLI, Cdr. M. S.

●174. Nine Atop Everest. Story of the Indian Ascent. New Delhi, 1969. xxviii + 384 pp, 16 pp. col. ills, 40 pp. b/w ills, drgs, maps.

KOTANI, A. and YASUHISA, K. (photographers)

●175. Japan Everest Skiing Expedition. Tokyo, 1970. 4to, 10 + 118 + 16 pp, 90 col. plts. Photo album, text in

Japanese, summary in English.

KRUPARZ, H.

●176. Shisha Pangma. Reisebilder aus Indien, Nepal und Tibet. Vienna, 1954. 190 pp, 8 ills, 2 maps. Text in German.

KURZ, M.

●177. Die Erschliessung des Himalaya. Bern, 1933. 68 pp, 16 plts, 2 f/maps. Paper covers. Text in German. A Limited edn. of 150 numbered copies, contents extracted from Die Alpen Vol. 9 (Nos. 7, 9, 10, 11), 1933.
Liste Chronologique des Expéditions dans l'Himalaya. Supplementary list of 6 pages to accompany the above entry. Text in French.
Chroniques Himalayennes. For subsequent chronicles see SWISS ALPINE CLUB - LES ALPES/DIE ALPEN.

●178. Bibliographie de l'Himalaya. Published in Die Alpen Vol. 12 (pp. 275-280, No. 7 and p. 400, No. 10), 1936.

●179. Chronique Himalayenne. L'âge d'or, 1940-1955. Zurich, 1959. 4to, x + 444 pp, 69 ills, 16 maps, e/p maps. Text in French. Limited edn. of 600 numbered copies.

(as ed.) Berge der Welt - See SWISS FOUNDATION FOR ALPINE RESEARCH.

KYOTO, ACADEMIC ALPINE CLUB OF

●180. The First Ascent of Yalung Kang. Kyoto, 1975. 4to, 171 pp, 72 pp. ills. (8 pp. in col.), diags, f/chart, e/p maps. Text in Japanese.
Together with: Scientific Reports. 4to, 62 pp, 4 pp. col. ills, text ills, diags, f/chart. Paper covers. Text in Japanese.
The First Ascent of Yalung Kang. 4to, 12-page summary in English. Paper covers.

LAMBERT, R. and KOGAN, C. (transl. STYLES, S.)

●181. White Fury. Gaurisankar and Cho Oyu. (Record à l'Himalaya. Paris, 1955). 1956. 176 pp, 21 ills, sk. map.

Forerunners to Everest - See DITTERT, R.

LANDON, P.

●182. Nepal. 1928. 2 vol. Vol. I, xiv + 358 pp, 4 col. plts, 4 collotype plts, text ills, 5 maps and charts. Vol. II, viii + 364 pp, 2 col. plts, 4 collotype plts, text ills, 2 maps.

LEIFER, W. (transl. PRIDEAUX, U.)

●183. Himalaya: Mountains of Destiny. (Weltprobleme am

Himalaya. Goettingen, 1959). 1962. x + 176 pp, 15 ills.

LODGE, Sir Oliver

●184. Why I Believe in Personal Immortality. 1928. viii + 151 pp. An extremely restricted printing (probably not more than 10 copies, at least one of which was destroyed in the bombing of London) of the complete work was issued for selected circulation only. At the request of the Irvine family the eight pages referring to the loss of A. C. Irvine and G. L. Mallory were omitted from the published version.

LONGLAND, J. L. : COBHAM, Sir A. (and others)

●185. Tight Corners. Tales of Adventure on Land, Sea and in the Air. 1940. 265 pp, 7 ills, 2 maps. (Chap. 1, pp. 15-30, is "Caught in an Everest Blizzard" by J. L. Longland). T. B. C. edn. 1941. 265 pp, 7 ills, 2 maps.

LONGSTAFF, Dr. T. G.

●186. This My Voyage. 1950, repr. 1951. (xii) + 324 pp, 28 ills, 15 maps.

Mountaineering - See SPENCER, S. (ed.)

LOWE, W. G.

●187. Because It Is There. 1959. viii + 216 pp, 32 pp. ills, 6 maps, plans. (U. S. A. title: From Everest to the South Pole).

East of Everest - See HILLARY, Sir E. P.

LUNN, A.

●188. A Century of Mountaineering 1857-1957. 1957. 264 pp, 8 col. plts, 16 b/w plts.

MACINTYRE, N.

●189. Attack on Everest. 1936. viii + 172 pp, ill. (First published as a series of articles in The News Chronicle).

MALARTIC, Y. (transl. HELLER, J. B.)

●190. Tenzing of Everest. (La Conquête de l'Everest par le Sherpa Tensing. Paris, 1953). 1954. 285 pp, ills.

MARAINI, F. (transl. CADELL, J.)

●191. Karakoram. The Ascent of Gasherbrum IV. (Gasherbrum 4º. Bari, 1959). 1961. 320 pp, 108 ills. (col. and b/w), over 20 drgs, 4 maps, e/p maps.

MARKHAM, C. R.

●192. A Memoir on the Indian Surveys. 1871. xxv + 303 pp, map.

●193. A Memoir on the Indian Surveys, 1871-1878. 1878. xxix + 481 pp, map. (For third Memoir - See BLACK, C.E.D.).

MARSHALL, H.

●194. Men Against Everest. 1954. 64 pp, 27 ills, 2 maps.

MASON, K.

●195. The Exploration of the Shaksgam and Aghil Ranges 1926. Records of the S. O. I. Vol. 22. Dehra Dun, 1928. xii + 182 pp, 18 ills, map, f/map in end pocket.

●196. Abode of Snow. A History of Himalayan Exploration and Mountaineering. 1955, 2nd imp. 1955. xii + 372 pp, 21 ills, 16 maps and diags.

MATTHEWS, Dr. D. S.

●197. Medicine, My Passport. 1957. 256 pp, 29 ills.

MAZEAUD, P. (transl. SUTTON, G. J.)

●198. Naked Before the Mountain. (Schritte Himmelswärts. Munich, 1968. Montagne pour un Homme. Paris, 1971). 1974. 256 pp, 33 ills.

MAZUCHELLI, E. S. (Nina)

●199. The Indian Alps and How We Crossed Them. 1876. 4to, xiii + 612 pp, 10 chromo-litho col. plts, text drgs, f/map.

McCALLUM, J. D.

●200. Everest Diary. Based on the personal diary of Lute Jerstad. Chicago, 1966. vi + 213 pp, 32 pp. ills, 4 sk. maps.

McCORMICK, A. D.

●201. An Artist in the Himalayas. 1895. xii + 306 pp, over 100 text ills. and plts. drawn by the Author, f/map.

McMORRIN, I.

World Atlas of Mountaineering - See NOYCE, C. W. F.

MEADE, C. F.

●202. Approach to the Hills. 1940, repr. 1941. viii + 266 pp, 16 ills, 2 maps. Albermarle Library edn. 1948. viii + 266 pp, 9 ills, 2 maps.

MERKL, W.

● 203. Himalaja Bibliographie (1801-1933). Munich, 1934.
48 pp. Paper covers. Text in German.

MESSNER, R.

●204. Die Rote Rakete am Nanga Parbat. Munich, 1971.
224 pp, 58 ills. (col. and b/w), maps. Text in German.
(Following legal proceedings the book was withdrawn from
circulation shortly after publication).

●205. Sturm am Manaslu. Munich, 1972. 157 pp, 4 col.
ills, 32 b/w ills, pan, 4 diags, map. Text in German.
Stiff paper covers.

●206. (transl. BOWMAN, E. N. and SALKELD, A.) The
Challenge. (Die Herausforderung. Munich, 1976). 1977.
206 pp, 16 pp. col. ills; text ills, drgs. and maps.

MIDDLETON, D.

●207. Victorian Lady Travellers. 1965, 2nd imp. 1965.
xiii + 182 pp, 12 pp. ills. (inc. F. Bullock Workman).

MILL, Dr. H. R.

● 208. The Record of the Royal Geographical Society, 1830-
1930. 1930. xvi + 288 pp, 35 ills.

MILLER, L.

●209. On Top of the World. Five Women Explorers in Tibet.
1976. 222 pp, 18 text ills, 7 sk. maps, e/p map. (I. Bird
Bishop, A. David-Neel, E. S. Mazuchelli, A. Taylor,
F. Bullock Workman).

MILNE, M.

●210. Book of Modern Mountaineering. 1968. 4to, 304 pp,
many ills. (col. and b/w).

M'INTYRE, Flt. Lt. D. F.

The Pilots' Book of Everest - See DOUGLAS and CLYDES-
DALE, Sq. Ldr. the Marquess of.

MOLLIER, C.

●211. Everest 74. Le Rendez-vous du Ciel. Paris, 1975.
248 pp, 16 pp. col. ills. Text in French.

MONTAGNE DEL MONDO - See SWISS FOUNDATION FOR
MONTAGNES DU MONDE   ALPINE RESEARCH

MONZINO, G.

● 212.   La Spedizione Italiana all'Everest 1973. Bologna,
1976. Large 4to. Italian text - pp. 1-158 + 10. English text
- pp. 159-248. 23 col. plts, 2 b/w plts, pan, text drgs, 2
d/page maps. Bound in full leather, in slip case. For presentation only.

MORDECAI, D.

● 213.   The Himalayas. An Illustrated Summary of the World's
Highest Mountain Ranges. Calcutta, 1966. 60 pp. inc. 57
ills. (col. and b/w) and 1 drg. + pan. with profile on verso.
(Oblong, 30. 8 x 18. 2 cm.).

MORIN, M.

● 214.   Everest: From the First Attempt to Final Victory.
(Everest, du Premier Assaut à la Victoire. Paris, 1953).
1955. 205 pp, 54 ills. (some in col.), 10 maps.

MORRIS, James.

● 215.   Coronation Everest. 1958. 146 pp, 8 plts, 3 text
maps. School edn. 1970. 146 pp, plts, text maps.

MORRIS, John.

● 216.   Hired to Kill. 1960. 272 pp, 3 sk. maps.

MOUNTAIN

● 217.   A magazine first published Jan. 1969 (formerly
Mountain Craft). Generally bi-monthly. Dec. 1977 was
No. 58.

MOUNTAIN WORLD, The - See SWISS FOUNDATION FOR
ALPINE RESEARCH

MULGREW, P.

● 218.   No Place for Men. (Wellington and Sydney, 1964).
1965. 199 pp, 24 pp. ills, text drgs. and diags. e/p map.
(U. S. A. title: I Hold the Heights).

MULLICK, B. N.

● 219.   The Sky Was His Limit. The Life and Climbs of
Sonam Gyatso. Dehra Dun, 1970. 200 pp, 19 ills.

MUMM, A. L.

● 220.   Five Months in the Himalaya. A Record of Mountain
Travel in Garhwal and Kashmir. 1909. xvi + 264 pp, 24
full-plts, 48 ills. mounted in text, 4 pans, 2 maps (on one
plate), 2 f/maps.

• 221. The Alpine Club Register, 1857-1863. 1923. viii + 392 pp. (inc. H.H. Godwin Austen).
The Alpine Club Register, 1864-1876. 1925. viii + 376 pp. (inc. 10 pp. of Addenda and Corrigenda to Vol. I). (Inc. D. W. Freshfield).
The Alpine Club Register, 1877-1890. 1928. viii + 352 pp. (inc. W. M. Conway, G. Hastings, A. L. Mumm, A. F. Mummery, V. Sella).

MUMMERY, A. F.

• 222. My Climbs in the Alps and Caucasus. 1st edn. May, 1895, 2nd imp. June, 1895, 3rd imp. July, 1895; 2nd edn. (4th imp.) July, 1908. (The 2nd and 3rd imps. are shown confusingly as 2nd and 3rd edns.).
1st edn. xii + 360 pp, 2 litho. plts. in col., 9 plts, 21 other ills.
2nd edn. xl + 362 pp, frp. portrait of Author, 2 litho plts. in col., 8 plts, 22 other ills. (The 2nd edn. and the following Nelson and Blackwell edns. contain an Appreciation of the Author by J. A. Hobson and an Introduction with extracts from the Author's last letters sent during the ill-fated Nanga Parbat expedition, by his wife, Mrs. M. Mummery).
Limited edition - 1895. 24 numbered copies signed by the Author. xii + 360 pp, 2 litho plts. in col., 9 plts., 21 other ills. Printed on Japan paper. 8 photogravure plts. printed on Japan silk tissue, mounted. Bound in half-leather.
Nelson ('pocket') Library edn. N. d. (c. 1910). 379 pp, frp. portrait of Author.
Blackwell's Mountaineering Library edn. 1936, repr. 1946. xxiii + 256 pp, 16 plts.

MURRAY, W. H.

• 223. The Story of Everest. April, 1953. x + 193 pp, 24 pp. ills, 14 maps and diags, e/p map.
Revd. May 1953. x + 195 pp, 24 pp. ills, 14 maps and diags, e/p map.
Revd. July 1953, repr. Aug. 1953. x + 198 pp, 24 pp. ills, 14 maps and diags, e/p map.
Revd. Nov. 1953. x + 218 pp, 24 pp. ills, 14 maps and diags, e/p map.
Revd. 1954. x + 230 pp, 24 pp. ills, 14 maps and diags, e/p map.
R. U. edn. July 1953. x + 198 pp, 24 pp. ills, 14 maps and diags, e/p map.

NANGERONI, G.

Lhotse '75 - See CASSIN, R.

NATIONAL GEOGRAPHIC MAGAZINE

• 224. First published in 1888. A monthly magazine issued

in Washington, D. C. , U. S. A. Dec. 1977 was Vol. 152, No. 4.

NEVE, A.

• 225. Thirty Years in Kashmir. 1913. viii + 316 pp, 24 ills, f/map.

NEVE, E. F.

• 226. A Crusader in Kashmir. Being the Life of Dr. Arthur Neve. 1928. 218 pp, 9 plts.

NEWBY, E.

• 227. Great Ascents. A Narrative History of Mountaineering. 1977. 208 pp, 157 ills. in col. and b/w, text maps.

NICOLSON, N.

• 228. The Himalayas. World Wild Life Series. 1975. 4to, 184 pp, over 100 ills, maps in col.

NOEL, Capt. J. B. L.

• 229. Through Tibet to Everest. Oct. 1927, repr. Dec. 1927. 302 pp, 22 ills, 4 drgs. Kingfisher Library edn. 1931. 302 pp, 19 ills, 7 drgs. (U. S. A. title: The Story of Everest).

NORTHEY, Major W. B.

• 230. The Land of the Gurkhas. Or the Himalayan Kingdom of Nepal. N. d. (1937). x + 248 pp, 77 ills, f/map.

NORTON, B. P. (transl. DELGOVE, H.)

• 231. Mémoires d'un Sherpa. Paris, 1954. 210 pp, 10 ills, 5 maps. Text in French. (Apparently no edn. in English). (As told by Ang Tharkey).

NORTON, Lt. Col. E. F. (and others)

• 232. The Fight for Everest: 1924. 1925. xii + 372 pp, 8 col. plts. from paintings by T. H. Somervell, 24 b/w plts, d/p pan, f/map.

NOYCE, C. W. F.

• 233. South Col. One Man's Adventure on the Ascent of Everest, 1953. 1954. xx + 303 pp, 4 col. plts, 48 pp. ills, 16 drgs, 5 maps.
R. S. edn. 1955. xx + 249 pp, frp. in col, 48 pp. ills, 5 text maps.
New Windmill edn. 1956, repr, 1962. 145 pp, 16 pp. ills, 8 drgs, 3 maps.

• 234. The Springs of Adventure. 1958. xii + 240 pp, 21 ills.

- 235. <u>Climbing the Fish's Tail</u>. 1958. xiv + 150 pp, 34 ills, 2 maps.

- 236. (and McMORRIN, I. - eds.) <u>World Atlas of Mountain-eering</u>. 1969. 224 pp, 25 col. ills, many b/w ills. in text, 32 principal and 18 text maps, e/p map.

- 237. (and TAYLOR, R.) <u>Everest Is Climbed</u>. Puffin Picture Book No. 100. For children. 1954. 32 pp, drgs. in col. Paper covers.

ORMEROD, A.

<u>Don Whillans, Portrait of a Mountaineer</u> - See WHILLANS, D. D.

PARAGOT, R. and SEIGNEUR, Y.

- 238. <u>Makalu, Pilier Ouest</u>. Paris, 1972. 264 pp, 35 ills. (col. and b/w), 8 sk. maps. Text in French.

PARES, B.

- 239. <u>Himalayan Honeymoon</u>. 1940. 301 pp, 8 pencil portraits, 16 ills, 60 text drgs, map, route profile.

PECCHIO, C. O.

- 240. <u>La Lunga Strada agli 8000</u>. Ivrea, 1971. 4to, x + 256 pp. ills. in col. and b/w, line drgs, route maps, maps. Text in Italian.

PEOPLES' PHYSICAL CULTURE PUBLISHING HOUSE

- 241. <u>Mountaineering in China</u>. Peking, 1965. 4to, 95 pp. text and ills. (col. and b/w). Stiff paper covers.

PETZOLDT, P.

- 242. <u>On Top of the World</u>. My Adventures with My Mountain-Climbing Husband. (New York, 1953). 1954. 254 pp, 9 ills. P/back edn. 1958.

PHILLIMORE, Col. R. H.

- 243. <u>Historical Records of the Survey of India</u>. Vol. I - 18th Century. Dehra Dun, 1945. 4to, xx + 416 pp, 19 plts, 2 e/p maps.
Vol. II - 1800-1815. Dehra Dun, 1950. 4to, xxviii + 478 pp, 22 plts, 2 e/p maps.
Vol. III - 1815-1830. Dehra Dun, 1954. 4to, xxii + 534 pp, 22 plts, 2 e/p maps.
Vol. IV - 1830-1843. <u>George Everest</u>. Dehra Dun, 1958. 4to, xviii + 493 pp, 21 plts, 2 e/p maps.

PROGRAMME (NOYCE. C. W. F. and others)

• 244. <u>Ascent of Everest 1953.</u> N. d. (Oct. 1953). 4to, 20 pp, ills. (The Programmes were obtainable at the public lectures).

PUSKAS, A. and URBANOVIC, I.

• 245. <u>Nanga Parbat 8125m.</u> Bratislava, 1974. 4to, 182 pp, 145 ills. (col. and b/w), 4 maps. Text in Czechoslovakian. Summaries and captions in English and German.

PYE, D.

• 246. <u>George Leigh Mallory.</u> A Memoir. 1927. x + 184 pp, 6 ills.

RÉBUFFAT, G. (transl. SUTTON, G. J.)

• 247. <u>Mont Blanc to Everest.</u> (Du Mont Blanc à l'Everest. Paris, 1955). 1956. 158 pp, 69 ills and pans. (8 in col.).

RISLEY, H. H. (ed.)

• 248. <u>The Gazetteer of Sikhim.</u> Calcutta 1894. 4to, xxii + 392 pp, 21 ills. diags. (several folded), 2 f/maps in front pocket.

ROBERTS, D.

• 249. <u>I'll Climb Mount Everest Alone.</u> The Story of Maurice Wilson. 1957. 158 pp, 19 ills.

ROBERTSON, D.

• 250. <u>George Mallory.</u> 1969. 279 pp, 21 ills, 5 maps.

ROCH, A.

• 251. <u>Karakoram Himalaya.</u> Sommets de 7000m. Neuchâtel, 1945. 188 pp, frp. in col, 30 pp. ills, 3 maps. Paper covers. Text in French.

• 252. <u>Everest 1952.</u> Geneva, 1952. 4to, 110 pp. inc. 8 pp. col. ills, 86 pp. b/w ills, route diag, map and facsimile letter. Stiff paper covers. Text in French.

RONALDSHAY, Earl of.

• 253. <u>Lands of the Thunderbolt; Sikhim, Chumbi and Bhutan.</u> 1923, repr. 1928, 1931. xviii + 267 pp, 32 plts, f/map.

ROWELL, G.

• 254. <u>In the Throne Room of the Mountain Gods.</u> (San Francisco, 1977). 1977. 4to, x + 326 pp, 48 pp. col. ills, many text ills, d/page map.

ROYAL GEOGRAPHICAL SOCIETY

● 255. Proceedings of the RGS (Old Series). 1855-1878.
Issued at intervals. 22 vols.

● 256. Index published 1920.

● 257. Proceedings of the RGS (New Series). 1879-1892.
Issued monthly. 14 vols.

● 258. Index published 1896.

● 259. Journal of the RGS. 1830-1880. 50 vols. published.

● 260. In addition: 5 Indexes:
1831-1840 published 1844   1861-1870 published 1881
1841-1850 published 1853   1871-1880 published 1884
1851-1860 published 1867

● 261. Geographical Journal. First issued in 1893. Issued
at varying intervals; at present (1977) every 4 months.
1977 completes Vol. 143.

● 262. In addition: 7 Indexes:
1893-1902 published 1906 Vols. 1-20
1903-1912 published 1925 Vols. 21-40
1913-1922 published 1930 Vols. 41-60
1923-1932 published 1935 Vols. 61-80
1933-1942 published 1951 Vols. 81-100
1943-1954 published 1959 Vols. 101-120
1955-1964 published 1971 Vols. 121-130

RUTTLEDGE, H. (and others)

● 263. Everest 1933. Oct. 1934, repr. Oct. 1934, Nov. 1934,
Dec. 1934. xvi + 390 pp, 59 plts. (2 d/page), 3 diags, chart,
3 f/maps.
Popular edn. (Observations omitted). 1936. xix + 291 pp,
17 ills, f/map.
Black Jacket edn. (Observations omitted). 1938, repr. 1940,
1943, 1944, 1947. 254 pp, 10 ills, map. (U.S.A. title:
Attack on Everest).

● 264. Everest: The Unfinished Adventure. 1937. xvi + 296
pp. + 128 pp. of ills. and captions; 13 portrait drgs,
2 f/maps.

SAVOIA-AOSTA, A. di

La Spedizione Geografica Italiana al Karakoram - See
SPOLETO, Duke of.

SAYRE, W. W.

● 265. Four Against Everest. (New York, 1964). 1964.
251 pp, 12 pp. ills, 2 maps.

SCHLAGINTWEIT, H. , A. and R. von

● **266.** Results of a Scientific Mission to India and High Asia undertaken between the years 1854 and 1858. Leipzig and London. Four 4to vols. and a folio Atlas.
Vol. I - Astronomical determinations of latitudes and longitudes and magnetic observations during scientific mission to India and High Asia, preceded by general introductory reports. 1861. xii + 494 pp.
Vol. II - General hypsometry of India, the Himalaya, and Western Tibet with sections across the chains of the Karakorum and Kuen-luen. 1862. xvi + 549 pp.
Vol. III - Route book of the western parts of the Himalaya, Tibet and Central Asia; and geographical glossary from the languages of India and Tibet. 1863. xx + 293 pp.
Vol. IV - Meteorology of India and analysis of the physical conditions of India, the Himalaya, Western Tibet and Turkistan. 1866. xvi + 586 pp.

● **267.** Atlas of Panoramas and Views, with geographical, physical, and geological maps. Title sheet imprint: Leipzig and London, 1861. Folio, 4 parts, comprising:
(i) 34 col. litho ills. on 27 sheets, "Panoramas and Views of India and High Asia".
(ii) 7 tinted panoramic profiles, "Hypsometry, Vol. II".
(iii) 3 col. magnetic survey maps, "Physical Maps nos. 1-3", and "Geographical Map no. 1" also col.
(iv) 3 uncol. maps, "Geographical Maps nos. 2-4 (3 and 4 on one sheet). Published 1863.
(v) One meteorological chart, "Met. Maps and Tables no. 1" (actually a sheet of tables).
(vi) 3 col. meteorological maps, "Met. Maps and Tables nos. 2-4".

SCHLAGINTWEIT, H. von

● **268.** Reisen in Indien und Hochasien. Reultate der Wissenschaftlichen Mission von Hermann, Adolph und Robert von Schlagintweit, ausgeführt in den Jahren 1854-8. Jena. Four 8vo. vols. Texts in German.
Vol. I - Indien. 1869. 586 pp, 2 maps.
Vol. II - Hochasien I. Der Himalaya von Bhutan bis Kashmir. 1871. xviii + 476 pp, 7 ills, 3 tables.
Vol. III - Hochasien II. Tibet, zwischen der Himalaya und der Karakorum-Kette. 1872. 366 pp, 3 profiles, map.
Vol. IV - Hochasien III. Ostturkestan und Umgebungen. 1879. 323 pp, ill.

SCHMUCK, M.

● **269.** Broad Peak, 8047m. Meine Bergfahrten mit Hermann Buhl. Stuttgart, 1958. 359 pp, 60 ills, 5 maps. Text in German.

SCHOMBERG, Col. R. C. F.

● 270.   Unknown Karakoram.   1936.   244 pp, 24 ills, f/map
in end pocket.

SCHNEIDER, E.

Mount Everest - See HAGEN, T.

SCOTT, Col. R. L.

● 271.   God is My Co-Pilot.   1st edn.   Charles Scribner & Sons
(U. S. A.) 1943.   2nd edn.   Blue Ribbon Books (U. S. A.) 1944.
vii + 277 pp, 13 ills, e/p map.

SEAVER, G.

● 272.   Francis Younghusband.   Explorer and Mystic.   1952.
xii + 392 pp, 13 ills, 5 maps.

SÉGOGNE, H. de (and others)

● 273.   Himalayan Assault.   The French Himalayan Expedition
1936.   (L'Expédition Française à l'Himalaya 1936.   Paris,
1938).   1938.   xvi + 204 pp, 59 ills, 4 maps and diags.

SEIGNEUR, Y.

Makalu, Pilier Ouest - See PARAGOT, R.

SERRAILLIER, I.

● 274.   Everest Climbed.   1955.   vii + 60 pp, drgs.   (Anthology
and poem on 1953 ascent).

SHERWILL, Capt. W. S.

● 275.   Notes upon a Tour in the Sikhim Himalayah Mountains,
undertaken for the purpose of ascertaining the geological
formation of Kunchinjinga and of the perpetually snow-covered
peaks in its vicinity.   Calcutta, 1852.   Privately printed.
60 pp, 1 eng. plt.
Reprinted in JASB 22 (1854) as Notes of a Journey in the
Sikhim Himalayas.   pp. 540-611.

● 276.   In addition: Notes upon some Atmospherical Pheno-
mena.   (1852).   9 pp, f/diag. in col. of a Fog Bow.

SHIPTON, E. E.

● 277.   Blank on the Map.   1938.   xv + 299 pp, 51 ills, drgs.
in text, 2 maps, f/map (1/250,000 by M. Spender).

● 278.   Upon That Mountain.   Oct. 1943, repr. Dec. 1943,
1944, 1947.   222 pp, 31 ills, 4 maps.
R. U. edn. 1945.   248 pp, 31 ills, 4 maps.   P/back edn. 1943.
216 pp, 30 ills, 4 maps.   (With additional note on the

Abominable Snowman).

● 279. The Mount Everest Reconnaissance Expedition 1951.
1952, repr. 1953. 4to, 60 pp. text, 68 pp. ills, diags, panoramic views, 2 maps.

● 280. The True Book about Everest. 1955. 142 pp, text
drgs. (For children). (U. S. A. title: Men against Everest).

● 281. Mountain Conquest. (New York, 1966). 1967. 153 pp,
many text ills. (col. and b/w).

● 282. That Untravelled World. 1969, repr. 1970. New edn.
1977. 286 pp, 27 ills, text drgs, 6 maps, 2 e/p maps.
T. B. C. edn. 1970. 286 pp, text drgs, 6 maps.

SHIRAKAWA, Y.

● 283. The Himalayas. 1974. Large 4to, 300 pp, 284 col.
ills.

SINGH, Brig. G.

● 284. Lure of Everest. Story of the first Indian Expedition.
Delhi, 1961. xiv + 212 pp, frp. in col, 40 pp. ills, text
drgs, 2 maps, e/p map.

SIRCAR, S. J.

● 285. The Himalayan Handbook. Annotated Index of the
named Peaks over 6095m. (19,998') of Afghanistan and the
Indian Subcontinent. Calcutta, 1974. Vol. I - 36 pp. Paper
covers. (Vol. II in preparation).

SMITH, B. W.

● 286. True Stories of Modern Explorers. 1930, repr. 1931,
1934; revd. 1936. 221 pp, 8 ills. (One chap. on Mt. Everest).

● 287. Pioneers of Mountaineering. N. d. (1933). 224 pp,
8 plts, 8 text drgs. and maps. (2 chaps. on the Himalaya).

SMYTHE, F. S.

● 288. The Kangchenjunga Adventure. 1930, repr. Jan. 1931.
Cheap edn. Oct. 1931, 4th imp. Jan. 1932, 5th imp. Nov.
1932, 6th imp. 1934. 464 pp, 48 ills, 8 text maps.
Black Jacket edn. 1946. 344 pp, 8 ills, 8 text maps.

● 289. The Spirit of the Hills. 1935, 2nd edn. 1945. xiv +
308 pp, 36 ills.
Black Jacket edn. Oct. 1937, Dec. 1937, 1938, 1940, 1941,
1944. 320 pp, 1 drg.
Uniform edn. Feb. 1946. xii + 308 pp, 36 ills.
Popular edn. Aug. 1946, 2nd imp. 1950.

● 290. Camp Six. An Account of the 1933 Mount Everest

Expedition. 1937. xii + 308 pp, 36 ills.
Black Jacket edn. 1938, repr. 1941. 316 pp, d/p route diag.
New edn. 1956. x + 219 pp, 8 ills.

● 291. The Mountain Scene. 1937, repr. 1938. 4to, xii +
154 pp. inc. 78 ills. from photographs by the Author.

● 292. The Adventures of a Mountaineer. 1940, 2nd imp.
1941, 3rd imp. 1945. viii + 228 pp, 17 ills.

● 293. The Mountain Vision. 1941, repr. 1942. xii + 308 pp,
16 ills. Uniform edn. 1946, repr. 1950. viii + 240 pp, 16
ills.

● 294. British Mountaineers. 1942, 2nd edn. 1946 (corrected).
48 pp, 9 col. ills, 24 b/w ills. and drgs. It was included
complete (but 6 col. ills, 22 b/w) in the collection entitled:
British Adventure (W. J. Turner, ed.). 1957. 324 pp, 48
col. ills, 120 b/w ills. and drgs. in text.

SNAITH, S.

● 295. At Grips with Everest. 1937. xvi + 240 pp, 8 ills.
2nd edn. 1945. xi + 164 pp, 8 ills.

SOMERVELL, T. H.

● 296. After Everest. The Experiences of a Mountaineer
and Medical Missionary. 1936. xiv + 340 pp, frp. in col,
21 ills, map, e/p map.
Black Jacket edn. 1938, repr. 1939, 1947, 1950. 320 pp,
2 drgs, 2 maps.

SPENCER, S. (ed.) (and many contributors)

● 297. Mountaineering. Lonsdale Library. N. d. (1934 and
later). 384 pp, 102 ills, 9 f/maps. (7 chaps. on Himalaya
by Dr. T. G. Longstaff).

SPOLETO, S. A. R. AIMONE DI SAVOIA-AOSTA, Duca di,
and DESIO, A.

● 298. La Spedizione Geografica Italiana al Karakoram (1929).
Storia del viaggio e risultati geografici. Rome/Milan, 1936.
xxiv + 568 pp. and Appendix li pp. Portraits, ills; pans,
4 maps (1/250,000 and 1/75,000 on 3 sheets) in separate
case. Published also as a Special Edition, limited to 50
copies. Milan, 1936. Text in Italian.

STEELE, Dr. P.

● 299. Doctor on Everest. 1972. 222 pp, 32 ills, 16 text
drgs, 3 maps. R. U. edn. 1973. 222 pp, 32 ills, 16 text
drgs, 3 maps.

STOBART, T.

● 300.   Adventurer's Eye. 1958. 256 pp, 41 pp. ills.
P. B. C. edn. 1960. 248 pp, 23 ills.

STURM, G.

● 301.   Erfolg am Kantsch. 8438m. Munich, 1975. 142 pp,
8 pp. col. ills, 8 pp. b/w ills, pan, text diags. and maps.
Stiff paper covers. Text in German.

STYLES, S.

●302.   The Moated Mountain. 1955. 255 pp, frp. in col,
32 ills, 13 text drgs, e/p panoramic diag.

●303.   Mallory of Everest. 1967. 157 pp, 17 ills, maps.

304.   On Top of the World. 1967. 4to, xx + 278 pp, 32 col.
plts, 158 b/w ills, 12 diags. and sk. maps.

●305.   First on the Summits. 1970. 157 pp, 15 ills, diags.
Q. B. C. 1971. 157 pp, 15 ills, diags.

●306.   The Forbidden Frontiers. The Survey of India from
1765 to 1949. 1970. 160 pp, 12 ills, 2 maps.

SUNDAY TIMES MAGAZINE

● 307.   Interview of Capt. J. B. L. Noel by P. Gillman.
28th September, 1969. 4to, pp. 32-43, ills. in col.

●308.   Man at the Top. The Everest Assault in Colour.
26th October, 1975. 4to, pp. 44-51, ills. in col.

SUWATA, E. and YAKUSHI, Y.

● 309.   Contents and Index to the Himalayan Journal. Vol. 1
(1929) to Vol. 21 (1958). Kyoto, 1960. 72 pp. Privately
printed. Limited to 200 copies. Paper covers.

SWINSON, A.

● 310.   Beyond the Frontiers. The Biography of Colonel
F. M. Bailey, Explorer and Special Agent. 1971. xiv + 246
pp, 17 ills, 4 maps.

SWISS ALPINE CLUB

●311.   Katalog der Zentralbibliothek des S. A. C. Zurich,
1925. 140 pp. Paper covers.
1st Supplement, 1926-1930. 1931. 58 pp. Paper covers.
2nd Supplement, 1931-1941. 1943. 104 pp. Paper covers.
3rd Supplement, 1942-1951. 1954. 114 pp. Paper covers.
4th Supplement, 1952-1963. 1965. 98 pp. Paper covers.

●312.   Les Alpes/Le Alpi/Las Alps/Die Alpen. Bern, first
issued Jan. 1925. It amalgamated the Annuaire du C. A. S.

(Jahrbuch), L'Écho des Alpes (of Geneva) and Alpina (of Bern).
Originally issued monthly, at present quarterly with a month-
ly Bulletin. 4to magazine. Articles published variously in
French, Italian, Romanche and German.
Chroniques Himalayennes by M. KURZ: (Subsequent to Die
Erschliessung des Himalaya by the same author, q. v.).
Published in the following numbers -
L'Himalaya en 1934. 1934/11
Himalaya 1933-1935. 1936/1
Expéditions mineures dans l'Himalaya entre 1932 et 1935.
1936/6
Himalaya 1935-1936. 1937/11 and 12
Himalaya 1937. 1939/1
Himalaya 1936 (Supplement). 1939/2
Himalaya 1938. Vol. 16 (pp. 27-35 and 67-76), 1940
The chronicles for 1939-1946, 1947-1950 and 1951-1952 were
continued in Berge der Welt, Montagnes du Monde and The
Mountain World, 1947 to 1954. The 'Golden Age 1940-1955'
was consolidated and continued in his two volumes Chronique
Himalayenne (q. v.).
Chroniques Himalayennes by G. O. DYHRENFURTH: Pub-
lished in the following numbers -

1958.	1959/4	1967.	1968/4
1959-1961.	1962/2	1968.	1969/4
1962.	1963/4	1969.	1970/4
1963.	1965/1	1970.	1971/4
1964.	1965/3	1971.	1972/4
1965.	1966/4	1972.	1973/4
1966.	1967/4		

SWISS FOUNDATION FOR ALPINE RESEARCH

313. Berge der Welt. Zurich, 1946 and annually until 1955,
then biannually until 1968/69. Chief Editor: M. KURZ (until
1960/61). 17 vols. in German. Index inc. in the final vol.
also published separately.

●314. Montagnes du Monde. 1946, 1947, 1953, 1954. Texts
in French.

●315. Montagne del Mondo. 1954, 1955. Texts in Italian.

●316. Mountain World. Editor: M. BARNES. 1953 - 220 pp,
64 ills. (inc. f/ills), pan, 12 maps and sketches.

●317. 1954 - 224 pp, 64 ills. (inc. f/ills), 12 maps and
sketches.

●318. 1955 - 222 pp, 64 ills. (inc. f/ills), 12 maps and
sketches.

●319. 1956/57 - 200 pp, 68 ills. (inc. f/ills), 8 text ills,
11 maps and sketches.

●320. 1958/59 - 208 pp, 52 ills. (inc. f/ills), drg, 5 maps
and sketches, f/map.

- 321.   1960/61 - (viii) + 262 pp, 63 pp. ills, 9 maps and sketches, f/map; separate f/map of Mt. McKinley, 1/50,000 in end pocket.

- 322.   1962/63 - (viii) + 240 pp, 64 pp. ills. (12 in col.). 4 text ills, 7 maps.

- 323.   1964/65 - (x) + 216 pp, frp. in col, 62 pp. ills, 6 text ills, 2 pp. facsimile letter, 10 maps and sketches; separate f/map of Panta, Cordillera Vilcabamba, 1/25,000, in end pocket.

- 324.   1966/67 - (x) + 228 pp, frp. in col, 56 pp. ills, text ill, 12 maps and sketches.

- 325.   1968/69 - 188 pp, frp. in col, 52 pp. ills. (4 in col.). 12 maps and sketches.

- 326.   The First Ten Years of the Swiss Foundation for Alpine Research. Zurich, 1951. 4to, 48 pp, col. plt, 12 ills, f/map. Limited edn. of 750 copies.

- 327.   Everest: The Swiss Everest Expeditions. (Everest: ein Bilderbericht. Zurich, 1953). 1954. 4to, 37 pp. text, 8 col. plts, 144 pp. ills, 2 diags, 3 route drgs, 2 maps.

SYMONDS, J.

- 328.   The Great Beast. Life and Magick of Aleister Crowley. 1971. ix + 413 pp, ill. (A revised and expanded version of The Confessions of Aleister Crowley, 1969).

TAYLOR, P.

- 329.   Coopers Creek to Langtang II. 1965. 239 pp, 38 ills, e/p maps.

TAYLOR, R.

Everest is Climbed - See NOYCE, C. W. F.

TEMPLE, P.

- 330.   The World at Their Feet. The Story of New Zealand Mountaineers in the Great Ranges of the World. Christchurch, 1969. 250 pp, 4 col. plts, 54 ills, 4 maps.

TENZING NORGAY

Man of Everest - See ULLMAN, J. R.
After Everest - See BARNES, M.

TERRAY, L. (transl. SUTTON, G. J.)

- 331.   Conquistadors of the Useless. (Les Conquérants de l'Inutile. Paris, 1961). Sept. 1963, repr. Sept. 1963, 1975. 351 pp, 84 pp. ills, 8 maps and diags.

TICHY, H. (transl. CREIGHTON, B.)

● 332. Cho Oyu, By Favour of the Gods. (Cho Oyu; Gnade der Götter. Vienna, 1955). 1957. 196 pp, 4 col. plts, 32 pp. ills, 2 sk. maps.

● 333. (transl. RICKETT, R. and STREATFIELD, D.) Himalaya. (Vienna, 1968). 1971. 4to, 176 pp, 61 col. plts, 84 ills, drgs.

TILMAN, H. W.

● 334. When Men and Mountains Meet. 1946, repr. 1947. x + 232 pp, 54 ills, 6 maps.

● 335. Mount Everest, 1938. March, 1948, repr. Nov. 1948. x + 160 pp, 49 ills, 2 maps, 2 diags.

● 336. Nepal Himalaya. 1952. xii + 272 pp, 62 ills, 7 maps.

TIMES, The

● 337. Mount Everest Reconnaissance Expedition 1951. Dec. 1951. Newspaper tabloid, 16 pp, ills. A Special Supplement, text mainly by E. E. Shipton.

● 338. Challenge to Mount Everest. 5th May, 1953. Newspaper tabloid, 8 pp, ills. A Special Supplement, text mainly by H. C. J. Hunt and E. E. Shipton.

● 339. The First Ascent of Everest. July, 1953. Newspaper tabloid, 32 pp, ills, maps. A Special Supplement.

● 340. Everest 1953. Royal 4to, 24 pp, ills, maps. A Special Colour Supplement.

TOMBAZI, N. A.

● 341. Account of a Photographic Expedition to the Southern Glaciers of Kangchenjunga in the Sikkim Himalaya. Bombay, 1925. 4to, x + 73 pp. + 4 Appendices and Index, 62 mounted photographs, f/map in end pocket. Privately printed. Limited edn. of 150 numbered copies.

TUCKER, J. W.

● 342. Kanchenjunga. 1955. 224 pp, 40 ills, 2 diags, 4 maps. P/back edn. 1957. 224 pp, 8 pp. ills, 2 diags, 4 maps.

ULLMAN, J. R.

● 343. High Conquest. The Story of Mountaineering. (Philadelphia, 1941). 1942. 320 pp, 16 pp. ills, 5 maps and sketches. T. B. C. edn. 1943. 300 pp, 16 pp. ills, 5 maps and sketches.

● 344. Kingdom of Adventure: Everest. A Chronicle of

Man's Assault on the Earth's Highest Mountain. (New York, 1947). 1948. 320 pp, 29 ills, 4 maps and diags.

● 345. Man of Everest. The Autobiography of Tenzing.
(Tiger of the Snows. New York, 1955). 1955, repr. 1955.
320 pp, 49 ills. (4 in col), 4 maps and sketches.
R.S. edn. 1956. 320 pp, 29 ills, 4 maps and sketches.
New and revd. edn. 1975. 320 pp, 32 pp. ills, text diags.

● 346. The Age of Mountaineering. 1956. 384 pp, 27 ills,
4 maps and sketches. (An extended version of High Conquest,
with one chap. on British Mountains by W.H. Murray).

● 347. (and others) Americans on Everest. (Philadelphia,
1964). 1965. xxiv + 430 pp, 56 pp. ills. (8 pp. in col.),
1 drg, map, e/p panoramic drg. of route.

UNSWORTH, W.

● 348. Tiger in the Snow. The Life and Adventures of A.F.
Mummery. 1967. 126 pp, 11 ills, 5 maps and diags.

● 349. Because It Is There. Famous Mountaineers 1840-1940.
1968, repr. 1973. 144 pp, 12 ills. (Bruce, Collie, Conway,
Eckenstein, Mallory, Mummery, Smythe).

● 350. Encyclopaedia of Mountaineering. 1975. 272 pp, 34
ills, text drgs. and maps. Penguin p/back edn. 1977 (Revised). 398 pp, 16 pp. ills, text diags. and maps.

URBANOVIC, I.

Nanga Parbat 8125m. - See PUSKAS, A.

VERGHESE, B.G. (ed.)

● 351. Himalayan Endeavour. The Story of Indian Mountaineering. Bombay, 1962. x + 155 pp, 26 ills. (6 in col.),
4 maps, f/map. Paper covers.

VIGNE, G.T.

● 352. Travels in Kashmir, Ladak, Iskardo and the Countries
adjoining the Mountain Course of the Indus, and the Himalaya,
north of the Punjab. 1842, 2nd edn. 1844. 2 vols. Vol.I,
xlviii + 406 pp, 5 plts, 6 vignettes in text, f/map in end
pocket. Vol.II, x + 464 pp, 7 plts, 6 vignettes in text.

VISSER, Ph. C.

● 353. Wissenschaftliche Ergebnisse der Niederländischen
Expeditionen in den Karakorum und die Angrenzenden Gebiete
in den Jahren 1922, 1925, 1929/30 und 1935. Vol.II (of III)
- Glaziologie. Leipzig and Leiden, 1938. 4to, viii + 216 pp,
98 ills. and diags, 3 f/maps, 1 table. Text in German.

WADDELL, Major L. A.

● 354. Among the Himalayas. 1899, 2nd edn. 1900, 3rd edn. (1909?). xvi + 452 pp, 105 plts., text ills. and maps, f/map.

WARD, F. Kingdon.

● 355. Modern Exploration. 1945. 124 pp, 2 text figs. R. U. edn. 1946. 124 pp, 2 text fig. (one chap. on Mountain-eering).

WARD, Dr. M. P.

● 356. In This Short Span. 1972. 304 pp, 40 ills, 5 maps. Penguin p/back edn. 1973, repr. 1976.

WHILLANS, D. D. and ORMEROD, A.

● 357. Don Whillans, Portrait of a Mountaineer. 1971. 266 pp, 25 ills. Penguin p/back edn. 1973, repr. 1976. 302 pp, 12 pp. ills.

WHITE, J. C.

● 358. Sikhim and Bhutan: Twenty-One Years on the North-east Frontier, 1887-1908. 1909. xx + 332 pp, 40 ills, map. (Reprinted in India, 1971).

WIBBERLEY, L.

● 359. The Epics of Everest. 1955. 218 pp, many text drgs.

WIESSNER, F.

● 360. K2, Tragödie und Sieg am Zweithöchsten Berg der Erde. Munich, 1955. 56 pp, 16 ills, 2 maps. Text in Ger-man.

WILLIAMS, C.

● 361. Women on the Rope. The Feminine Share in Mountain Adventure. 1973. 240 pp, 8 pp. ills.

WILSON, A.

● 362. The Abode of Snow. Observations on a Journey from Chinese Tibet to the Indian Caucasus, through the Upper Valleys of the Himálaya. 1875. xxvi + 476 pp, frp. in col, title page vignette, f/map. 2nd edn. 1876. xxviii + 436 pp, frp. in col, title page vig-nette, f/map.

WINTERHALTER, K.

● 363. Der Letzte Achttausender. Dhaulagiri-Expedition 1958. Bern, 1959. 199 pp, 15 col. ills, 23 b/w ills, text diag. and maps. Text in German.

WOLF, J.

● 364. Reka Jmenem Cervankya. Prague, 1975. 80 ills, text sketches, maps. Text in Czechoslovakian.

WOLLASTON, M.

● 365. Letters and Diaries of A. F. R. Wollaston. 1933. xvi + 261 pp, 4 portrait photos.

WOOD, Capt. H.

● 366. Report on the Identification and Nomenclature of the Himalayan Peaks, as seen from Katmandu, Nepal. Calcutta, 1904. 4to, iv + 8 + iv pp, 3 profiles, map.

WOOD, H. B.

● 367. Nepal Bibliography. Eugene, 1959. 108 pp.

WORKMAN, F. Bullock and W. H.

● 368. In the Ice-World of Himalaya. Among the Peaks and Passes of Ladakh, Nubra, Suru and Baltistan. 1900, 2nd edn. 1901. xvi + 204 pp, 67 ills, 3 f/maps.

● 369. Two Summers in the Ice-Wilds of the Eastern Karakoram. The Exploration of Nineteen Hundred Square Miles of Mountain and Glacier. 1917. 296 pp, 141 ills. and pans, 3 f/maps.

● 370. Illustrations of Ice-Wilds of Eastern Karakoram. N. d. (1917?). 133 plts, 3 maps (1 folding), no text. Issued by the Authors for presentation. (The illustrations appear to be all from the previous entry).

YAKUSHI, Y.

● 371. Catalogue of the Himalayan Literature. Kyoto, 1972. 343 pp. The Foreword and the details of books in Japanese are given in Japanese and in English; the rest of the bibliography is in English. Privately printed, limited to 500 copies.

The Himalaya from the Air - See YAMADA, K.

YAMADA, K. and YAKUSHI, Y.

● 372. The Himalaya from the Air. Tokyo, 1975. 4to, 112 pp. inc. 35 d/p views in b/w and 1 d/page pull-out in col.; f/map in end pocket. Text in Japanese, names of peaks shown also in roman script.

YASUHISA, K.

Japan Everest Skiing Expedition - See KOTANI, A.

YODA, T.

- 373. Ascent of Manaslu in Photographs 1952-1956. Tokyo, 1956. 4to, 9 pp. Japanese text, 5 pp. English text, 8 pp. col. ills, 96 pp. b/w ills, map.

YOSHIZAWA, I. (Chief Ed.)

- 374. Mountaineering Maps of the World: Himalayas.
Vol. 1 - Bhutan, Sikkim, Nepal, Garhwal, Kashmir. Tokyo, 1977. 4to, 328 pp. inc. 196 pp. text, 32 pp. col. ills, 52 pp. maps. Text in Japanese. Place names on maps shown in roman script.
Vol. 2 - Karakoram, Hindu Kush. (due for publication mid-1978).

YOUNGHUSBAND, Sir F. E.

- 375. The Heart of a Continent: A Narrative of Travels in Manchuria, across the Gobi Desert, through the Himalayas, the Pamirs, and Chitral, 1884-1894. 1896, 2nd edn. 1896, 3rd edn. 1896. xx + 410 pp, 18 plts, 4 f/maps.
Revd. edn. 1937. xvi + 246 pp, 4 ills, map.

- 376. The Epic of Mount Everest. Oct. 1926, repr. Nov. 1926, April 1927, Aug. 1927, 1928, 1929, 1931, 1934, 1942. (In smaller format) 1943, repr. 1945. 320 pp, 16 plts, 2 maps.
E. P. reprint 1974. 320 pp, 16 plts, 2 maps.
School edn. 'English Literature' Series. 1931, 1932, 1933 (twice), 1935, 1938, 1939, 1946, 1951, 1953 (twice), 1954. 320 pp, 8 ills, 2 maps.

- 377. Everest: The Challenge. 1st edn. March, 1936. 2nd edn. April, 1936 with Chap. 5 rewritten to include an account of the 1936 expedition. x + 244 pp, 16 plts, 3 maps, e/p map.
Nelson 'Travel and Adventure' Series. 1941, repr. 1942, 1943, 1944, 1945 (twice), 1948, 1949. x + 244 pp, 16 plts, 3 maps, e/p map.

ZURBRIGGEN, M.

- 378. From the Alps to the Andes, Being the Autobiography of a Mountain Guide. 1899. xvi + 269 pp, 30 plts, 25 text ills.

□

SUPPLEMENT

for the end of 1977 and for 1978.

The presentation of the Chronicles and of the Bibliography is identical to that of the original book (pages 53 to 314).

Some chronicles of expeditions that took place during the latter half of 1977 and about which little information was available when the original book was written have been enlarged upon and are included in this Supplement. Books listed under 'Additional Books' and followed by 'PSR' are recommended Principal Source References to the expeditions indicated and already chronicled in the original book.

The Addenda to the Bibliography that had appeared on pages 315 and 316 of the original book has been interpolated into the Supplementary Bibliography. Some books published in 1979 have been included as they refer to expeditions of 1977 and 1978 or earlier.

Louis Baume

KANGCHENJUNGA

1977 THIRD ASCENT: Indian Army expedition, 16 members, leader Col. N. Kumar; the plan was to climb the mountain by the N.E. Spur (1929 and 1931 route). They left Lachen March 7 and having passed through Sikkim established Base Camp near the Green Lake (Zemu gl.) at 4940m. on March 24; an Advance Base Camp was sited a little higher up. Camp 3 was placed on the crest of the N.E. Spur at 6300m., April 30; Camp 6 was erected just short of the Spur's highest point, at 7630m., May 24. The steep snow slope where the N.E. Spur joins the North Ridge, which had rebuffed the Germans in 1931, provided no great obstacle on this occasion. On May 30 Camp 7 was pitched on the main ridge at 7990m. The following day Major P. Chand and Sherpa Naik Nima Dorje, using oxygen, reached the summit – or rather, within 2m. of it. A second pair was prevented from repeating the ascent by bad weather. Havildar Sukhvinder Singh had been killed early in April in a fall below Camp 2. (39)

1978 Kangchenjunga South, FIRST ASCENT, and Kangchenjunga Central, FIRST ASCENT: A Polish expedition of 25 members (including J.A. Brady and C. Tobin from America) and six Sherpas, leader P. Mlotecki (leader of the first ascent of Kangbachen, 7902m., in 1974), had received permission to climb the South Summit (8476m.) by its south flank. They left Dharan Bazar March 14 but were delayed during the approach march by bad weather; it was not until April 10 that the first two tents were pitched on the site of their Base Camp. Finding the prospects of an attempt by the South Ridge somewhat daunting, they followed the original British 1955 route as far as the Great Shelf, where Camp 3 was erected, April 27, at 7150m. Camp 4 at 7600m. was pitched at the base of the summit's west wall and from there, May 19, E. Chrobak and W. Wroz succeeded in reaching the top; the following day they descended to Camp 3. In Camp 3 was the second team: W. Branski, Z. Heinrich and K. Olech. These three changed plan and decided to attempt the Central Summit, which the Spanish climbers had failed to reach on May 18 (see below).

From the abandoned Spanish camp at the base of the long snow couloir (about 7550m.), the three Polish climbers managed to reach the highest of the Central Summit's three 'tops' – 8496m. – on May 22. Three days later M. Janas and M. Malatynski climbed the 8430m. 'top'. As the Poles did not have permission to climb the Central Summit, the Nepalese Government imposed a ban on them. (40)

1978 A Spanish expedition, leader J. Piera, had received permission to attempt Yalung Kang. Because of various delays this climb was abandoned and the Spanish decided instead to make a bid for Kangchenjunga Central, still unclimbed. They followed the route established by the Poles as far as the Great Shelf where they erected a Camp 3 at about 7200m. Camp 4 (referred to above) was placed at the foot of the long snow couloir leading up to the ridge between the Main and Central summits. From there, May 18, N.S. Comerna and Sherpa Phuri tried to reach the summit. It seems that the climbers were unable to find the way and reports vary as to exactly where or how high they reached; certainly not the Central Summit itself. As the Spanish did not have permission for this mountain, the Nepalese Government imposed a ban on them also. (41) (42)

Principal Source References:

(39) Kumar Kanchenjunga. First Ascent from the North East Spur
(40) Brniak "Five Treasuries of Great Snow" AAJ 1979 pp. 36-44
(41) ....Yalung Kang (Kangchenjunga West) 8438m.
(42) AAJ 1979 p. 259

MAKALU

1977 A mainly American expedition of 15 members (nine climbers and six in support), leader J. Long (Am). The intention was to climb the mountain by its West Face, using neither oxygen nor Sherpas. Base Camp was finally established at 5610m. on April 1. Two more camps were set up: Camp 1 at 6400m., April 10, and Camp 2 at 6700m., April 18. But by then seven members (of whom five were climbers) had departed, chiefly because of illness. Rockfalls, the destruction of Camp 1 on May 10 by fire, and the wrecking of Camp 2 on May 11 by an avalanche, all added to the difficulties; the attempt was called off on May 12. High point reached - by B. Krivic and M. Malezic (both Yugoslavian) - was 6950m. (23)

1978 11th, 12th, 13th ASCENTS: An International expedition - three Germans, one Austrian, three Nepalese and one Swiss - of whom Dr. H. Warth (Ger) was leader, K. Diemberger (Aus), deputy-leader and Sirdar Ang Chappal. They planned to traverse the mountain: ascending the S.E. Ridge and descending by the French 1955 route. They took no high-altitude Sherpas. Another innovation was that all food was purchased in Nepal in order to help the country's economy. They left Tumlingtar March 11 and established Base Camp twenty days later, having lost some time because of heavy snow on the way. Conditions on the south side being particularly bad, the idea of making a traverse was abandoned and the ascent and descent were made more or less along the original French route. Camp 3 was erected on the Makalu La, April 24, and Camp 4 at 7950m., April 30. Three teams in all reached the summit. May 1: Warth and Ang Chappal, the latter without using oxygen; May 10: H. von Känel (Sw), Dr. K. Landvogt (Ger) and Nga Temba (Nep); May 21: Diemberger and Nawang Tenzing (Nep). (24) (25)

1978 Polish expedition, 19 members (including two women), leader J. Kurczab. They set off to attempt the climb by the N.W. Ridge. Four camps were established, the highest at 7400m. But the climbers were unable to continue much beyond there and the attempt

was called off October 27. Earlier, October 6, one
member was killed by an avalanche - apparently while
asleep in his tent at Base Camp. (26)

Principal Source References:

(23) AAJ 1978 pp. 591-593
(24) Warth Makalu. Expedition in die Stille
(25) AAJ 1979 pp. 259-261
(26) AAJ 1979 p. 261

Additional Books:

GÁLFY & KRISSAK Makalu (1973, 1976) PSR

MOUNT EVEREST

1977 New Zealand expedition, eight members including A.
Twomey (Can), leader K. Woodford. The plan was to
climb the mountain via the South Col without employ-
ing Sherpas. Base Camp was established at 5400m.,
March 10, and Camp 5 - the highest - was placed at
7565m. on the Lhotse Face, April 25. M. Brown and
M. Mahoney reached the South Col on May 14. The
undertaking, however, proved to be beyond the power
of the expedition and no further progress was
made. (57)

1977 22nd ASCENT: South Korean expedition, 16 members,
leader Young-do Kim. Base Camp was established at
5400m., August 9. Camp 4 was sited on the South Col
September 7, and Camp 5 was placed at 8500m. the day
after. Two climbers, Sang-ryel Park and Sherpa Ang
Phurba (the climbing Sirdar), made a bid for the
summit September 9 (10?) but had to turn back when
about 100m. from the top owing to oxygen failure;
they were obliged to bivouac on their return at

8610m. A second attempt was made by Sang-don Ko and Sherpa Pemba Norbu on September 15; they did reach the top. The weather throughout the expedition was the best ever; the same could not be said for the oxygen equipment selected. There is some uncertainty as to whether any other South Koreans managed to reach Camp 4. (There are a few minor differences of detail between the report received by the author from Korea and that received by the AAC from Katmandu). (58)

1978 23rd, 24th, 25th, 26th ASCENTS: An Austrian expedition, ten climbing members, leader W. Nairz, with Ang Phu as Sirdar. Attached to the expedition as a separate team were P. Habeler and R. Messner. It had been agreed that these two would make the first attempt on the summit and this by the South Ridge and without oxygen; the others would follow the customary S.E. Ridge using oxygen. Base Camp was established at the foot of the ice-fall during March. Camp 2, the Advanced Base Camp, was set up April 2, and Camp 4 on the South Col, April 17. During these operations the independent pair noticed that the South Ridge was covered with bare ice so they decided to make their attempt from the South Col. They left Base Camp, to which they had returned, April 21 and reached Camp 3, on the Lhotse Face at 7200m., two days later. The following day Habeler, afflicted with food poisoning, was obliged to return to Camp 2. Messner, with two Sherpas, pushed on to the South Col from where they were forced to retreat after two nights of atrocious weather. The initial attempt having failed, H. Bergmann, W. Nairz and R. Schauer of the main party, with Ang Phu, set off for the summit. A Camp 5 was placed on the S.E. Ridge at 8500m. and on May 3 the four climbers reached the top through deep snow. The following day H. Hagner, Dr. R. Margreiter and H. Schell left Camp 3 for their attempt but they were obliged to turn back on account of the very deep snow. On May 7 Habeler and Messner, accompanied by the cameraman E. Jones (Br), climbed back to the South Col. The following day Habeler and Messner reached the summit without using oxygen, taking nine hours for the round trip. It was

Messner's fourth 8000m. peak. Dr. O. Ölz and R. Karl (Ger) gained the summit May 11 and F. Oppurg got to the top on his own on May 14; Oppurg and J. Knoll had reached Camp 5 the previous day and had stayed there overnight but as Knoll's oxygen equipment was found to be faulty on the morrow he was forced to renounce the climb. Sherpa Dawa Nuru was killed in the ice-fall on April 18. (59) (60)

1978 27th, 28th, 29th, 30th ASCENTS: A joint Franco-German expedition. A French party of 14 members (including K. Diemberger from Austria), leader P. Mazeaud, and a German party of 16 members (including R. Allenbach from Switzerland and the Polish woman climber W. Rutkiewicz), leader Dr. K.M. Herrligkoffer, left their respective countries in the first days of August. Base Camp was established about four weeks later. Four further camps were set up, the last on the South Col, October 13, by H. Engl (Ger), Diemberger, H. Hillmaier (Ger), J. Mack (Ger) and Mazeaud. The following day Engl (without oxygen), Hillmaier and Mack reached the summit. On the morrow, October 15, Diemberger (aged 46 and this his fourth 8000m. summit) and Mazeaud (aged 49) reached the top in eleven hours; the other team to climb the mountain that day was J. Afanassieff and Dr. N. Jaeger (both French). Then, October 16, six more climbers gained the summit: Allenbach, S. Hupfauer (Ger), W. Klimek (Ger), Rutkiewicz, Sherpa Ang Dorje and Sherpa Mingma. Finally two more trod the summit snows on October 17: B. Kullmann and G. Ritter (both German). It was a successful and harmonious international expedition. (61) (62)

Principal Source References:

(57) AAJ 1978 pp. 588-589
(58) AAJ 1978 pp. 589-590
(59) Nairz Gipfelsieg am Everest
(60) Messner Everest. Expedition to the Ultimate
(61) Mazeaud Everest '78
(62) AAJ 1979 p. 264

Additional Books:

AHLUWALIA Faces of Everest
BHANJA Lure of the Himalaya
CARR The Irvine Diaries
CLARKE Everest
FAUX Everest. Goddess of the Wind
HABELER Everest. Impossible Adventure (1978)
HUNT Life is Meeting (part, 1953)
JAPANESE ALPINE CLUB Mount Everest 1975 PSR
MIURA & PERLMAN The Man who Skied down Everest
   (1970) PSR
MOON Man of Everest (part)
RAWLING The Great Plateau (1904) PSR
RIDGEWAY The Boldest Dream (Americans 1976)
   PSR
ROBERTSON, M Mountain Panorama (part, 1953)
TOKYO ROCK CLIMBING CLUB Everest (1973) PSR

LHOTSE

1977 2nd, 3rd, 4th ASCENTS: German expedition, 13
members (including two Austrian and one Swiss),
leader Dr. G. Schmatz, succeeded in climbing this
peak for the first time in 21 years. Their line of
ascent was up the N.W. Face from the West Cwm. Base
Camp was established at 5300m. during mid-March;
five more camps were set up, the last at 7800m. on
the Lhotse Face. After a first abortive attempt at
the end of April, the expedition withdrew to Base;
bad weather set in. Finally three teams (10 climbers in all) achieved success. May 8 - H. von Känel
(Sw), Dr. H. Warth and Sirdar Urkien; May 9 - G.
Sturm, P. Vogler and F. Zintl; May 11 - M. Dacher
(without oxygen), M. Lutz, and Peter and Sebastian
Wörgötter (from Austria). Unfortunately Lutz fell
and was killed while descending from the summit.
(17)

1978 Swiss expedition, eight members, leader J. Fauchère, made a winter attempt to climb the mountain by its S.E. Face. Base Camp was established close to Island Peak at 5300m., November 16. They had to contend with very strong winds and finally abandoned the attempt on November 24, having reached barely higher than 6300m. (18)

Principal Source References:

(17) AAJ 1978 p. 590
(18) AAJ 1979 p. 267

MANASLU

1977 A German expedition, nine members (including one Nepali), leader G. Lenser. They attempted the ascent by the N.E. (East?) Ridge. Base Camp was established March 28; three more camps were set up, the third at 6400m. on April 24. H. Baumann, W. Heitzmann and M. Holz reached 6800m. but turned back on May 3. Heavy snow fell and the expedition was abandoned. (19)
(T. Braham "Chronique Himalayenne" Les Alpes 1978/2 p.77 describes this as a new route; he refers to the 1956 Japanese expedition as having been up the East Face and the 1976 (sic) Spanish expedition as having been along the East Ridge. Both in fact were on the northern route, and the German route - if indeed the East Ridge - had been attempted by the Japanese 1974 expedition).

1977 A small French expedition of five members, leader J. Fréhel, hoped to climb the East Face in alpine style without oxygen. However, conditions were severe and the attempt was abandoned after one pair - P. Béghin and T. Leroy, who both suffered severe frost-bite - had reached about 7560m., October 26. (20) (21) (M & A refers to East Face; AAJ and M 59 refer to East Ridge. Probably neither but the usual northern route).

1978 American expedition, nine climbing members and two base-camp managers, with five Sherpas, was led by G. Porzak. Manaslu was not immune from the heavy snows of early 1978; in fact it appears to have had more than its fair share. Base Camp was established March 10 at 3840m., presumably near the tongue of the Manaslu glacier. The attempt was made by the usual northern route and by March 23 Camp 2 had been placed at the Naike Col (5600m.). Then the stormy weather worsened; during the expedition's first month on the mountain six metres of snow fell. Eventually, April 10, Camp 3 was sited at 6490m. and, April 15, Camp 4 from which the summit assault was due to be made was sited at 7315m. Heavy snow storms raged again, forcing the climbers back to Camp 2 which on April 22 was buried by a snowfall of over two metres. A week later the party was obliged to concede defeat, thwarted by atrocious conditions and the resulting dangers of avalanches. (22)

1978 Japanese expedition, leader S. Shimizu, made an attempt on the mountain by the original 1953 route. The summit pair, Y. Kato and Shimizu, managed to reach 8000m., October 7, but could make no further progress because of the deep snow. As with the previous expedition, the provisioning of the higher camps became extremely difficult. (23) (AAJ refers to the route as the North East Face).

Principal Source References:

(19) AAJ 1978 p. 593
(20) M & A 1978/1 p. 277
(21) AAJ 1978 pp. 593-594
(22) AAJ 1979 pp. 271-272
(23) AAJ 1979 p. 272

ANNAPURNA

1977 FOURTH ASCENT: Dutch expedition, 11 members, X.
Verrijn-Stuart, leader, and Mingma Tenzing as
Sirdar. Base Camp was established September 6 on
the north side of the mountain in the customary
area, at 4400m.; Camp 2 was pitched three days later
at about 5800m., a little lower than previous Camp 2
sites. From there the route ascended by the shorter
and sharp ridge leading up towards the snow slopes
to the east of the "Sickle" (this ridge lies between
the N.E. Buttress attempted by the British Army
expedition in 1970 and the original French route of
1950). Fixed ropes were installed along this
ridge as far as Camp 3, near the top, at 6500m.,
September 30. Two more camps were placed above Camp
3, the higher one at 7350m., October 11. Oxygen was
used in Camp 5 and the following day when M. van
Rijswick and Mingma Tenzing set off for the summit,
which they failed to reach by about 200m. However,
the following day, October 13, van Rijswick made a
second attempt, accompanied by Sherpa Sonam, and
this time the pair was successful; oxygen was used.
(14) (15)

1978 Austrian expedition, leader E. Gritzner. They
approached the mountain early in the year from the
north, following the original French 1950 route.
Unfortunately between Camps 2 and 3 – a notorious
avalanche zone – an avalanche struck and R. Widmann
was injured. The attempt was abandoned May 8.
(16)

1978 FIFTH ASCENT: American women's expedition, ten
members, two film crew and a Base Camp manageress,
with Lobsang Tsering as Sirdar and five other
high-altitude Sherpas, was under the leadership of
A. Blum. They also planned to climb the mountain
from the north. They left Pokhara August 15 and
reached Base Camp, 4360m., eleven days later. From
Camp 2, positioned on the site of the Dutch camp
September 3, possible routes were inspected;
it was decided finally to follow the Dutch route up
the short sharp ridge. Hampered by snow and avalanches, they did not erect Camp 3 (at 6400m.) until

September 27. Camps 4 and 5, at 7000m. and 7300m. respectively, followed on October 8 and 13. On October 15 V. Komarkova, I. Miller and the two Sherpas Chewang Rinzing and Mingma Tsering (the latter without oxygen) reached the summit. They returned the same evening to Camp 5 and on the following day went down to Camp 4 where they met up with the second summit team of A. Onyszkiewicz (from Poland), V. Watson and Sherpa Wangel. October 17 the two women left for Camp 5 but Wangel, feeling ill, descended to Camp 3 with the others. Just before dark the summit pair was seen within about 100m. of the Camp 5 tents. There was no further contact from the climbers and no movement was observed around Camp 5 during the next two days. Finally, October 20, Sherpas Lakpa and Mingma were persuaded to go up from Camp 2 to Camp 5 to investigate. Just below Camp 4 they saw Onyszkiewicz's body; a taut rope led from her into a near-by crevasse. The two climbers must have slipped and fallen just after they were seen approaching Camp 5 three days previously. The expedition was called off. (Alison Onyszkiewicz, née Chadwick, was the English-born wife of the Polish mountaineer Janusz Onyszkiewicz; in 1975 they had climbed together on Gasherbrum II and III, g.v.). (17)

Principal Source References:

(14) Verrijn-Stuart Annapurna, 8091 meter
(15) AAJ 1978 p. 594
(16) AAJ 1979 p. 274
(17) Komarkova "American Women's Himalayan Expedition, Annapurna I" AAJ 1979 pp. 46-58. And AAJ 1979 pp. 345-348

Additional Books:

KENNETT The Story of Annapurna (1950)
MACHETTO & BINI Annapurna (1973) PSR
PONS Annapurna Este (1974) PSR

DHAULAGIRI

1977 A small team of mixed nationalities, four climbers, leader R. Messner, attempted to find a route up the South Face. They approached the mountain by the Thula Khola and established Base Camp at 4000m., April 2. The planned route just left of the centre of the main face proved too dangerous so the team switched its attention to the south pillar on the extreme left (west) of the face. This also was too risky and the attempt was abandoned in late April. The conclusion arrived at was that the entire South Face was fraught with difficulty and danger. (18)

1977 A Japanese expedition of 13 members, leader Dr. Y. Tsukazaki, came to the mountain during the post-monsoon period to make an attempt by the S.W. Buttress of the West Face. Base Camp was established August 15 at 3500m. in the Mayangdi Khola. Camps 1 (4120m.) and 2 (4950m.) were sited on the glacier flowing down from the South Ridge and Camps 3, 4 and 5, on the Buttress itself — Camp 5 being erected at a height of 6200m., October 3. On October 9 a high point of 6550m. was attained but the attempt was given up. (19)

1978 6th and 7th ASCENTS: Japanese expedition, 12 members, leader T. Amamiya, set off to attempt the mountain again by the 1975 route i.e., by the South Buttress rising on the extreme left of the South Face (it has been described variously as the South Ridge, South Pillar and South West Pillar). Base Camp, above the Mayangdi Khola, was established at 3660m. on March 11. Five more camps were set up: Camp 1 at 5180m. March 28; Camp 2 at 5790m. April 7; Camp 3 (above a 250m. section of rock of great severity and requiring the use of wire ladders) at 6500m. April 17; Camp 4 at 7150m. May 3; and Camp 5 (atop another section of near vertical rock) at 7500m. May 5. From this high camp T. Kobayashi and T. Shigeno reached the summit on May 10. The next day Y. Kato, S. Shimuzu, H. Yoshino and Sherpa Ang Kami (the last using no oxygen) repeated the ascent. Earlier, April 21, K. Naganuma had died of exhaustion while climbing above Camp 3. (20)

1978 French expedition, ten members, leader Y. Pollet-Villard, left Pokhara September 8 with the intention of climbing the South Buttress (but not the same route as the one followed by the Japanese in the spring). The French South Buttress lies further west of what is elsewhere referred to as the Japanese South Ridge route, and rises from the snow plateau forming the South Col – now quoted as 5200m. Base Camp was established September 22 at 3600m. Camp 1 was placed on the South Col three days later. Camp 2 was erected at 5650m. on October 2, and Camp 3 at 6100m., October 9. The site of Camp 4 (at 6900m.?) was reached October 20 but the camp was not set up until October 25. Between then and November 4 several attempts were made to surmount the steep and extremely difficult face above but to no avail. The onset of severe winter conditions resulted in the attempt being called off. The high point reached was about 7200m. (A picture showing the Japanese 1978 and the French routes appeared in M 65 p. 11). (21) (22)

1978 8th and 9th ASCENTS: Japanese expedition, 18 members, under the leadership of S. Tanaka. Their intention was to climb the mountain by its S.E. Ridge, attempted unsuccessfully by the Americans in 1973. Disaster struck between Camps 4 and 5 when an avalanche overwhelmed and killed three climbers on September 23; they were H. Akuzawa, Y. Fukasawa and K. Kobayashi. Despite this rebuff the assault continued and six climbers in two teams gained the summit on October 19 and on October 20. This praiseworthy achievement was marred by a second fatal accident that befell the climbing leader, K. Kogure, who fell while ferrying loads and died suspended from the fixed ropes between Camps 4 and 5. (23)

Principal Source References:

(18) Messner The Big Walls
(19) AAJ 1978 pp. 596-598
(20) AAJ 1979 pp. 276-277
(21) Les Alpes/Die Alpen, Bulletin Mensuel No. 2,

February 1979, pp. 27-28
(22) AAJ 1979 p. 277
(23) AAJ 1979 p. 278

Additional Books:

HARVARD & THOMPSON   Mountain of Storms   (1969,
    1973) PSR

NANGA PARBAT

1977 Two Americans, A.D. Wadeford and another, carried out a reconnaissance from the north. They are reported as having reached about 7000m. (36)

1977 An American expedition, 14 members including the three leaders G. Bogel, D. Bunce and J.M. Hellman. They left Rawalpindi June 30 by bus, Balikot July 1 by jeep, and Jal the following day on foot. Base Camp was established at the head of the Diamir valley on July 9. Four days later Camp 1 was set up below the Diamir Face. A pulley system was constructed on Depot Rock at 5880m. to haul up sleds loaded with 50 kg.; this saved a great deal of time and effort. Camp 2 was sited on a ridge above at 6580m. by July 31. That evening a 30m. high slab of rock broke away from the face and fell onto the tent at Depot Rock in which were Bogel and R. Broughton. Both were killed instantly, and equipment was scattered over the mountainside. The expedition was abandoned. (37)

1977 A Polish expedition, 14 members including A. Precht and W. Sucher both from Austria, leader A. Zyzak, arrived at their Base Camp in the Rupal valley (3575m.) September 1 with the intention of climbing

the Rupal Face, using neither porters nor oxygen.
They followed the 'Kinshofer Way' and placed five
camps in all: Camp 4 at 7500m. and Camp 5, erected
by the summit team (J. Kukuczka, M. Piekutowski and
M. Pronobis) during their attempt, at about 7680m.
The team managed to gain the col (7800m.) at the top
of the 'Merkl Couloir', October 14, but were unable
to continue much further. (The report in the AAJ
says they reached the col via the 'Merkl Couloir';
this seems unlikely as the Kinshofer route follows
generally the S.W. Ridge). Intense cold and strong
storms made the descent off the mountain difficult.
Base Camp was evacuated October 18. (38)

1978 German expedition, seven members, leader A. Kraus,
made an unsuccessful attempt on the south-west side
of the mountain by the 'Kinshofer Way'. The high
point reached was 6800m. (39)

1978 SEVENTH ASCENT: R. Messner (Aus) made a solo ascent
of this peak which he had traversed in 1970. This
time he went up the west wall from the Diamir gl.
well to the right of Mummery Rib; his line was to
the right of the very evident lip of the hanging
glacier below the West Saddle (6940m.) then left, in
the direction of the summit. He left his Base
Camp, established July 20 at about 4000m., on August
6 taking with him only 15 kg. of gear - enough
for ten days and including a mini-tent and a sleeping bag. He did not take oxygen nor did he have any
climbers in support. He made three bivouacs: at
4800m., 6400m. and 7400m. A local earthquake in the
early morning of August 8 caused widespread ava-
lanching of the snow slopes below his 6400m. encamp-
ment but he himself was unaffected and was able to
proceed up through deep snow to his third bivouac.
On August 9 he attained his goal and stood for the
second time on the summit of Nanga Parbat. He
returned to his tent at 7400m. but was obliged to
remain there the following day because of adverse
weather. The morning of August 11 was better so,
leaving behind most of his equipment, he set off for
the descent of nearly 3500m. back to Base, which he
reached about nine hours later having come down by a
different route closer to the Mummery Rib. This
unprecedented achievement proved to be, in his

estimation, "the ultimate in pure mountaineering". (40) (41)

1978 8th and 9th ASCENTS: An Austrian expedition of six members, leader R. Wurzer, set out to climb the mountain by the Diamir Face without the help of high-altitude porters. They followed the German 1962 route as far as 7200m. (the German Camp 4 site on the edge of the Bazhin hollow). The Austrians pitched their third camp at 6800m., August 11. From a higher Camp 4, A. Imitzer and A. Indrich made a bid for the summit on August 20 but were obliged to turn back by bad weather on reaching 8000m. Three days later W. Bauer, R. Streif and Wurzer reached the top. Imitzer and Indrich repeated the ascent on August 28. (42)

Principal Source References:

(36) Braham "Chronique Himalayenne" Les Alpes 1978/2
     p. 82
(37) AAJ 1978 pp. 626-627
(38) AAJ 1978 p. 627
(39) AAJ 1979 pp. 307-309
(40) Messner Alleingang Nanga Parbat
(41) Messner "Solo" M 65 pp. 18-21
(42) AAJ 1979 p. 309

Additional Books:

MESSNER The Big Walls (briefly, 1970)

GASHERBRUM I

1977 FOURTH ASCENT: A Yugoslavian expedition, eight members, leader J. Loncar. The ascent was made from the South Gasherbrum gl. by a new route up the S.W. Ridge leading directly to the summit. This route led into a small cirque beneath the South Face (where Camp 1 was placed) then up a steep couloir and eventually up to "White Dome" on the main S.W. Ridge; Camp 2 had been erected lower down at about 5760m. Camp 3 was erected on "Black Cap", further along the ridge, at about 6340m. A. Stremfelj and N. Zaplotnik came up from Base Camp to Camp 3 then continued up via the West Face; an uncomfortable Camp 4 was pitched on this face. The following morning, July 8, the two climbers continued up the steep face in worsening weather conditions and reached the summit soon after noon. They returned in a snowstorm to their Camp 4 where they were joined by D. Bregar who had come up from one of the lower camps. The following morning the successful pair descended to Camp 1; Bregar did not accompany them, preferring to stay in the hope that the bad weather might improve and that he could make a solo bid for the summit. Radio contact between Base and Bregar could not be established on July 10. The weather improved so an attempt was then made to reach Bregar. But on the 14th it began to snow again and the bad weather persisted for another five days. Bregar was not found and was never seen again. (13)

1977 An expedition from Iran is reported to have attempted an ascent of the mountain by the American 1958 route but to have reached no more than about 6300m. (14)

Principal Source References:

(13) AAJ 1978 pp. 616-619
(14) Braham "Chronique Himalayenne" Les Alpes 1978/2 p. 82

GASHERBRUM II

1978 SIXTH ASCENT: A small expedition of two Germans and two Austrians established Base Camp on the Abruzzi gl. at 5100m., July 26, then ascended the South Gasherbrum gl. at the top of which, at 6100m., they set up a camp on August 1. The two Austrians, A. Hosp and O. Zöttl, returned to the Base Camp. G. Brosig and A. Fischer then climbed the mountain by the S.W. Ridge, following the Austrian 1956 route. They bivouacked at 6500m., August 7, and at 7300m., August 8. the following day Fischer, unwell, had to give up but Brosig continued alone and gained the summit by the S.E. Ridge. No oxygen was used. (10)

Principal Source Reference:

(10) AAJ 1979 pp. 298-300

Additional Books:

FRÉSAFOND   Expédition au Gasherbrum II   (1975) PSR

BROAD PEAK

1977 SECOND ASCENT: A Japanese expedition of 13 members, leader M. Yasua, arrived on the Godwin-Austen gl. with the intention of climbing the mountain by the Austrian 1957 route. Base Camp was established at about 4900m. on July 7. Four further camps were set up along the route, the last at 7500m., August 2. From there three climbers - K. Noro, T. Ozaki and Y. Tsuji - reached the summit on August 8. (13)

1978 THIRD ASCENT: A French expedition of four members left Skardu on May 15 and established Base Camp on the Godwin-Austen gl. at 4800m., May 27. Two days later G. Bettembourg, Y. Seigneur and cameraman G. Sourice set off to climb Broad Peak by the Austrian 1957 route and bivouacked at 6100m. but the weather turned foul and they had to withdraw to Base. On June 2 they set off once more for their bivouac site and the day after they continued up to 7500m. where they bivouacked again. On June 4 Bettembourg and Seigneur reached the summit and came down again to their high bivouac. The following day they went down to Base Camp. (14) (15)

Principal Source References:

(13) AAJ 1978 p. 616
(14) M & A 1978/4 p. 444
(15) AAJ 1979 p. 298

K2

1977 SECOND and THIRD ASCENTS: A strong Japanese expedition of 55 members, including three Pakistani climbers and 10 television and cameramen, general leader I. Yoshizawa, leader I. Shinkai, set off from Skardu on May 26. The party, with nearly 900 porters, 15 tractors and 20 jeeps, travelled up the Baltoro gl. to the Godwin-Austen gl. where Base Camp was established June 11, altitude about 5200m. The ascent by the Abruzzi Ridge started June 16. Only six camps were set up along the route; they were at 5530m., 6260m., 6850m., 7460m., 7920m. and 8130m., the last on August 3. The following day the first summit party (five men) reached 8300m. before being turned back by a violent storm. The second summit party — S. Nakamura, T. Shigehiro and T. Takatsuka —

left Camp 6 on August 8 and reached 8550m.; there Nakamura fell through a crevasse and a precious hour was lost while his rescue was effected. However the three reached the summit early in the evening and came down to Camp 5, arriving shortly after midnight, August 9. Oxygen had been used. That same day a third party - A. Aman (Pak), M. Hiroshima, M. Onodera and H. Yamamoto - set off from Camp 6 and reached the summit in the early afternoon. A fourth summit party (eight men) was poised ready for another bid on August 10, but the weather changed and it was recalled from Camp 6. Base Camp was vacated August 22. (20)

1978 British expedition, eight members, leader C.J.S. Bonington. The plan was to climb by a new route up the West Ridge, the ridge rising from the Savoia gl. through Pts. 6212 and 8230. They left Skardu May 16 and established Base Camp at the foot of the ridge June 2, altitude 5400m. A reconnaissance of both sides of the ridge convinced them that the best prospects lay with an ascent up the south side. Camp 1 was placed just below the crest of the ridge at 6000m., June 4. Camp 2 was sited at 6500m. just short of the Pear Buttress by the First Step, June 7; it was on the far side of an easy 30° snow slope. Snow fell for a couple of days then the tasks of load carrying and of pushing the route up the First Step resumed. On June 12 N.J. Estcourt and D.K. Scott, with the Hunza porter Kamajan, set off to carry loads up to Camp 2. While crossing the snow slope Scott ran out a hand rail as a protection. He had just about reached the far side and Estcourt was about half way across when the entire slope above them avalanched. Estcourt was swept to his death and Scott only just escaped when the rope to which he was attached broke almost at the last moment. The expedition was abandoned. High point reached, about 6700m. (21)

1978 FOURTH and FIFTH ASCENTS: American expedition, 14 members (including three women), leader J. Whittaker, set forth to climb this mountain whose summit had so often and so tragically eluded American climbers over the last 40 years. They had four high-altitude Hunza porters and, as liaison officer,

Subadar-Major Mohammed Saleem Khan. The intention
was to climb the N.E. Ridge, attempted by the Poles
in 1976. Advanced Base Camp was established close
to Conway's "Possible Saddle" at 5350m., July 8.
Camp 1, and Camps 2 and 3 (6800m.) on the ridge,
followed during the next ten days. Ahead lay one of
the most difficult parts of the climb: the mile
long traverse of the steep ridge leading to the Camp
4 site. Harrassed and delayed by heavy storms, Camp
4 at 6950m. was not occupied until August 7; Camp 5
was placed at about 7680m., August 18.   After
another seven days of storm C. Anderson, L.F.
Reichardt, Whittaker and his wife Dianne Roberts,
and J. Wickwire occupied Camp 5. The following day,
August 29, Reichardt and Wickwire pushed on to the
site of Camp 6 at about 8000m. - two weeks later
than the Poles - but the advantage could not be
pressed home and they had to retreat. It was not
until September 2 that two assault parties were able
to set off once again for Camp 5. T. Bech and his
wife Cherie Bech, Reichardt and Wickwire, having
decided that the upper reaches of the N.E. Ridge
were not feasible, began a traverse to the top of
the Abruzzi Ridge September 4; but the snow was so
deep that they were obliged to withdraw once more to
Camp 5. The next day, Bech, Reichardt and Wickwire,
undaunted, tried again and succeeded in pitching a
tent on the Abruzzi Ridge (Camp 6) at 7850m.   On
September 6 Reichardt and Wickwire made a bid for
the summit, taking one oxygen cylinder each; Wickwire started using his at 8075m., Reichardt found
that his was not working and so dumped it.   They
reached the top at 17.20 hours. Reichardt did not
stay long and managed to get back to Camp 6 despite
the darkness; there he found R. Ridgeway and J.
Roskelley. Wickwire stayed to take photographs but
delayed his return too long; he bivouacked for the
night at about 8460m. - the highest solo bivouac
yet. His oxygen had given out but the next morning
he was able to reach Camp 6.

During this time Ridgeway and Roskelley had, September 4, continued up the N.E. Ridge and reached their
Camp 6. The following day they tried to go for the
summit but decided that the conditions in sunlight

were too dangerous and returned to their tent. They set off again in the very early hours of the morning of September 6, hoping conditions would be better; they were not so the two climbers were forced yet again to return to their Camp 6. They then resolved to move boldly across to the Abruzzi Ridge in a final effort to snatch success. They reached the other Camp 6 where they were able to welcome Reichardt on his return late that evening. Next morning, September 7, Ridgeway and Roskelley, without using oxygen, managed to gain the summit by mid-afternoon and return to Camp 6 before dusk. A near disaster occurred when they burnt down their tent and some of their equipment when changing fuel cartridges while another stove was alight. After a very cramped and sleepless night jammed in one tent, the four climbers began the descent; four days were required to reach Camp 1. The following day, September 12, they all returned to Base Camp. Wickwire, suffering from delayed multiple pulmonary embolli, had to be carried down to Concordia; finally he was evacuated from Paiju by helicopter. (22)

Principal Source References:

(20) AAJ 1978 pp. 614-616
(21) Bonington "British K2 Expedition" AAJ 1979 pp. 20-23
(22) Reichardt "K2: The End of a 40-Year American Quest" AAJ 1979 pp. 1-18

Additional Books:

NATIONAL GEOGRAPHIC MAGAZINE   Volume 155 No. 5 May 1979 (1978)

SUPPLEMENT BIBLIOGRAPHY

A.

GENERAL WORKS

ASAHI SHIMBUN	The Magnificence of the Himalayas
CLEARE, J.S.	Collins Guide to Mountains and Mountaineering
ETHERTON, Col. P.T.	The Last Strongholds
KEAY, J.	The Gilgit Game
MacGREGOR, J.	Tibet. A Chronicle of Exploration
MOORCROFT, W. and TREBECK, G.	Travels in the Himalayan Provinces of Hindustan and the Panjab; in Ladakh and Kashmir, in Peshawar, Kabul, Kunduz and Bokhara, from 1819 to 1825

B.

BIBLIOGRAPHIES AND CATALOGUES

NEATE, W.R.	Mountaineering and its Literature

C.

BIOGRAPHICAL

HILLARY, E.P.	See: MOON, K.	Man of Everest
HUNT, H.C.J.	ROBERTSON, M.	Mountain Panorama
IRVINE, A.C.	CARR, H.R.C.	The Irvine Diaries

MAIN BIBLIOGRAPHY

AHLUWALIA, Major H.P.S.
. 2a. Faces of Everest. Delhi, 1978. 4to, xxvi + 238 pp.
Ills. in col. and b/w, diags, maps.

ASAHI SHIMBUN (Publishers)
. 12a. The Magnificence of the Himalayas. Tokyo, 1978.

4to, vii + 219 pp, inc. 164 pp. of ills. (mainly in col.).
Explanatory text in Japanese. 2-page intro. in English,
also List of Illustrations and picture captions. F/pano-
rama in col. of the Himalaya and beyond.

BAUME, L.C.
- 18a. Sivalaya. The 8000-metre peaks of the Himalaya.
1978. 316 pp. Frp., 29 maps and diags.

BHANJA, Dr. K.C.
- 22a. Lure of the Himalaya, embodying accounts of Mount
Everest expeditions by land and air. Darjeeling, 1944.

BINI, G.
Annapurna - see MACHETTO, G.

BONATTI, W.
- 24. On the Heights. Diadem p/back edn. 1979. 248 pp.
16 ills.

BONINGTON, C.J.S.
- 26. The Next Horizon. Arrow p/back 2nd imp. 1978.
- 28. Everest The Hard Way. Arrow p/back 2nd imp. 1977.

BRAHAM, T.
Chronique Himalayenne. See SWISS ALPINE CLUB - LES ALPES/
DIE ALPEN.

CARR, H.R.C.
- 47a. The Irvine Diaries. Andrew Irvine and the enigma
of Everest 1924. 1979. 128 pp, 13 ills, line drgs.

CLARKE, C.
- 56a. Everest. 1978. 4to, 64 pp. of text and col. ills.
Epic Adventure Series.

CLEARE, J.S.
- 57a. Collins Guide to Mountains and Mountaineering.
1979. 4to, 208 pp, 16 pp. col. ills, 170 b/w ills,
many text maps.

ETHERTON, Col. P.T.
- 89a. The Last Strongholds. 1934. 298 pp, 79 ills.

FAUX, R.
- 96a. Everest, Goddess of the Wind. 1978. 4to, (15)

SUPPLEMENT BIBLIOGRAPHY

+ 115 pp. B/w ills, diags.

FELLOWES, Air-Commodore P.F.M.
. 98. First Over Everest. Cherry Tree p/back edn. N.d.
(c. 1938). 176 pp, 2 ills. Dust-jacket.

FINCH, G.I.
. 103. Climbing Mount Everest. 3rd edn. 1933, repr. 1935.

FRÉSAFOND, J-P
. 109a. Expédition au Gasherbrum II. Lyon Premier 8000.
Paris, 1977. 192 pp, 19 ills. in col. 3 maps. Text
in French.

GÁLFY, I. and KRISSAK, M.
. 112a. Makalu. Bratislava, 1978. 4to, 220 pp, inc. more
than 160 ills. (of which 30 in col.), some d/page; charts.
Text in Czechslovakian; summary of text and captions to
ills. in Russian, German, English and French.

HABELER, P. (transl. HEALD, D.)
. 123a. Everest. Impossible Victory. (Everest. Der einsame
Sieg. Munich, 1978). 1979. 224 pp, 23 col. ills, many
in b/w.

HAGEN, T.
. 124. (Nepal. Königreich am Himalaya. Bern, repr. 1979).

HARVARD, A. and THOMPSON, T.
. 128a. Mountain of Storms. The American Expeditions to
Dhaulagiri 1969 and 1973. New York, 1974. 4to, 222 pp,
16 col. ills, 77 b/w ills, 3 maps.

HERRLIGKOFFER, K.M.
. 135a. Mount Everest. "Thron der Götter". Sturm auf den
höchsten Gipfel der Welt. Stuttgart, 1973. 4to, 232
pp, 6 col. plts, 36 pp. b/w ills, map, e/p map. Text
in German.

HILLARY, Sir E.P.
. 139. Nothing Venture, Nothing Win. Q.B.C./T.B.C. edn.
1976, 2nd imp. 1977.

HIMALAYAN CLUB
. 142. The Himalayan Journal. Vols. 1 to 15 were reprinted
in Japan in 1978. Limited to 300 sets.

HOOKER, Sir J.D.
. 146. Another edn., 2 vols. in one, 1974.
        An earlier edn., n.d., similar to the Minerva 1 vol.
but in a different binding was published by the Grand
Colosseum Warehouse Co., Glasgow.

HOUSTON, C.S. and BATES, R.G.
. 148. K2, The Savage Mountain. Seattle and London, 1979.
P/back enlarged edn. 400 pp, 45 ills, drgs, 16 diags.
and maps. (The col. ills. of the 334-page New York
1954 edn. are reproduced in b/w).

HUNT, Brig. Sir H.C.J.
. 150. The Ascent of Everest. P/back edn. also 1957.
. 151a. (as Lord Hunt of Llanfair Waterdine) Life is
Meeting. 1978. 286 pp, 24 ills. 11 maps.

JAPANESE ALPINE CLUB
. 167a. Mount Everest 1975. Tokyo 1975 (?). 4to, 100
pp. of ills. in col. Text under ills. also in English.
Paper covers.

KEAY, J.
. 170a. The Gilgit Game. The Explorers of the Western
Himalaya 1865-95. 1979. 278 pp, 16 pp. of ills, 3
drgs, 3 maps.

KENNETT, J.
. 171a. The Story of Annapurna. Bombay, 1955. 72 pp,
figs. Adaptation from HERZOG's Book (No. 136).

KNIGHT, E.F.
. 172. Edns. also in 1896 and 1916.

KRISSAK, M.
Makalu. - See GÁLFY, I.

KUMAR, Col. N.
. 176a. Kanchenjunga. First Ascent from the N-E Spur.
New Delhi, 1978. 4to, 156 pp, inc. 42 pp. col. ills
and text b/w ills. Text maps.

KURZ, M.
. 177. Later published in its original French version

in Alpinisme (the French journal, merged with La
Montagne in 1955, with the title "Le Problème
Himalayen"; journals 1933/2, 3 and 4, and 1934/1 and
2.

. 179a. Chronique Himalayenne. Supplément. Zürich,
1963. 4to, viii + pp. 443-562, 18 ills, 1 route
diag, 8 maps. Text in French. Limited edn. of
600 numbered copies.

MacGREGOR, J.
. 188a. Tibet. A Chronicle of Exploration. 1970.
viii + 374 pp, 28 ills, 8 maps.

MACHETTO. G. and BINI, G.
. 188b. Annapurna. Spedizione italiana nel Nepal 1973.
Pero, 1974. 4to, 192 pp, 142 col. plts. Text in
Italian.

MAGNANI, A.E.
. 189a. Argentinos al Himalaya. Buenos Aires, 1955.
228 pp, ills, map. Text in Spanish.

MAZEAUD, P.
. 198a. Everest '78. Paris, 1978. Text in French.

MESSNER, R.
. 206a. (transl. SALKELD, A.) The Big Walls. (Die
grossen Wände. Munich 1977). 1978. 4to, 144 pp.
Ills. in col. and b/w, route diags, e/p diag.
. 206b. (transl. SALKELD, A.) Everest. Expedition to
the Ultimate. (Everest. Expedition zum Endpunkt.
Munich 1978). 1979. 256 pp, 32 pp. col. ills,
numerous b/w ills, maps, diags.
. 206c. Alleingang Nanga Parbat. Munich, 1979. 272
pp, 50 pp. col. ills, b/w ills, maps, diags.

MIURA, Y. and PERLMAN, E.
. 210a. The Man who Skied down Everest. San Francisco,
1978. xii + 170 pp, 8 pp. col. ills, b/w ills, map.

MONZINO, Count G.
. 212. La Spedizione Italiana all'Everest 1973. Also
issued as described but cloth bound, in slip case.
Another edn. with 165 pp, 23 col. plts, 2 b/w plts,
pan, figs, etc., 2 d/page maps. In protective sleeve.

MOON, K.
. 212a. Man of Everest. The Story of Sir Edmund Hillary.
1962. 96 pp, portrait in col. (For children).

MOORCROFT, W. and TREBECK, G. (H.H. WILSON)
. 212b. Travels in the Himalayan Provinces of Hindustan
and the Panjab; in Ladakh and Kashmir, in Peshawar,
Kabul, Kunduz and Bokhara, from 1819 to 1825. 1841.
2 vols. Vol. I, lvi + 460 pp, ills, map. Vol. II,
viii + 508 pp, ills, map.
Reprinted in India in one vol., 1971. lvi + 967 pp,
ills, map.

MORAVEC, F.
. 212c. Dhaulagiri; Berg ohne Gnade. Vienna, 1960.
224 pp, 16 ills. Text in German.

NAIRZ, W.
. 223a. Gipfelsieg am Everest. Vienna, 1978. Ills.
Text in German.

NEATE, W.R.
. 224a. Mountaineering and its Literature. 1978.
4to, 166 pp. Ills. and sketch maps.

PERLMAN, E.
The Man who Skied down Everest. - see MIURA, Y.

PONS, J.
. 243a. Annapurna Este. Un 8.000 Virgen. Barcelona 1977.
176 pp, 4 col. plts, 16 pp. b/w ills, 3 text maps. Stiff
paper covers. Text in Spanish (Castillian). First appeared (1976?) in Spanish (Catalan) under the title
Annapurna Est; transl. into Castillian by QUADRAS, M.
de.

RAWLING, Capt. C.G.
. 246a. The Great Plateau. Being an Account of Exploration
in Central Tibet 1903, and of the Gartok Expedition, 1904-
1905. 1905. xii + 320 pp, 57 ills, 2 f/maps.

RIDGEWAY, R.
. 247a. The Boldest Dream. The story of twelve who climbed
Mount Everest. New York, 1979. 264 pp, 19 b/w ills, diag.

ROBERTSON, M. (ed.)
. 250a. Mountain Panorama. A book of winter sport and climb-

ing. 1955. 128 pp. with ills. (Includes biographical chapter on Sir John Hunt).

ROYAL GEOGRAPHICAL SOCIETY
. 262. 8th Index: 1965–1974 published 1977 Vols. 131–140.

SÉGOGNE, H. de (and others)
. 273. The title of the French Limited Edn. (1000 numbered copies) is as shown. The title of the ordinary edn. is Karakoram. Expédition Francaise à l'Himalaya 1936.

SHIRAKAWA, Y.
. 283. The Himalayas. (Tokyo, 1971) New York, 1971. Large 4to, 282 pp, 168 pp. of col. plts, 40 pp. of plans, maps.
Deluxe edn. With 93 col. plts, 26 b/w plts. Commentary in Japanese and in English.
Concise edn. New York, 1977. Large 4to, 128 pp, inc. 64 pp. col. plts, 15 pp. b/w ills. and 6 of maps.

STAMMBERGER, F.
. 298a. Todeszone. St. Ottilien, 1972. 124 pp, 4 col. ills, 4 pp. b/w ills. Stiff paper covers. Text in German.

STYLES, S.
. 304. The first copies issued had wrong pagination in the Index; they were mostly withdrawn.

SWISS ALPINE CLUB
. 312. Chroniques Himalayennes by G.O. DYHRENFURTH: Published also:
1956. 1957/1
1957. 1958/3
1973. 1975/1
        Chronique Himalayenne by T. BRAHAM:
1977. 1978/2
1978. 1979/2

SWISS FOUNDATION FOR ALPINE RESEARCH
. 327a. Schweizerischen Stiftung für Alpine Forschungen, 1939 bis 1970. Rückblick auf ihre 30 jährige Tätigkeit. Zürich 1972. 4to. (6) + 149 pp, 8 ills. Text in German.

THOMPSON. T.
Mountain of Storms. - see HARVARD, A.

TOKYO ROCK CLIMBING CLUB
• 340a. Everest. The preliminary Report of the Japanese
Expedition to Mount Everest (8848m.), 1973. Tokyo (?).
About 50 pp. with 12 pp. b/w ills. Subtitles and
Chronological List at end in English.

TREBECK, G.
Travels in the Himalayan Provinces - See MOORCROFT, W.

ULLAH, M.A.
• 342a. Citizen of Two Worlds. New York, 1960. xii +
286 pp, ills.

VERRIJN-STUART, X.
• 351a. Annapurna, 8091 meter. Nederlandse Klimmers in
de Himalaya. Bussum, 1978. 298 pp, 16 pp. col. ills,
b/w ills, diags, sk. maps. Text in Dutch.

WARTH, H. & D.
• 356a. Makalu. Expedition in die Stille. St. Ottilien,
1979. 144 pp, 16 pp. of ills, drgs. Text in German.

YOSHIZAWA, I. (Chief Ed.)
• 374. Mountaineering Maps of the World: Himalayas.
Vol. 2 - Karakoram, Hindu Kush, Pamir, Tien Shan.
Tokyo, 1978. 4to, 350 pp, inc. 32 pp. col. ills,
54 pp. maps; b/w ills, diags. Text in Japanese.
Place names on maps and mountain names under col.
ills. in roman script.

• • • • • • • •
• Yalung Kang (Kangchenjunga West) 8438m. Expedicion
Himalaia 1978. Terrassa, 1978. 4to, 20 pp, 13 ills,
map. Text in Spanish.

LOUIS BAUME

Louis Baume first began mountaineering in 1937 and has climbed extensively in the Alps, as well as the Julian Alps, the Pyrenees, and on Corsica. During 1955-1956 he was a member of the South Georgia Survey Expedition, in the Antarctic, whose object was exploration and mapping. A major peak overlooking the head of the Novosilski glacier, Mount Baume, was subsequently named after him.

The Baume family was one of the earliest watch and chronometer makers in the Franches Montagnes of Switzerland. Louis, part of the family firm for many years, is a Fellow and past Chairman of the British Horological Institute and a long-time Governor of Hackney Technical College.

In 1967, Baume resigned from the family business to devote full time to his 30-year avocation of collecting books. He purchased the stock of mountaineering books of Thomas J. Gaston, London, to start Gaston's Alpine Books, and three years later co-founded Gastons-West Col Publications. Baume has written many articles on technical, travel and mountaineering subjects and is a book restorer and binder as well as collector and dealer. He has edited about 12 books to date, but *Sivalaya* is the first to appear under his own name.

HAVE YOU SEEN THESE BOOKS FROM THE MOUNTAINEERS?

STORM AND SORROW IN THE HIGH PAMIRS. Robert W. Craig describes a tragic summer where climbing, the primary objective, became secondary to survival.

THE CHALLENGE OF RAINIER. Dee Molenaar documents every significant event in the climbing history of Mt. Rainier. Sketches by the author and more than a hundred photos give the climber's perspective.

CHALLENGE OF THE NORTH CASCADES. Fred Beckey chronicles three decades of adventures among these rugged peaks, including numerous first ascents. Photos, maps, and a list of more than 500 ascents by the author.

MOUNTAINS OF THE WORLD. Handy, compact guide to climbing routes on every continent, on islands large and small, in regions seldom thought of as even having mountains, let alone climbing.

THE ASCENT OF DENALI. Original account of the first complete climb of Mt. McKinley together with the previously unpublished diary of Walter Harper, the first man to stand on the highest point in North America.

THE UNKNOWN MOUNTAIN. Discovery and exploration of Mt. Waddington, the "Mystery Mountain" that turned out to be the highest peak in Canada's Coast Range.

TALES OF A WESTERN MOUNTAINEER. Fascinating first-hand accounts of early climbs on Mt. Adams, Rainier, Baker, Glacier Peak, Hood, Stuart, and Shasta, combined with recently uncovered details of the author's eventful career.

For complete list, write:

The Mountaineers, 719 Pike Street
Seattle, Washington 98101